This book is dedicated to all the hard-working teachers I have had the privilege to work with through the years.

READY-TO-USE
Lessons & Activities
for the
INCLUSIVE
PRIMARY CLASSROOM

E I L E E N   K E N N E D Y

**THE CENTER FOR APPLIED
RESEARCH IN EDUCATION**
West Nyack, New York 10994

Library of Congress Cataloging-in-Publication Data

Kennedy, Eileen
    Ready-to-use lessons & activities for the inclusive primary classroom /
Eileen Kennedy
      p. cm.
    ISBN 0-87628-754-2 (spiral-wire). — ISBN 0-87628-506-X (paperback)
    1. Education, Primary—Activity programs—Handbooks, manuals, etc.
2. Inclusive education—Handbooks, manuals, etc. I. Title.
LB1537.K46 1997   96-50116
372.24'1—dc21   CIP

Printed in the United States of America

10 9 8 7 6 5 4 3 2

ISBN 0-87628-754-2 (spiral)   ISBN 0-87628-506-X (pbk)

**THE CENTER FOR APPLIED RESEARCH
IN EDUCATION**
West Nyack, NY 10994
A Simon & Schuster Company

On the World Wide Web at http://www.phdirect.com

Prentice Hall International (UK) Limited, *London*
Prentice Hall of Australia Pty. Limited, *Sydney*
Prentice Hall Canada Inc., *Toronto*
Prentice Hall Hispanoamericana, S.A., *Mexico*
Prentice Hall of India Private Limited, *New Delhi*
Prentice Hall of Japan, Inc., *Tokyo*
Simon & Schuster Asia Pte. Ltd., *Singapore*
Editora Prentice Hall do Brasil, Ltda., *Rio de Janeiro*

Acknowledgments

Many thanks to Ellen, Karen, both Freds, Susan, Dorothy, Stephanie, Tanar, Terry, my son Michael, my brother Joe, my editor Susan Kolwicz, and everyone who helped along the way.

About the Author

Eileen Kennedy holds two teaching licenses—Special Education and Common Branches in the Day Elementary Schools. The Special Education license serves kindergarten through sixth grade and she has taught all of these grades. She is also a qualified Educational Evaluator in New York City. She has been teaching in the New York City Schools over a period of seven years in special education and inclusion classrooms, and substituted over a period of two years as a general education teacher. She has taught learning disabled, emotionally disturbed, mentally retarded, and multiply handicapped students. She is a delegate to her school-based management committee.

She holds a Master of Science degree in Special Education from Brooklyn College and an undergraduate degree from the University of Missouri in Journalism. She has worked professionally for a daily and a weekly newspaper as well as holding several jobs in publishing.

Eileen Kennedy has written and published several children's stories and served as a report writer under an education grant for Earthwatch for a California wildlife study. She takes an ongoing writer's workshop at Bank Street College. She lives with her 13-year-old son in Brooklyn.

About This Book

Inclusion can be a scary proposition for many professional educators today. It is a term that causes much controversy and confusion for teachers and administrators alike. Confusing the issue further is a lack of legal mandate, precise definition, or clear standards on what inclusion is or how it should be implemented. The issue is so complicated that a separate section on it is at the end of the introduction.

On a national average, about 44 percent of disabled children are in the general education classroom today. In 1995, this figure was only about 40 percent and in 1990, it was about 32 percent.[*]

Some advocates of inclusion insist that the disabled child belongs only in the general education classroom, some insist that special children remain in the general education classroom and be pulled for appropriate supplementary services, and others concludes that the disabled child needs a separate classroom. By all indications there is a national trend to expand the opportunities for inclusion of children in the general classroom, and the earlier grades are feeling the most pressure.

Ready-to-Use Lessons & Activities for the Inclusive Primary Classroom was written to assist teachers in their regular lesson planning, integrating special education children with inclusion techniques. These ready-to-use activities should help not only the regular classroom teacher, but administrators, special education teachers, librarians, supplementary service providers, and paraprofessionals who deal with special children.

I have modeled the book around seven content areas in the primary classroom: social activities, communication arts, mathematics, science, social studies, the arts, and health and physical education.

The first is not usually considered a content area in the primary curriculum, but it is hoped that these social activities will help integrate the child with special needs into the general classroom population. These children are often cited for poor interpersonal skills, and many classroom teachers are wary of including them because of their negative impact on classroom interactions and management. This section will give the classroom teacher strategies for improving interpersonal interactions and managing overall classroom behavior.

There are 122 ready-to-use lessons in a wide range of areas, with accompanying reproducible activity sheets. These activities are designed to be used in any of three ways:

- The first is to use a lesson with the entire class, including the special child in the activity.

- The second is to use the lesson separately for the special child while the rest of the class is working on an overall lesson.

- The third is to use it for both—first including the special child in the overall lesson and then having the special child work on the special project as a supplementary, reinforcement activity.

---

[*]17th Annual Report to Congress on Implementation of Individuals With Disabilities Education Act: 1996.

The lessons can be driven by the general education teacher or the special education teacher, if available.

Lessons are divided into general activities and special projects for the special child. Additionally, I have provided a section on specific overall strategies (see Specific Strategies below) for assessing and dealing with the special child, which can be applied in any area. An Assessment Sheet, ready for use, is also included here.

The classroom teacher can decide, after a basic assessment, which learning mode will be the best approach for the child with special needs. All activities can be adapted to a wide range of disabilities; for example, the child who is a poor writer can draw in most lessons. I have also assumed, in this time of shrinking funding and personnel cuts, that there is not a paraprofessional or other teacher on the scene. If one is available to work with the special child, all the better.

Using *Ready-to-Use Lessons & Activities for the Inclusive Primary Classroom* will inspire the professional educator to help the special child adapt and thrive in the general classroom. From my years of having the privilege of working with learning disabled, mentally disturbed, and emotionally and multiply handicapped students, I know that they are special in more ways than one, and that they can add a unique new dimension to the classroom atmosphere.

SPECIFIC STRATEGIES

. . . all that is valuable in human society depends upon the opportunity for development accorded the individual.
—Albert Einstein

The special child in the regular education classroom is one of the biggest challenges facing the general education teacher, the special education teacher, and administrators. Teaching them can also be one of the most rewarding experiences.

Intellectually gifted children are known to be unbalanced in their "giftedness"; children with advanced mathematical skills may have problems in verbal areas, or children who read very early may not be able to calculate. So too with the special child. The special child may not be able to focus on a math problem, but may be able to draw for hours. He or she may not be able to read letters accurately, but may excel in schoolyard basketball. Finding the strengths and weaknesses of this child is a first step in the process of moving him or her successfully into your classroom.

Assessment is a basic start when introducing the child to your classroom. Every child who has been placed in special education must, by federal law, have an Individualized Education Plan (IEP).

Try to get a copy of the IEP and check out the formal testing that was done on the child, particularly in reading and mathematics. Also check the suggested goals on the IEP.

You should also do some informal testing of your own. A good place to start is with class workbooks or textbooks, asking the child to do a sample of work that would be common in your everyday class routine. This will give you an idea of where he or she is in relationship to the rest of the class. When you are testing reading, remember to look at independent reading, silent reading, and oral listening comprehension.

A basic assessment sheet for the primary grades that may help you find out some basic things about the child is included in this section.

It may seem like an overwhelming task to assess the special child while continuing the regular classroom lesson, but this can be one of the most valuable aids for the special child.

Here are just some of the things that you could observe during a regular lesson:

- the child's learning rate
- the child's interests
- the child's learning modality (see Section 1, Social Activities, for more specifics on this)
- the child's difficulties
- how the child interacts with peers (see Section 1, Social Activities)
- what the child requires to learn

Now that you have an idea of the child's strengths and weaknesses, remember the most important rule of thumb in dealing with the special child: "don't give up."

If plan 1, 2, or 3 does not work, go on to plan 4. Success with the special child will require flexibility and commitment and going frequently back to the drawing board. Just remember, when you finally do succeed, it's a true moment of triumph for both of you.

Success itself should be judged in a different way for the special child than for the general education child. Set your standards for success for the special child after careful evaluation. The objectives set up in the activities can be valuable guidelines in this area.

Failure syndrome is a large problem with special children (see Section 1, Social Activities, for more detailed instructions on how to handle this). Here are a few overall tips for building self-esteem:

- Give quick feedback and encouragement.
- Give classwork in the same format as that of the eventual test. Special children often know the information but don't recognize it in a different form.
- Emphasize what the special child has done right—then address the errors.

Student attention is another problem that plagues the special child, who often distracts other classmates along with himself or herself. Here are some suggestions for keeping the special child's attention:

- Seat the special child close to you and keep up frequent eye contact.
- Clear the desk of extra books and materials each time you start a new activity so there are no distractions.
- Surround the special child with attentive, well-focused students.
- Be as concrete as possible. Use pictures, manipulatives, music, and so forth.
- Point to the visual material you want students to see as you are using it. Be sure to write instructions, as well as saying them.
- Keep steps short and memorable.

Name _____

ASSESSMENT SHEET

Below are different questions. If you can't write the answers, you can draw on the back of this page or tell the teacher:

Name the days of the week:

1. _____

2 _____

3. _____

4. _____

5. _____

6. _____

7. _____

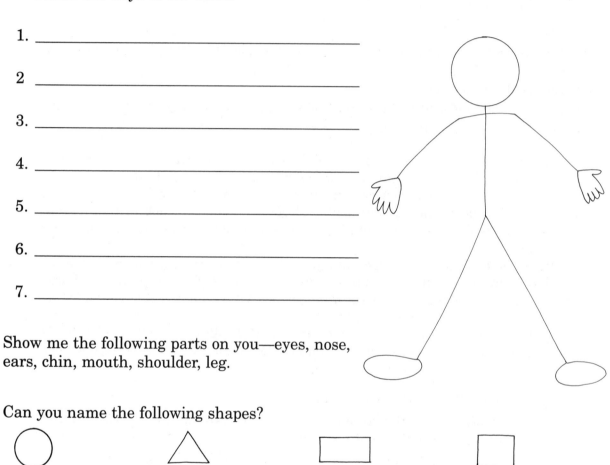

Show me the following parts on you—eyes, nose, ears, chin, mouth, shoulder, leg.

Can you name the following shapes?

Write the letters of the alphabet.

Write a story about yourself and draw a picture.

ON INCLUSION

The term *inclusion* itself causes much confusion with classroom teachers and administrators alike. While there is no legal mandate, concise definition, or clear standards on what it is or how it should be implemented in the schools, there is a national trend toward expanding the opportunities to have disabled students in the general education classroom.

Proponents of "full inclusion" believe that all students, regardless of the nature or severity of their disability, should be educated in a general education classroom. Other proponents of inclusion believe that the child's primary placement should be in the general education classroom, but that the child may be removed from the classroom to receive supplementary services as needed.

The Education for all Handicapped Children Act, PL 94-142 of 1975, revamped as the Individuals with Disabilities Education Act of 1990, guarantees students with disabilities the right to a free, appropriate public education in the least restrictive environment.

The federal "least restrictive environment (lre)" mandate aims at guaranteeing that children with disabilities are educated with their nondisabled peers to the maximum extent appropriate. It puts into place a continuum of alternative placements, from hospitals and institutions at one end to the general education classroom on the other. It also calls for additional personnel or related services to assist the child in the educational setting.

Mainstreaming stems from the concept of education in the least restrictive setting. Again, the term has different meanings in different settings and school systems. Mainstreaming usually means the placement of disabled students into a general education classroom for a portion of the day, based on their educational and social needs. Mainstreaming differs from inclusion in that the mainstreamed child is still in a separate self-contained class, whereas the inclusion model has the child in the general education classroom.

The lre mandate requires that the general education classroom be the first consideration for all students with disabilities, and the most pressure seems to be on the earlier grades to comply. This book is not meant to advocate inclusion, but simply to support those professionals involved in the process. It is my hope that *Ready-to-Use Lessons & Activities for the Inclusive Primary Classroom* will help that innovative classroom teacher make a smooth transition into inclusion.

Eileen Kennedy

Contents

About This Book • ix

Note: *Each activity contains the following parts—Aim, Performance Objectives, Performance Objectives for the Special Child, Materials Needed, Motivation, Do Now, Development, Individual Project for the Special Child, Summary, Summary for the Special Child, and Homework.*

SECTION 1
Social Activities • 1

SECTION 2

Communication Arts • 75

SECTION 3
Mathematics • 133

SECTION 4
Science • 193

SECTION 5
Social Studies • *255*

SECTION 6
Arts • 311

SECTION 7
Physical and Health Education • 367

SECTION 1
Social Activities

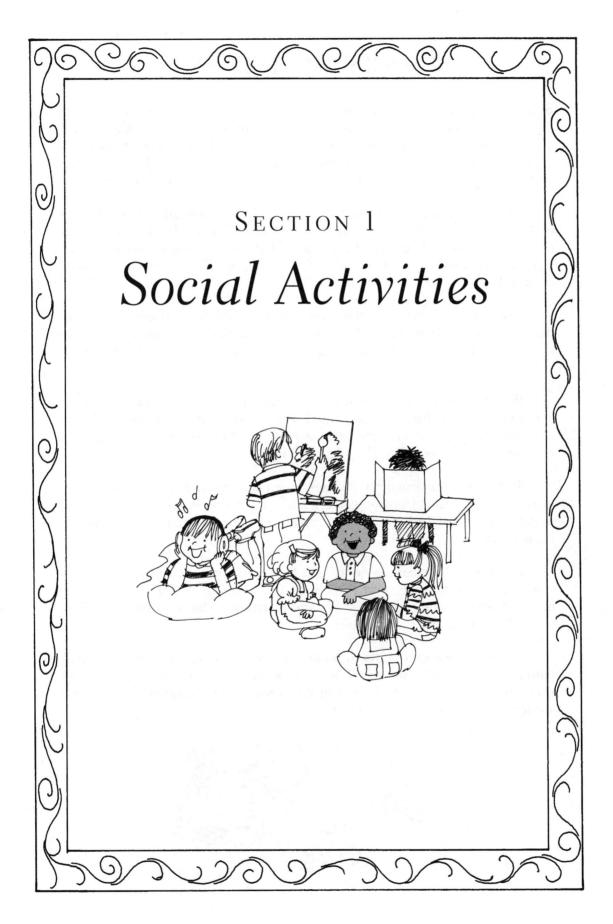

SOCIAL ACTIVITIES

Social acculturation into the classroom is probably the most important issue for the special child, who can't learn without finding a place socially in your class. From the general education teacher's point of view, a behavior management plan that incorporates the special child into your classroom successfully is a cornerstone of your classroom program for the school year.

In this section, a classroom discipline plan is presented with records and positive recognition for students who follow rules and consequences for students who do not. Information is provided for creating a separate discipline contract for the special child who is having difficulty with the classroom rules.

Listening, a basic skill that some special and general education students lack, is explored in relationship to the teacher and to peers, to set up a framework for direction following and mutual respect within the classroom.

Positive repetition techniques and modeling, important basics for the special education child, are presented to reinforce the classroom discipline program. There are even some suggestions for reinforcement techniques to deter aberrant behavior in the special child.

Techniques for transitional times, when classroom discipline often lags, are examined. Also, attention-getting and focusing techniques are explored, using whole-class techniques that encourage all children in the class to focus together.

Building self-esteem is addressed for those special children who have the "I can't" syndrome, and strategies for building "I can" feelings are demonstrated. Organizational skills and learning styles are investigated as ways of reaching the special child.

Appropriate social skills to make and keep friends are explored next, emphasizing the need to know how to play and work together in a positive way. Cooperative learning is presented as an optimal strategy for keeping student involvement and attention.

Activity 1
BONDING WITH THE CLASS

Aim:

How can we make our class year special?

Performance Objectives—Students will be able to:

- bond with the class as a group.
- take ownership of the classroom.
- understand that they will be spending a full school year together.

Performance Objectives for the Special Child:

- identify a "special" friend
- share a friendship experience with the class

Materials Needed:

- MY CLASS Activity Sheet
- crayons
- copy of a book about friendship, like *The Little Prince*, by Auguste St. Exupery. Harcourt Brace Jovanovich: San Diego, 1993
- sentence strips with lines
- pictures of each child in the class—using an instant camera or asking children to bring them from home
  (*Note:* This activity is best done at the beginning of the school year.)

Motivation:

Tell students they will be hearing a story about friendship today.

Do Now:

Write or draw in your notebook any people in the class.

Development:

1. Review the "Do Now." Find out exactly how many students in your class know one another.
2. Have students introduce themselves to the class and say their names.

3. Tell students they will be hearing a book about friendships today because you are hoping that many friendships will be made over the course of the year. Remind students that they will be spending a whole school year together and that you want to make it "special."

4. Read *The Little Prince* or another friendship book aloud to the class. In *The Little Prince*, read the section in the book on the conversation between the little prince and the fox when they are parting.

5. In this section, the fox says that although they will be apart, the beautiful things in the world around him will always remind him of his friendship with the little prince.

6. Explain to the class that you would like to make this year in the classroom as special for them as this friendship was to the fox.

7. Take the children's photos or collect the photos the children have brought in. Write each child's first name on a sentence strip. Put each child's name on the chalkboard.

8. Attach the child's photo and name to his or her desk. This way, the child, and other children, will associate the picture with the desk. It will also help children remember where they sit.

9. Next, ask children where they would like to set up different things in the room. If you have certain centers in mind, discuss with children the logical places they should be; for example, the library center should be off to the side where the bookshelves are. Then set up centers.

10. Have children help with setting up the bulletin board. Then discuss with children that this is the place where their work will be displayed.

11. Pass out MY CLASS Activity Sheets and crayons. Read the directions aloud.

12. Have the children copy down the names from the chalkboard of all the children in the class and draw in some of their faces.

13. Have student volunteers share their Activity Sheets.

14. Create a bulletin board called "My Class." Hang the children's Activity Sheets on the bulletin board.

Individual Project for the Special Child:

- Have the special child choose a "special" friend. Ask each of the children to do something nice for the other child. Then have them share their experience with the class.

Summary:

1. What class do you belong to?
2. Where does your work hang in this classroom?
3. How long will this class be together?

Summary for the Special Child:

1. Who is your special friend?
2. Can you share with the class your friendship experience?

Homework:

List or draw as many of your classmates as you can remember.

Name _____

MY CLASS

Below are some faces. Draw some of your classmates' faces and write the name under the face.

_____   _____

_____   _____

Activity 2
CLASSROOM BEHAVIOR

Aim:

Are class rules necessary?

Performance Objectives—Students will be able to:

- recognize that class rules are necessary.
- discuss classroom rules.
- think about possible behaviors.

Performance Objectives for the Special Child:

- work together with other classmates on a role play
- recognize that rule breaking could lead to chaos

Materials Needed:

- ACTING OUT Activity Sheet
- crayons
- a copy of a peer pressure book, such as *The Berenstain Bears and the Double Dare* by Stan and Jan Berenstain, Random House: New York, 1988

Motivation:

Tell students they will be discussing how they would behave in certain situations today.

Do Now:

Write or draw about any rules you can think of.

Development:

1. Review the "Do Now." List on the chalkboard any rules the children name; for example, crossing the street on a green light.
2. Read aloud a book on peer pressure, such as *The Berenstain Bears and the Double Dare*.
3. Discuss the consequences of giving in to peer pressure when you know something is wrong.

4. Discuss how Brother violates the "No Trespassing" sign and what happens to him, or some other problem in the book you are reading.

5. Discuss why rules are necessary and why the class as a whole needs to follow them.

6. Pass out ACTING OUT Activity Sheets and crayons. Read directions aloud.

7. Read each situation aloud and have students discuss how they would handle each situation.

8. Have students work on their Activity Sheets and put down their solutions.

9. Have student volunteers share their Activity Sheets with the class.

Individual Project for the Special Child:

• Put the special child into a small group of classmates. Have the group work together on doing a role play of one of the problems on the ACTING OUT Activity Sheet and one solution to the problem.

Summary:

1. Are classroom rules necessary?

2. Can you tell me about classroom rules?

3. Can you tell me about some of the ways you would react to classroom rules?

Summary for the Special Child:

1. Can you show me the classmates you worked with?

2. Can you perform your role play for the class?

Homework:

Draw a picture or write a story about the class, following a classroom rule.

Activity 2
ACTING OUT

Below are certain problems that could arise in the classroom. Write or draw your solution to the problem.

The class is supposed to go to gym. The teacher asks the class to line up, but several children are running around the room and refuse to line up. One of these children taps you on the back. What do you do?

You have been given a group assignment. No one in your group wants to be a recorder. What do you do?

You have been given an assignment you don't understand. You want to speak to your teacher, but she is speaking to another student. What do you do?

Activity 3

CLASSROOM RULES

Aim:

Can we make and follow class rules?

Performance Objectives—Students will be able to:

- create rules for the classroom.
- learn rules for the classroom.
- follow rules for the classroom.

Performance Objectives for the Special Child:

- learn one classroom rule
- draw a picture of a child observing that rule

Materials Needed:

- CLASSROOM RULES Activity Sheet
- crayons
- a book about responsibility, like *The Berenstain Bears' Trouble With Pets* by Stan and Jan Berenstain, Random House: New York, 1990

Motivation:

Tell the class they will be working on making their own rules today.

Do Now:

Write or draw in your notebook any job or responsibility you may have at home.

Development:

1. Review the "Do Now." Write on the chalkboard any responsibilities the children may have at home, for example, taking out the garbage or feeding the family pet.
2. Discuss that responsibilities are jobs that make everything run smoothly, as taking out the garbage helps keep the kitchen clean and provides a nice place to sit and eat.
3. Explain that the classroom operates in the same way. Discuss that everyone has responsibilities in the classroom to each other to work together and make it an enjoyable place to learn and be with one another.
4. Read your book on responsibility, such as *Trouble With Pets*, aloud to the class. Discuss what you read with the class.

5. Discuss what the children think would make the classroom environment a good place to be in. Ask the children how they think they could accomplish this.
6. Explain to the class that if they all did what they wanted, when they wanted, the class would be in chaos—total disorder. Tell the class they will be making, learning, and following class rules.
7. Start a class discussion of class rules. Guide the children into suggesting rules. If the class does not come up with an obvious rule, suggest it.
8. When you make the rules, make sure they are observable, that they apply to the whole day, and that they are clear.
9. Here are some examples of rules that are appropriate for kindergarten to second grade:
   * Follow directions.
   * Do not leave the room without permission.
   * Raise your hand before leaving your seat.
   * Keep hands, feet, and objects to yourself.
10. Pass out the CLASSROOM RULES Activity Sheet and crayons.
11. Have the class copy down the rules on the CLASSROOM RULES Activity Sheet.
12. Have volunteers share their Activity Sheets with the class.
13. Have student volunteers role-play the rules. For instance, have one student be the teacher and one student be the student who wants to leave his or her seat. Then have the student raise a hand to get permission and have the other student give permission to leave the seat.

Individual Project for the Special Child:
* Ask the special child to draw a picture of a child observing one classroom rule.

Summary:
1. Can you show me the Activity Sheet of rules we made up for the class?
2. Can you tell me what those rules are?
3. Can you do a role play of what following one rule would be like?

Summary for the Special Child:
1. Can you name one classroom rule?
2. Can you show me the drawing of what it looks like to follow that rule?

Homework:
Take your Activity Sheet of classroom rules home. Ask your parent or guardian to read the classroom rules and sign them. Then sign them yourself.

Name _____

Activity 3

CLASSROOM RULES

Below please list the classroom rules that we have agreed on for the year:

1. _____

2. _____

3. _____

4. _____

5. _____

I have read the classroom rules and agree to them

_____
My name

I have read the classroom rules for my child's class

_____
Parent / Guardian

©1997 by The Center for Applied Research in Education

Activity 4
REWARDS AND CONSEQUENCES

Aim:

What are the rewards for following, and the consequences for breaking, class rules?

Performance Objectives—Students will be able to:

- identify that there are rewards for following rules.
- understand that there are consequences for breaking rules.
- learn both the rewards and consequences associated with classroom rules.

Performance Objectives for the Special Child:

- suggest separate rewards and consequences for following the rules
- create a contract for the teacher and himself or herself to sign

Materials Needed:

- REWARDS AND CONSEQUENCES Activity Sheet
- BEHAVIOR AWARD Sheet
- pencils
- lined paper
- a copy of a book on breaking a rule, like *The Berenstain Bears and the Truth* by Stan and Jan Berenstain, Random House: New York, 1983
- poster for star chart

Motivation:

Tell students they will be making up their own rewards and consequences in the classroom today.

Do Now:

Think of any rewards you would like to see for rule following and list or draw them in your notebook.

Development:

1. Review the "Do Now." List on the chalkboard any rewards children can think of. List all of them, even if they seem inappropriate.

2. Tell children that together you will be making the rewards for following class rules and the consequences for not following rules.

3. Read a book about breaking a rule, like *The Berenstain Bears and the Truth*.

4. Discuss the book. How was the bears' behavior at the beginning of the book? How was it different at the end? Why?

5. Now discuss how you think rewards and consequences may help students to follow rules.

6. Form a student rewards list. The first reward should always be positive recognition and the second could be a communication home to the parent or guardian.

7. A sample rewards list for students might look like this:

    1. Praise
    2. Good note home
    3. Behavior Award
    4. Star-chart rewards

8. Show students the BEHAVIOR AWARD Sheet.

9. Set up the star chart with each child's name. Tell students they can earn stars on their star chart for following the rules.

10. Go back to the chalkboard. Look at the rewards the children suggested. Guide the students in picking appropriate rewards. Then determine the number of stars it will take to earn each reward. List the rewards and the stars on the chalkboard.

11. A sample star/rewards list might include:

    - a sticker—5 stars
    - a pencil—10 stars
    - a toy—20 stars
    - a book—25 stars

12. Next discuss consequences. Ask the students what they think is fair. Make sure the consequences are tangible and consistent. They don't have to be severe, but students do have to know that the consequences are inevitable.

13. Here is a sample consequences list:

    If a student breaks a rule, the following will happen:

    - first time—reminder
    - second time—warning
    - third time—five-minute timeout (You should establish a place in the classroom for the timeout.)
    - fourth time—phone call home
    - fifth time—sent to principal
    - sixth time—meeting of parent, principal, and student.

    Whatever you decide on, list it on the chalkboard.

14. Pass out the REWARDS AND CONSEQUENCES Activity Sheet and pencils. Read the directions aloud and have students complete them.

Individual Project for the Special Child:

- Tell the special child that in addition to participating in the class rewards and consequences system, he or she will have a separate rewards and consequences system for behavior in the class. Ask the special child to think about what reward or consequence he or she would think appropriate; for example, a reward would be a special job as a class monitor, and a separate consequence would be ten minutes in timeout. Write down the contract, then both you and the special child sign it.

Summary:

1. Are there rewards for following the rules?
2. Are there consequences for breaking the rules?
3. What are they?

Summary for the Special Child:

1. What is the reward and consequence we decided on for your behavior?
2. Where is the contract we made?

Homework:

Go home with your REWARDS AND CONSEQUENCES Activity Sheet and have your parent or guardian sign it.

Name _____

REWARDS AND CONSEQUENCES

Below, please list the rewards and consequences of the class:

If I follow the rules, I will earn:

1. _____
2. _____
3. _____
4. _____
5. _____
6. _____

If I break the rules, the following will happen:

1. _____
2. _____
3. _____
4. _____
5. _____
6. _____

Parent/Guardian Signature _____

BEHAVIOR AWARD

The following student _____
was caught being good.

Signed _____

BEHAVIOR AWARD

The following student _____
is a star of the star chart.

Signed _____

17

Activity 5

CLASS REWARDS AND CONSEQUENCES

Aim:

Can we earn class rewards for following the directions and class consequences for not following directions?

Performance Objectives—Students will be able to:

- create rewards for the class following directions.
- create consequences for not following directions.
- learn class rewards and consequences associated with the following directions.

Performance Objectives for the Special Child:

- identify one of the rewards for the class following directions
- participate in a role play about the class following directions

Materials Needed:

- CLASS REWARDS AND CONSEQUENCES Activity Sheet
- JOURNAL OF BEHAVIOR Activity Sheet
- pencil
- star chart

Motivation:

Tell students you will be discussing class rewards today.

Do Now:

Think of some class rewards that you would like. List or draw them in your notebook.

Development:

1. Review the "Do Now." List whatever rewards the children can think of for the class on the chalkboard.
2. Discuss with the class that it is important to the well-being of the classroom that the class follow directions.
3. Choose a few volunteers to do a role play. Be sure to include the special child. Have one child be the teacher and several students be classmates.

4. Give them a class situation, such as the teacher's calling for the class to line up. The first time they do it, have the classmates not cooperate. Have one student sit at his desk and refuse to move. Have another two argue over who should be first on line.

5. Discuss the problems with this particular behavior. For instance, if the class refuses to line up, they will not be able to get to their next activity on time and they could lose valuable time in the gym, lunch room, art room, and so on.

6. Next, have the class do the same role play, only cooperating immediately and getting into a quiet, orderly line. Discuss with the class how much better this is for the functioning of the class.

7. Discuss with the class that in addition to individual rewards, the class can earn rewards for following directions.

8. Discuss that there will also be consequences if the class, as a whole, does not follow directions.

9. Show the class that there will be a star chart for class behavior also. As the class follows directions, stars will be given. Set up the star chart, next to the chart for individuals.

10. Next, go back to the chalkboard and list of rewards that the children said they would like. Select some that are appropriate and select the number of stars it will take to earn the rewards.

11. You can follow this sample class rewards list:
    - class stickers—5 stars
    - special activity—10 stars
    - extra outdoor recess—20 stars
    - a video—30 stars
    - a video with popcorn—50 stars

12. Next, discuss the class consequences for not following directions. Try to use class suggestions.

13. A sample class consequences list might look like this:
    - First time—a reminder
    - Second time—a warning
    - Third time—entry in the behavior journal in class
    - Fourth time—entry in the behavior journal for homework
    - Fifth—loss of a special activity, for example, outdoor recess

14. Do a role play with the class. Have a student volunteer be teacher. Have the teacher tell the class it is time to gather round the reading corner and read a story. Have the class scatter in all directions as the volunteer teacher tries to read the story.

15. Next, have the class cooperate and gather around the volunteer teacher in a quiet circle on the floor while the story is read.

16. Discuss the differences in the children's behavior.

17. Pass out the CLASS REWARDS AND CONSEQUENCES Activity Sheet and pencils. Have children write down the class rewards and consequences.
18. Have student volunteers share their Activity Sheets.

Individual Project for the Special Child:

- Ask the special child and several other children to work on a role play together. Have them work out a role play where the teacher is trying to explain some addition problems and no one is paying attention. Then ask the same group to role-play a lesson where the whole class is paying attention to the teacher.

Summary:

1. Do we have rewards for the class's following directions?
2. Do we have consequences for the class's not following directions?
3. What are the class rewards and consequences?

Summary for the Special Child:

1. Can you tell me what one class reward is?
2. Can you do the role play for the class of the students not paying attention?
3. Can you do the role play of the class paying attention?

Homework:

Bring home your CLASS REWARDS AND CONSEQUENCES Activity Sheet. Have your parent or guardian sign it.

Activity 5
JOURNAL OF BEHAVIOR

Date _____

The directions I did not follow were _____

_____

_____

_____

The consequences of my action were _____

_____

_____

_____

I could have handled this situation differently by _____

_____

_____

_____

Name _____

Activity 5
CLASS REWARDS AND CONSEQUENCES

These are the rewards the class can earn for following directions:

1. _____

2. _____

3. _____

4. _____

5. _____

6. _____

These are the consequences if the class does not follow directions:

1. _____

2. _____

3. _____

4. _____

5. _____

6. _____

Parent/Guardian Signature _____

©1997 by The Center for Applied Research in Education

Activity 6
AT HOME AND AT SCHOOL

Aim:

Can we tell the difference between home and school rules?

Performance Objectives—Students will be able to:

- identify that there are rules at home and rules at school.
- recognize that rules at school must be obeyed at school, even if they differ from the rules at home.
- distinguish between home and school rules.

Performance Objectives for the Special Child:

- learn a rule from home
- learn a rule from school

Materials Needed:

- AT HOME AND AT SCHOOL Activity Sheet
- crayons
- a book about home rules, like *The Berenstain Bears Trick or Treat* by Stan and Jan Berenstain, Random House: New York, 1991

Motivation:

Tell students they will be hearing a story about home rules today.

Do Now:

List or draw in your notebook any rules you may have at home.

Development:

1. Review the "Do Now." List any home rules the children may name on the chalkboard.
2. Talk about how school rules are applicable at school and home rules are applicable at home.
3. Discuss how students must follow school rules in school, even if they are different from home rules.

4. Read aloud the book you have chosen about home rules, such as *The Berenstain Bears Trick or Treat*.

5. Discuss the rules in the book you read. In *The Berenstain Bears*, Mama Bear lays out special rules for Halloween. Discuss these rules and why there are certain rules needed in certain situations.

6. Ask the children to name the class rules. They can read them from the class chart or they can name them from memory.

7. Write the class rules on the chalkboard.

8. Pass out the AT HOME AND AT SCHOOL Activity Sheet and crayons.

9. Read directions aloud.

10. Have children mark school rules with the appropriate drawing, then do the same with the home rules.

11. Have student volunteers share their Activity Sheets with the class. Check for accuracy.

Individual Project for the Special Child:

- Ask the special child to draw or list one rule from home. Then draw or list one rule from school.

Summary:

1. Are there rules for home and rules for school?

2 Which rules must be obeyed at school?

3. Can you show me your Activity Sheet where you identify school and home rules?

Summary for the Special Child:

1. Can you name one rule for home?

2. Can you name one rule for school?

Homework:

Go home and discuss home rules with your parent or guardian. Discuss them tomorrow with the class.

Activity 6

AT HOME
AND
AT SCHOOL

Below are listed different rules. Draw a house next to the ones that apply to home and a school next to the ones that apply to school.

1. Do not leave the room without permission. _____

2. Put your dirty dishes in the sink. _____

3. Ask permission before you invite a friend to play. _____

4. Follow directions. _____

5. Take out the garbage. _____

6. Brush your teeth. _____

7. Raise your hand before leaving your seat. _____

8. Ask permission before going to the bathroom. _____

9. Make your bed. _____

10. Keep your room clean. _____

Activity 7
LISTENING

Aim:

Can we listen carefully?

Performance Objectives—Students will be able to:

- understand that listening is an important skill.
- recognize that the teacher is the most important person in the room to listen to.
- listen carefully.

Performance Objectives for the Special Child:

- create some sample teacher instructions with a group
- participate in a role play about listening to instructions

Materials Needed:

- LISTENING Activity Sheet
- crayons
- a book about listening, like *The Berenstain Bears and the Missing Honey* by Stan and Jan Berenstain, Random House: New York, 1987

Motivation:

Tell students they will be hearing a mystery story today.

Do Now:

Close your eyes and listen to the sounds you hear. Open your eyes and draw in your notebook what you think you hear.

Development:

1. Review the "Do Now." List on the chalkboard all the things the children thought they heard.
2. Read a story about listening, like *The Berenstain Bears and the Missing Honey.*

3. Discuss with the class the importance of listening in the context of the story; for example, Papa Bear would have known from the beginning who the thief was if he had listened to the owl.

4. Discuss the importance of listening in the classroom.

5. Discuss why the most important person to listen to in the classroom is the teacher.

6. Pass out the LISTENING Activity Sheet and crayons.

7. Read the directions from the Activity Sheet aloud to the children. All of the directions will not be on the Activity Sheet, because you will want them to have to listen in order to complete the sheet.

8. Read the following rhyme to them first, and ask the children to complete it with the appropriate letters:

> There was a girl named ____am. (Pam)
> Who liked to eat ____am. (jam or ham)
> Out to the raft she ____am. (swam)
> Where she saw a soft-shell ____am. (clam)

9. Next, ask the children to draw four items. You can make up items or use the following.

- First, draw an apple with a green stem.
- Second, draw a dog with an orange hat.
- Third, draw a purple house with flowers all around.
- Fourth, draw yourself listening carefully in class.

10. After the children have finished, have student volunteers share their Activity Sheets. Check for accuracy.

Individual Project for the Special Child:

- Select a group of children, including the special child, to work on a role play. Ask the class to create instructions that a teacher might give. Then have the group demonstrate what it is like when the group listens to the teacher's instructions and when it doesn't.

Summary:

1. Why is it important to listen?

2. Who is the most important person to listen to in the classroom?

3. Can you show me the LISTENING Activity Sheet where you followed the verbal instructions?

Summary for the Special Child:

1. Can you tell me the instructions you made up to do in your role play?
2. Can you do your role play for the class?

Homework:

Listen to and follow some instructions from your parent or guardian at home. Then come in tomorrow and tell us about it.

Name _____

Activity 7
LISTENING

Below is a rhyme that needs to be completed. Listen to your teacher say it, and then complete it. Then, listen to your teacher's instructions and draw in the four boxes below.

There was a girl named ____am.

Who liked to eat ____am.

Out to the raft she ____am.

Where she saw a soft-shell ____am.

1.	**2.**
3.	**4.**

29

Activity 8
LISTENING TO EACH OTHER

Aim:

Can we listen to each other?

Performance Objectives—Students will be able to:

- sit quietly while another student speaks.
- look at the person who is speaking.
- listen to the student who is speaking.

Performance Objectives for the Special Child:

- create a role play for the class to listen to
- perform a role play for the class to listen to

Materials Needed:

- COLOR ME PRETTY Activity Sheet
- crayons
- a story about listening, like *Oasis of Peace* by Laurie Dolphin. Scholastic, Inc.: New York, 1993
- Good Listener Award
- sentence strips

Motivation:

Tell the class they will be hearing a special story today.

Do Now:

Draw things that make noise in the classroom in your notebook.

Development:

1. Review the "Do Now." List on the chalkboard any things the children can name that make noise.
2. Read the story aloud to the children. Have them listen closely for details. In *Oasis of Peace*, an Arab boy and Jewish boy in Israel form a friendship because they listen to each other.

3. Discuss with the class why listening is so important and what details they remember from the story about the boys' friendship.

4. Prepare the sentence strips. Have the children prepare the strips themselves, if they print well enough, or do them yourself in advance.

5. The sentence strips should read:
   - The kite is blue.
   - The cat is orange.
   - The book is yellow.
   - The feather is purple.
   - The apple is green.
   - The desk is brown.

6. Pass out the COLOR ME PRETTY Activity Sheets and crayons.

7. Read the Activity Sheet directions aloud.

8. Call student volunteers to the front. Have each one read his or her sentence strip to the class. Make sure the children watch as each one speaks. Do not have the child show the sentence strip until later. Give the children a chance to color in each item before you move on to the next sentence strip.

9. Have student volunteers come to the front and share their Activity Sheets. Check for accuracy.

10. Pass out Good Listener Awards to those children who listened well.

Individual Project for the Special Child:

- Ask several children in the class, including the special child, to create a role play in which they each choose an animal and describe it, without naming it to the class. Then the class guesses the animal.

Summary:

1. Can you sit quietly while a classmate speaks?
2. Can you look at the child who is speaking?
3. Can you listen to the child who is speaking?

Summary for the Special Child:

1. Can you show me the role play you created?
2. Can you perform it for the class?

Homework:

Go home and ask a family member to tell you how to do something. Then come back and explain it to the class.

Activity 8

COLOR ME PRETTY

Listed below are six things. Listen as your classmates tell you which color they should be and then color them in the correct color:

1. kite

2. cat

3. book

4. feather

5. apple

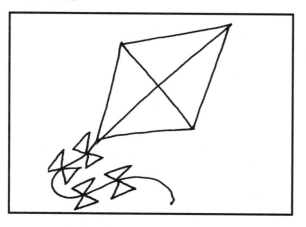

6. desk

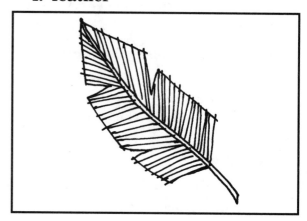

GOOD LISTENER AWARD

Name _____

is a good listener and has earned this award.

TEACHER _____

DATE _____

Activity 9
LET'S GET ORGANIZED

Aim:

Can we get organized?

Performance Objectives—Students will be able to:

- keep a weekly checklist of organizational behaviors.
- keep a schedule of upcoming assignments.
- get organized in class.

Performance Objectives for the Special Child:

- choose a classmate to work with
- participate in a peer study system

Materials Needed:

- LET'S GET ORGANIZED Activity Sheet
- crayons
- *Grandfather's Journey*, by Allen Say, Houghton Mifflin Company: Boston, 1993, or other sequential book

Motivation:

Tell students they will be filling out their own organization sheets this week.

Do Now:

List your schedule for the day in your notebooks.

Development:

1. Review the "Do Now." Ask students for details of their schedules and list them on the chalkboard.
2. Ask them if there is any part of the day that they might have left out. List this on the chalkboard.
3. Tell students that today they will be doing an exercise that will help them organize their day.
4. Next, list the schedule for the book reading on the chalkboard. Here is an example of a schedule:
    - Read questions.

- Listen to story.
- Answer questions.

5. Write questions on the chalkboard; for *Grandfather's Journey*, for example, try these questions:
    - Where was grandfather born?
    - Where did he go?
    - When did he return to his homeland?
    - Why did the author return to his homeland?

6. Read questions about your story aloud to the class.
7. Read story aloud to the class.
8. Ask students to answer questions about the story.
9. Tell students that it is useful to them to know what is coming up on the classroom schedule.
10. Pass out the LET'S GET ORGANIZED Activity Sheet and crayons.
11. Read directions aloud. Have students complete Activity Sheets. Ask student volunteers to share Activity Sheets.
12. Do a class activity list for the day. Have students copy it down.
13. Repeat as needed for reinforcement.

Individual Project for the Special Child:

- Ask the special child to choose a buddy. Pair the special child with the buddy in class to guide him or her through classroom activities. They should also exchange phone numbers for homework assignments.

Summary:

1. Can you show me your Activity Sheet?
2. Can you show me the schedule of upcoming assignments you copied from the chalkboard?
3. Are you more organized now?

Summary for the Special Child:

1. Can you show me your study buddy?
2. Can you show me what you two worked on together?

Homework:

Talk to your parent or guardian about your schedule at home. Come in tomorrow and share it with the class.

Activity 9
LET'S GET ORGANIZED

Below is a checklist set up by day, Monday to Friday. Each day, check off each item as you complete it. For example, when you come in, check off "Attended School." Check off each item as you go along and do this every day.

CHECKLIST BY DAY:

Date _____

Then list the following items down:

	Monday	Tuesday	Wednesday	Thursday	Friday
1. Attended School					
2. Completed Homework					
3. Followed Directions					
4. Completed Math Assignment					
6. Completed Reading Assignment					
7. Completed Other Assignments					
8. Raised My Hand to Answer Questions					
9. Got Along With Peers					

Activity 10

REINFORCEMENT AND MODELING

Aim:

Can we show what we have learned?

Performance Objectives—Students will be able to:

- demonstrate how to follow a direction.
- recognize when other students are following directions.
- draw themselves following directions.

Performance Objectives for the Special Child:

- use a cup and marble system to reinforce and repeat a good behavior
- purchase something with the chips he or she has earned from you

Materials Needed:

- LOOK AT ME BEING GOOD Activity Sheet
- crayons
- cup
- marbles
- camera, preferably a Polaroid™
- film with 36 exposures

Motivation:

Tell students they will have pictures taken today.

Do Now:

Imagine that you are following directions in the classroom. Now draw yourself doing this.

Development:

1. Review the "Do Now." List on the board any examples of following directions the children can think of.
2. Have student volunteers share their drawings with the class.

3. Give an instruction. Immediately look for a few students who are following that direction. Then acknowledge those students, for example, "Good, Debbie is already in line."

4. Tell students that you will be taking their pictures doing something right throughout the day.

5. Try to photograph each child doing something right throughout the day. Try to photograph particularly the behavior you want to reinforce.

6. When you get all the photographs of all the children, tape them to each desk. When you want to remind the child about that behavior, cue the child by walking over and pointing to the photo.

7. Be sure to photograph the whole class doing a few basic behaviors well, like lining up or sitting quietly and looking up at you. Display these photos around the room.

8. Point to the photo when students are not following directions the way you would like. Remind them that they have done this behavior successfully before. Be sure to follow up with class rewards for good behavior, like stars on the star chart.

9. Pass out the LOOK AT ME BEING GOOD Activity Sheet and crayons.

10. Read directions aloud.

11. Ask the children to draw themselves following directions. They can use the photos taped to their desks as models.

12. Have student volunteers share their Activity Sheets.

13. Make a bulletin board entitled "Here We Are Being Good." Place class photos in the middle and hang Activity Sheets all around.

Individual Project for the Special Child:

• Speak privately to the special child about some behavior that you both want to work on, for example, impulse control. Promise the special child a reward if he or she is successful. Then give the child a cup of marbles. Everytime he or she blurts out something without permission, quietly remove a marble. Make sure not to acknowledge the special child's blurted-out responses, and do call on him or her when the hand is raised. If the special child has enough marbles at the end of the day, he or she can "purchase" the reward. Set up the number of marbles the child needs to purchase the reward at the end of the day. Start small and gradually build up.

Summary:

1. Can you follow directions?

2. Can the class follow directions?

3. Can you show me the drawing of yourself following directions?

Summary for the Special Child:

1. Did you use the cup of marbles for your behavior today?
2. Do you have enough marbles to purchase your reward?

Homework:

Go home and follow your parent or guardian's directions. Draw yourself following the directions.

Name _____

LOOK AT ME BEING GOOD

Below, make a drawing of yourself following a direction from a teacher:

Below, make a drawing of the whole class following a direction from a teacher:

Activity 11
TRANSITIONS

Aim:

Can we move quickly and quietly between classroom activities?

Performance Objectives—Students will be able to:

- identify when students are engaged in good transitions and when they're not.
- recognize why smooth transitions are essential for class functioning.
- understand the class schedule and move with it.

Performance Objectives for the Special Child:

- visualize moving smoothly from one activity to the next
- move smoothly from one activity to the next

Materials Needed:

- SMOOTH MOVES Activity Sheet
- crayons
- cassette player
- classical music tape, for example, Vivaldi's *Four Seasons*
- a three minute timer

Motivation:

Tell students they will be playing a "cleanup" game today.

Do Now:

List in your notebook your favorite parts of the school day.

Development:

1. Review the "Do Now." List on the chalkboard the students' favorite parts of the day.
2. This is the start of your class schedule. Now fill in the parts the students did not mention.

3. Have students read the class schedule aloud.

4. Ask students what the most important thing is if the class is going to follow the schedule and finish all the activities on the schedule. Guide the discussion toward smooth transitions, for example, cleaning up after an art activity so everyone can go to lunch on time.

5. Ask some students, including the special student, to role-play cleaning up after an art activity. First, have students in the role play fool around and not cooperate. Time the activity with the timer. Next have students role-play cleaning up with cooperation. Time the activity again.

6. Discuss with the class their observations of the role play. Guide them in acknowledging that it is smoother and more time efficient to cooperate and move on quickly to the next activity.

7. Set up a class activity on the schedule, like art.

8. Tell students that you are going to play a game to see how long it takes to set up the activity. Play the music on the cassette player during the setup time. Time the setup with the timer.

9. Do the art activity. But this time, tell students that five minutes before cleanup, you'll begin the music tape. Then they will play a cleanup game and see how long it takes to clean up. Tell students if they do it within a certain amount of time, they will win the game.

10. Five minutes before cleanup, begin the music tape.

11. Time the class cleanup time. If the class succeeds in cleaning up in the time allotted, give the class a reward, like a star on the star chart. If not, tell them you will try the game again. Use this technique for all transitions that are appropriate.

12. Pass out the SMOOTH MOVES Activity Sheet and crayons. Read directions aloud. Have students work on their Activity Sheets and share them with the class.

Individual Project for the Special Child:

• Play the music on the cassette for the special child. Ask the child to breathe deeply and imagine that he or she is quickly and efficiently cleaning up after an activity. Then have him or her do a cleanup.

Summary:

1. Can you show me your Activity Sheet and tell me which students are cooperating and which are not?

2. Can you tell me why it is important to move quickly from one activity to another?

3. Can you tell me the class schedule?

Summary for the Special Child:

1. Can you visualize cleaning up?
2. Can you clean up?

Homework:

Find out your schedule for the family at home. Then bring it in and report to the class tomorrow.

Activity 11
SMOOTH MOVES

Shown below are different things that go on in the class between activities. Most students are cooperating, but one in each activity is not. Find the student who is not cooperating and cross him or her out. Then color in the students who are cooperating.

Activity 12
GETTING THEIR ATTENTION

Aim:

Can we pay attention during class?

Performance Objectives—Students will be able to:

- understand what is required in a lesson.
- stay on task with the class during a lesson.
- complete the assignment in the allotted time.

Performance Objectives for the Special Child:

- work within a group on a project
- complete the task with the group

Materials Needed:

- KEEP YOUR EYE ON THE BALL Activity Sheet
- crayons
- a timer
- a self-esteem book, like *Just Because I Am* by Lauren Murphy Payne, Free Spirit Publishing, Inc: Minneapolis, 1994

Motivation:

Tell students they will be working together today as a class.

Do Now:

Draw in your notebook any story you can remember about a character who feels good about himself or herself.

Development:

1. Review the "Do Now." Have students hold up their notebooks and show their drawings in unison. Make sure to keep eye contact with the special child, or any other children who have trouble staying on task.

2. Read aloud *Just Because I Am* or another book you may have on self-esteem. Make sure to show the class illustrations as you go and tell the class to pay attention to the illustrations.

3. Have the class draw their favorite illustrations from the story. Set the timer for ten minutes. When the class is finished, have them all hold up their drawings together. Scan the class and make sure everyone, including the special child, is on task.

4. Pass out KEEP YOUR EYE ON THE BALL Activity Sheets and crayons. Read directions aloud.

5. Make sure the whole class understands that the final instructions are not on the Activity Sheet; the class must listen attentively to get the instructions.

6. Set the timer for as much time as you think the class will need to complete the Activity Sheet.

7. Tell the class that if they finish the task on time they will receive a reward, like a star on their star chart, but emphasize that the whole class must be finished.

8. Now begin your verbal instructions. Tell the children to do the following:
   - Draw a hat on the dog.
   - Draw a tie on the giraffe.
   - Draw a bookbag on the back of the hippo.
   - Draw an umbrella on the monkey.

9. After you have given the class verbal instructions, write the instructions on the chalkboard for reinforcement.

10. After the class finishes, have them hold up their sheets.

11. Check to see if they completed the task in the allotted time. Give them the reward, or say something encouraging, like "maybe next time."

Individual Project for the Special Child:

- Choose several students, including the special child, for cleanup after this activity. Have them work together to clean up the crayons and timer, or whatever materials were used.

Summary:

1. Did you understand the instructions for the lesson?
2. Did you work along with the class?
3. Did you complete the assignment?

Summary for the Special Child:

1. Did you work with the group on cleanup?
2. Did you complete the task?

Homework:

Go home and do a household chore. Time yourself and see how long it takes. Report back to the class tomorrow.

Name _____

Activity 12
KEEP YOUR EYE ON THE BALL

Below are different animals. Listen to the instructions from your teacher and draw the things your teacher tells you to. Then color in the animals.

1. dog

2. giraffe

3. hippo

4. monkey

Activity 13
BUILDING SELF-ESTEEM

Aim:

Can we feel good about ourselves?

Performance Objectives—Students will be able to:

- make an "I can" with their names on it.
- write down the things they can do.
- share the things they can do with the class.

Performance Objectives for the Special Child:

- talk about his or her feelings in a group
- listen to and make suggestions for other students' problems

Materials Needed:

- LOOK AT WHAT I CAN DO Activity Sheet
- markers
- sentence strips
- a can for each child, for example, an empty frozen juice can
- glue
- construction paper
- small pieces of paper
- a competency book, like *The Little Engine That Could* by W. Piper, G.P. Putnam and Sons: New York, 1991

Motivation:

Tell children that they will be hearing a special story about doing things today.

Do Now:

List or draw in your notebook all of the things that you do well.

Development:

1. Review the "Do Now." List on the chalkboard anything the children can name that they feel they do well. If some children are too modest to do this, have their classmates help them to come up with things they do well.

2. Read a competency book, like *The Little Engine That Could*.

3. Talk about the many things that we don't even think about, that we can do. Make some sentence strips from the students' comments, for example:

    - I can tie my shoe laces.
    - I can read letters.
    - I can button my coat.
    - I can be a good friend.
    - I can feed my hamster.

4. Tell students that today we will be doing a special art project to help remind us about all of the things that we can do.

5. Pass out the cans, glue, construction paper, and markers. Tell students to wrap the can in construction paper and glue it on. Then print their names and draw an *I*.

6. Have students place their cans on their desks. Have them take small pieces of paper (have some available for them) and write down the things they do during the day and place them in the "I can."

7. Toward the end of the day, go back to this activity. Pass out LOOK AT WHAT I CAN DO Activity Sheets.

8. Read directions aloud from the Activity Sheet. Have students copy down from the papers in their "I cans" the things they accomplished that day.

9. Have student volunteers share their LOOK AT WHAT I CAN DO Activity Sheets with the class.

10. Repeat this activity periodically to build self-esteem.

Individual Project for the Special Child:

- Choose several students, including the special child, to form a sharing group. Have the children in the group take turns sharing a problem they have and see if the rest of the group can come up with solutions for the problem.

Summary:

1. May I see the "I can" you made?
2. May I see the Activity Sheet where you wrote down the things you can do?
3. Can you share one thing you can do with the class?

Summary for the Special Child:

1. Can you tell me the problem you shared with your group?
2. Can you tell me some of the suggestions that were made to solve the problem?

3. Can you tell me about some of the suggestions you made to solve other children's problems?

Homework:

Go home and listen to some of the problems in your family. See if you can come up with any solutions and share them in class tomorrow.

Name _____

Activity 13
LOOK AT WHAT I CAN DO

I can do many things. Here is a list and drawings
of just some of the things that I can do:

1. _____

2. _____

3. _____

4. _____

5. _____

6. _____

7. _____

8. _____

9. _____

10. _____

Activity 14
WE LEARN IN DIFFERENT WAYS

Aim:

Can we learn in different ways?

Performance Objectives—Students will be able to:

- choose a way of learning something.
- create a project choosing a learning style.
- choose more than one way of learning.

Performance Objectives for the Special Child:

- choose an individualized project
- choose a way of making the individualized project

Materials Needed:

- WE LEARN IN DIFFERENT WAYS Activity Sheet
- crayons
- a book about learning, such as *Life With Papa* by Stan and Jan Berenstain, Comes to Life Books. New York, 1993
- clay
- reading material on a project
- pictures relating to a project
- music relating to a project
- a study carrel
- math manipulatives

Motivation:

Tell students they will be choosing their own way of making a project today.

Do Now:

List or draw in your notebook the favorite projects you have done and how you did them.

Development:

1. Review the "Do Now." List on the chalkboard all the different projects the children enjoyed doing and how they did them.

2. Discuss how different children learn in different ways. Look at the different projects and ways they did them and identify seven learning styles:

   • the visual learner
   • the verbal learner
   • the logical learner
   • the kinesthetic learner
   • the auditory learner
   • the group learner
   • the individual learner

   Talk about what each word means.

3. Tell children that they will be assigned to make something, and that they can choose their own way of making it. Some suggestions for projects might be an environmental cleanup, or creating an original piece of art, and so on.

4. Read *The Berenstain Bears' Life With Papa*, or another book about learning.

5. Discuss how in *Life With Papa*, Papa learned to do things without Mama, or discuss the learning styles in the story you read.

6. Read directions from the WE LEARN IN DIFFERENT WAYS Activity Sheet aloud. Tell students they will make something and choose the way they will do it.

7. Make available to children clay, pictures, music, reading material, study carrel, math manipulatives, or other class materials you think might contribute to a creative project.

8. Tell children they can work in groups or alone.

9. Tell children that, whatever way they choose to do their projects, they must make their notes first on their Activity Sheets.

10. After children complete their Activity Sheets, have them share them with the class.

11. Have children work on their projects during free time from regular classroom activities.

12. Allow students to display their creative projects.

13. Ask students to suggest a second way they might have done the same project.

Individual Project for the Special Child:

• Give the special child a book of projects to choose from, like science projects. Have the child figure out the materials he or she needs. Assist the child in getting the materials. Then let the child work on the project.

Summary:

1. How do you want to learn something?
2. May I see your project?
3. Can you tell me another way you could have done the project?

Summary for the Special Child:

1. What is the project you chose?
2. How did you make it?

Homework:

Go home and ask your parent or guardian if you can help with a household chore. Then figure out how to do it.

Name _____

Activity 14
WE LEARN IN DIFFERENT WAYS

My project is _____

_____

_____

I made it by _____

_____

_____

_____

I could have made it another way by _____

_____

_____

_____

Activity 15
COOPERATIVE LEARNING

Aim:

Can we work together?

Performance Objectives—Students will be able to:

- work in a group on a project.
- work together with other children they do and do not like.
- learn to brainstorm to come up with a group idea.

Performance Objectives for the Special Child:

- create a role play in a group
- perform a role play in a group

Materials Needed:

- MYSTERY BOX Activity Sheet
- crayons
- timer for each group
- a story about group dynamics, like *The Berenstain Bears and the In-Crowd* by Stan and Jan Berenstain, Random House: New York, 1989
- shoe boxes with odds and ends, like keys, a food wrapper, a paper clip, other items

Motivation:

Tell students they will be working on a Mystery Box game today.

Do Now:

List or draw in your notebook your favorite people to work with in the class.

Development:

1. Review the "Do Now." Quietly go around the room and check the children's notebooks and see whom they like to work with.

2. Make notes about dividing the class into groups in which children are grouped with children they like to work with and children they don't like to work with. Groups can vary in size, but should be no larger than five.

3. Read the story to the class aloud. Discuss the problems of group dynamics, like how Sister Bear felt being left out of the group and how she didn't want to wear the same clothes as the others.

4. Divide the class into the groups you arranged previously. Give each group one timer and one MYSTERY BOX Activity Sheet.

5. Explain that each group needs to come up with a solution to the Mystery Box robbery. Tell students to pretend there was a robbery in the school the night before.

6. Pass out to each group a Mystery Box with objects inside. (Each group should have different objects in their boxes.) Tell the group that the only clues they have to find the robber are in the Mystery Box.

7. Tell each group to brainstorm to come up with a plot based on the clues in the box, and to come up with a robber.

8. Explain that brainstorming means that each member of the group gets to put in his or her ideas and that no one should say anything negative about any of the ideas.

9. Then read the directions on the MYSTERY BOX Activity Sheet. Have the children put together a plot from the ideas put forward.

10. One child must make notes on the Activity Sheet and another child must present the mystery plot for the group, but the group itself must decide who does what.

11. Walk around the room and check the dynamics. Compliment the good listeners and workers in the groups.

12. After each group is finished, have one member in each group come up with the Mystery Box and present the plot based on the clues in the box.

Individual Project for the Special Child:

- Assign the special child, and several other children, to create and perform a role play. Have them pretend they are playing a game. In one role play, have a student exhibit poor sportsmanship. In the second role play, have everyone play together well.

Summary:

1. Which group did you work with?

2. Which children did you enjoy working with?

3. Can you tell me about your Mystery Box plot?

Summary for the Special Child:

1. Can you tell me about the story you made up about playing badly on a team?
2. Can you show me how you acted out the story?

Homework:

Go home and make up a story with your family. Then tell it tomorrow in school.

Name _____

Activity 15
MYSTERY BOX

The items in my Mystery Box are as follows:

1. _____

2. _____

3. _____

4. _____

5. _____

6. _____

This is how my group thinks the mystery happened:

_____

_____

_____

_____

Activity 16
MAKING FRIENDS

Aim:

Can we make friends?

Performance Objectives—Students will be able to:

- interview another child to find out about him or her.
- form partners to find out some things they both like.
- make a poster showing their favorite things.

Performance Objectives for the Special Child:

- work with a small group to create a role play about making friends
- perform the role play for the class

Materials Needed:

- OUR FAVORITE THINGS Activity Sheet
- crayons
- oaktag
- magazines with pictures
- safety scissors
- glue

Motivation:

Tell students they will be making posters of their favorite things today.

Do Now:

Write or draw in your notebook the ways in which you would try to make a new friend.

Development:

1. Review the "Do Now." Talk about ways that are appropriate to make a new friend, for example, finding out about things you and the person may have in common.

2. Ask the class to divide themselves into pairs. Tell them that they will have a chance to interview or ask their partners questions to learn about each other.

3. Pass out the OUR FAVORITE THINGS Activity Sheets and crayons. Read directions aloud.

4. Read each question and then ask children to interview each other.

5. Next, ask children to find out the things they both like. Make notes of these things.

6. Pass out picture magazines, scissors, glue, and oaktag.

7. Ask each pair to come up with a poster of Our Favorite Things. Use the Activity Sheet to find the things they both like, and then draw or cut out pictures of those things and put them on the poster, along with their names.

8. Have each pair come to the front of the room and present their posters to the class.

Individual Project for the Special Child:

• Assign a small group, including the special child, to create a role play about making friends. Tell them to make up one about all the wrong ways to make a friend, such as insulting the child, or pushing him or her. Then ask them to make up a role play about the right way to make a friend, such as offering to help someone. Then have the group perform the role plays for the class.

Summary:

1. Which child did you interview to find out about favorite things?

2. What are the things you both liked?

3. Where is your poster?

Summary for the Special Child:

1. What is the play you made up about making friends?

2. Can you perform the play for the class?

Homework:

Go home and call a friend and work on your reading and math homework together.

Activity 16
OUR FAVORITE THINGS

Below are listed some questions you should ask your partner. Make notes of what he or she says. Then have your partner ask you the same questions and make notes on what you say.

Question	My Friend	Me
1. What are your favorite things to eat?		
2. What are your favorite things to do?		
3. What are your favorite subjects in school?		
4. What are your favorite television shows?		
5. Where are your favorite places to go?		

List below the things you both like:

_____

_____

_____

©1997 by The Center for Applied Research in Education

Activity 17
SHARING FRIENDS

Aim:

Can we share our friends?

Performance Objectives—Students will be able to:

- understand that a friend can be shared.
- identify ways that a friend can be shared with another person.
- recognize that we can have many friends.

Performance Objectives for the Special Child:

- choose two friends in the class for an activity
- decide on an activity with the two classmates and do it together

Materials Needed:

- SHARING FRIENDS Activity Sheet
- crayons
- a book about a group of friends, like *Friends* by H. Heine, Simon & Schuster: New York, 1982
- math manipulatives

Motivation:

Tell students they will be hearing a story about friends today.

Do Now:

List or draw in your notebook things you like to do with your favorite friends.

Development:

1. Review the "Do Now." List on the chalkboard all the different things the children can name to do with friends.
2. Talk about all the different things that groups of friends can do together.
3. Read aloud your story about friendship, like *Friends*. This is a story about the friendship between a mouse, a pig, and a rooster and what they do together.

4. Discuss how three, and even more, people can be close friends.

5. Discuss how, if you have a special friend, even a "best friend," you can still share this friend with others.

6. Pass out the SHARING FRIENDS Activity Sheet and crayons. Read directions aloud.

7. Have students draw their solutions to the problems.

8. Have student volunteers role-play the problem and the solution they came up with.

Individual Project for the Special Child:

- Have the special child choose two other students in the class to work with. Have the three students work up a solution to an addition problem with math manipulatives, for example, two pattern blocks plus two pattern blocks equal four pattern blocks.

Summary:

1. Can we share a friend?

2. Can we share a friend with another friend?

3. Can we have many friends?

Summary for the Special Child:

1. Can you show me the two friends you worked with?

2. Can you show me your solution to the problem?

Homework:

Ask your family to help you solve this problem. You have a plan to go swimming with a friend and another friend phones and asks you to go skating. What do you do?

Activity 17
SHARING FRIENDS

Below are different problems that friends can have. Write or draw a solution to each problem in the space provided. Then act it out for the class.

1. Your friend Bobby needs help with his math homework. Your other friend, Henry, calls and tells you he is going to the movies and would like to include you. What do you do?

2. The teacher lets you pick the monitors for the week. Two of your friends want to be chalkboard monitors, but there's only one job. What do you do?

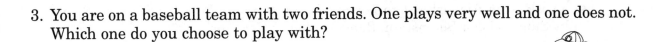

3. You are on a baseball team with two friends. One plays very well and one does not. Which one do you choose to play with?

4. You are playing outside with two hula hoops. Two friends want to play with the hula hoops. What do you do?

Activity 18
SPENDING TIME WITH FRIENDS

Aim:

Can we spend time nicely with our friends?

Performance Objectives—Students will be able to:

- realize that friends share something in common.
- recognize that a place to start making friends is where you have a common interest.
- list ways in which people might find time to spend together.

Performance Objectives for the Special Child:

- work with others to create a role play about friends spending time together
- perform the role play for the class

Materials Needed:

- SPENDING TIME WITH FRIENDS Activity Sheet
- crayons
- a book about friendship, like *The Berenstain Bears and the Trouble With Friends* by Stan and Jan Berenstain, Random House: New York, 1986

Motivation:

Tell children they will be guessing what friends are doing together from some word clues.

Do Now:

List in your notebook all the things you like to do with friends.

Development:

1. Read a book about friendship aloud, such as *The Berenstain Bears and the Trouble With Friends*.
2. Discuss how the friendship in the book began, for example, when a new cub moved in down the block from Sister Bear and how they both liked to jump rope.

3. Discuss any problems the friendship may have in the story, such as when the cubs had a fight over who was going to be teacher when they played school.

4. Review the "Do Now." List on the chalkboard all the things the children like to do with friends.

5. Discuss ways in which a person might seek to meet new friends, for example, Sister Bear found a new friend had moved into her neighborhood.

6. Pass out SPENDING TIME WITH FRIENDS Activity Sheets and crayons.

7. Read directions aloud. Have students draw or list ways in which they like to spend time with friends.

8. Have students share their Activity Sheets with the class. See if children in the class can match up their interests, such as jumping rope at recess.

Individual Project for the Special Child:

- Ask several students, including the special child, to make up three plays about friends spending time together, for example, playing baseball, riding bicycles, or playing a board game. Have students act out the play. See if the class can guess which activities the friends are engaging in.

Summary:

1. Who shares things in common?
2. Where would you start making a friend?
3. Can you name some of the ways that friends could spend time together?

Summary for the Special Child:

1. Can you work with others to create a role play?
2. Can you perform your role play for the class?

Homework:

Go home and figure out what you would like to do with a friend. Then call a friend and ask him or her to join you. Share it with the class the next day.

Name _____

Activity 18
SPENDING TIME WITH FRIENDS

List or draw below ways that you think friends might spend time together.

1	2
3	**4**

My favorite thing to do with friends is _____

Activity 19
GIRLS AND BOYS TOGETHER

Aim:
Can boys and girls do the same things?

Performance Objectives—Students will be able to:
- recognize that boys and girls can play the same sports.
- understand that men and women can have the same jobs.
- realize that any person, male or female, can be a caretaker.

Performance Objectives for the Special Child:
- identify a male who provides some caretaking for him or her
- identify a female who is actively engaged in working

Materials Needed:
- GIRLS AND BOYS TOGETHER Activity Sheet
- crayons
- drawing paper
- a book about gender, like *The Berenstain Bears: No Girls Allowed* by Stan and Jan Berenstain, Random House: New York, 1986

Motivation:
Tell students they will be doing surveys today.

Do Now:
List or draw in your notebook any sports that you like to play.

Development:
1. Review the "Do Now." List all the sports the children like to play, and their names, on the chalkboard.
2. Review with the class that both boys and girls like to play sports.
3. Discuss who takes care of them at home. If the mother is the primary caretaker, are there any ways that the father takes care of the children? Are there any ways grandfathers or other male family members or friends take care of them?

4. Discuss how both men and women are capable of caretaking as well as working.

5. Read aloud the story you have chosen about gender, like *The Berenstain Bears: No Girls Allowed.*

6. Discuss the problems in the book; for example, in *No Girls Allowed*, why did the boys want to exclude the girls? How did that make the girls feel? What did the girls do?

7. Discuss how some people are judged by what they are (boy or girl) rather than what they do. This is called prejudice. Talk about other forms of prejudice, like racial prejudice or prejudice against disabled people (particularly relevant if you have a special child with a visible disability).

8. Tell students that they will be doing a survey today. Explain that a survey is a detailed study in which you get people's opinions or feelings about things.

9. Pass out the GIRLS AND BOYS TOGETHER Activity Sheet and crayons.

10. Read directions aloud to the class and have each child choose an occupation he or she is interested in. Make two columns, one for girls and one for boys.

11. List which occupations each child is interested in. Then compare them. How many did boys choose? How many did girls choose? How many did both choose?

12. Discuss that girls and boys can do any job—that it's a matter of personal preference, not gender.

Individual Project for the Special Child:

• Give the special child drawing paper. On one side, ask the child to show some male relative helping him or her in some way. On the reverse side, ask the child to draw a female relative performing a job.

Summary:

1. Can boys and girls play the same sports?
2. Can men and women have the same jobs?
3. Can a male or female relative take care of you?

Summary for the Special Child:

1. Can you tell me about a man in your family who takes care of you?
2. Can you tell me about a female in your family who works?

Homework:

Draw a picture of the members of your household, male and female, helping out with a household chore. Put yourself in the picture and be sure to help out at home!

Name _____

Activity 19
GIRLS AND BOYS TOGETHER

Below are listed different jobs that you could do. Choose one from the list below and let your teacher know what it is:

- Farmer
- Artist
- Lawyer

- Doctor
- Banker
- Teacher

- Carpenter
- Custodian
- Entertainer

- Computer Programmer
- Other _____

This is the job I am interested in: _____

These are jobs both boys and girls were interested in:

_____

Activity 20
PERSONAL SPACE

Aim:

Can we identify personal space?

Performance Objectives—Students will be able to:

- understand that personal space is a necessary space around each student.
- become aware of personal space for themselves.
- recognize the importance of personal space.

Performance Objectives for the Special Child:

- work with other students on a personal space problem
- tell your results to the class

Materials Needed:

- PERSONAL SPACE Activity Sheet
- crayons
- stop sign made of oaktag

Motivation:

Tell students they will be playing games about personal space today.

Do Now:

Draw a picture of your personal space in school—your desk.

Development:

1. Review the "Do Now." Have student volunteers show pictures of their "personal spaces."

2. Discuss what a personal space is. Discuss how everyone needs a personal space at school, work, or home. Discuss how personal space is the space around the student that provides adequate room for movement.

3. Pass out PERSONAL SPACE Activity Sheets and crayons. Read directions aloud. Read each game description from steps 6, 7, 8, and 9 below. Have students color in games.

4. Have student volunteers display their Activity Sheets.

5. Push back desks. Have each child find a personal space to be in.

6. Play the first "personal space" game with students: Rocket Ship. In Rocket Ship a circle is formed by the children. A chosen child taps another child in the circle and returns to his or her original position unless caught. If caught, the chosen child continues to be the tapper. If not, the tapped child takes over as tapper.

7. Play the Cat and Mouse game. Choose two players—one to be cat and one to be mouse. Have the rest of the children form a circle with the cat on the outside and the mouse on the inside.

8. Have the cat chase the mouse, with the circle of players trying to stop the cat.

9. Red Light, Green Light, One, Two, Three is the third game to play. Choose one player as crossing guard and give him or her the stop sign and a vest, if one is available. Put the rest of the class about twenty feet from the goal desk, which is supposed to be the traffic light. The crossing guard counts from one to three and then says "stop" and displays the sign. Any child who is moving returns to the starting line. The first child to reach the crossing guard wins.

Individual Project for the Special Child:

- Choose several children, including the special child, to do a personal space experiment. Put four desks together to form an open square in the middle. Have the children cram into the middle space for a short time. Have them talk about how they felt having their personal space broken into. Have them report to the class.

Summary:

1. What is a personal space?
2. Where is your personal space in the classroom?
3. Why is personal space important?

Summary for the Special Child:

1. What is the personal space problem you had?
2. Can you tell the class about it?

Homework:

Draw a picture of your personal space at home, for example, your room or a portion of the room where you sleep.

Activity 20
PERSONAL SPACE

Below are three squares for you to draw a picture of each personal space game.

1. Rocket Ship

2. Cat and Mouse

3. Red Light, Green Light, One, Two, Three

1.

2.

3.

©1997 by The Center for Applied Research in Education

SECTION 2

Communication Arts

COMMUNICATION ARTS

Communication arts provide a multicultural, multidisciplinary approach to reading, writing, listening, and speaking with a whole-language plus skills emphasis. Activities are designed to help teachers plan integrated lessons that cover whole-class activities and special child objectives.

Listening skills are developed through stories read—aloud and to each other—as well as through everyday sounds in the environment. Speaking skills are encouraged in play dramatization, songs, and verbal reporting. Writing is emphasized in many lessons, including developing original books and biographies. Reading readiness, sound-symbol relationships of letters, and language experience approaches are all used to develop reading skills.

Activities for the special child include visual, auditory, kinesthetic, and tactile approaches to reading. There is also an emphasis on phonograms or word families—a technique that has proved particularly effective with special children.

Stories and poems from the Caribbean, Native American, Scandinavian, and African American cultures are included in lessons. Activities cross multidisciplinary lines and include such areas as math, science, and social studies.

Activity 1
THE WORDLESS STORY

Aim:

Can we read a wordless story?

Performance Objectives—Students will be able to:

- interpret pictures.
- tell a story from pictures.
- sequence a story.

Performance Objectives for the Special Child:

- make up a story about a picture
- dictate the story into a cassette player

Materials Needed:

- WORDLESS STORY Activity Sheet
- cassette player with blank tape
- photograph
- crayons
- a wordless book, like *Donkey Book* published by DLM: Allen, TX, 1990
- sentence strips
- safety scissors
- glue
- 3" × 5" index cards

Motivation:

Tell children they will be making up their own stories from pictures today.

Do Now:

Think of a story you would like to tell. Now draw the story in a picture without words.

Development:

1. Review the "Do Now." Ask student volunteers to show their pictures and tell their stories.

2. Tell children they will be making up their own story from pictures today.

3. Show the children the wordless book, for example, *Donkey Book*. Have the class discuss the pictures as you go through the pictures in order.

4. Turn on the cassette player. Go through the book in sequence again and record the children's interpretations of the pictures.

5. Play back the children's comments as you silently turn the pages of the book in order.

6. Play back the children's comments again, this time constructing a story and placing it on sentence strips under the appropriate pages in the book.

7. Now, go through the book again and have the children read back the sentence strips under the pictures in the book aloud.

8. This time, keep the book closed, and ask the children to repeat back the story on the sentence strips in order.

9. Pass out the WORDLESS STORY Activity Sheet, crayons, scissors, glue, and index cards. Read the directions aloud to the class.

10. Have students cut out the pictures, glue them on the index cards, and put them in the appropriate order.

11. Ask student volunteers to share their index cards with the class. Check for accuracy.

Individual Project for the Special Child:

- Give the special child the photograph and the cassette player. Have him or her make up a story about the picture and dictate it into the recording machine.

Summary:

1. Can you tell me about the pictures in this book?

2. Can you tell me a story about the pictures in this book?

3. Can you tell me what order the pictures are in from memory?

Summary for the Special Child:

1. Can you tell me about this photograph?

2. Can you play for me the story you dictated into the cassette player?

Homework:

Tell a story about something that happened at home in a picture or series of pictures without words.

Activity 1
WORDLESS STORY

Below are four pictures. Color them. Cut them out and glue them on index cards. Then put them in order.

Activity 2

VISUAL REALITY

Aim:

Can we find details in a picture?

Performance Objectives—Students will be able to:

- identify similarities and differences among objects.
- locate details in a picture.
- describe verbally the differences and similarities of objects.

Performance Objectives for the Special Child:

- assemble a simple picture puzzle
- describe verbally the picture in the puzzle

Materials Needed:

- CAN YOU FIND IT? Activity Sheet
- crayons
- a picture puzzle with 24 pieces
- a tray with coins, paper clips, buttons, and bottle caps
- a copy of a visual discrimination book, like *The Great Waldo Search* by Martin Handford, Scholastic: New York, 1989, or *Where's Waldo?* by Martin Handford, Little, Brown: Boston, 1987

Motivation:

Tell students they will be playing a tray game today with different objects.

Do Now:

Look at a picture in a book you are reading and imagine how you would describe it to someone who couldn't see it.

Development:

1. Review the "Do Now." Have children bring their pictures to the front and describe to the class what's in them. Check for details.

2. Tell the children that you will be looking for something in the pictures in a picture book today.

3. Show them *The Great Waldo Search* or *Where's Waldo?* or another picture book. Pass the book around and have them locate specific things in the pictures. As children find things that you name, such as Waldo, in the pictures, have them raise their hands and show the class.

4. Put the tray with the objects out. Ask for two student volunteers. Ask the first volunteer to go to the back of the room and look away while the other volunteer arranges two or three objects on the tray.

5. Ask the first volunteer to look at the tray and then go back to not looking.

6. Then have the second volunteer remove something from the tray and see if the first child can remember what object is missing. Rotate the players until all the children have had a turn to place objects and guess.

7. Next have children arrange objects that are similar or different on the tray; for example, the coins and the buttons are similar because they are round, paper clips are different because they are straight.

8. Have children take turns until everyone has had a turn.

9. Pass out the CAN YOU FIND IT? Activity Sheet and crayons.

10. Read directions aloud. Have children circle each item as they find it on the Activity Sheet.

11. Have volunteers share their Activity Sheets. Check for accuracy.

Individual Project for the Special Child:

- Give the special child a 24-piece puzzle. Have him or her put it together. Then ask the child to describe the picture.

Summary:

1. Can you find a detail in this picture and tell me about it?

2. Can you show me the things you grouped on a tray that are similar?

3. Can you tell me how they are similar and how they are different?

Summary for the Special Child:

1. Can you show me the picture puzzle you put together?

2. Can you tell me about the picture in the puzzle?

Homework:

Go home and look in a magazine. Bring in a picture of one of your favorite things.

Activity 2
CAN YOU FIND IT?

Look at this picture. See if you can find the following things and circle them:

- a kitten
- a chair
- a tulip
- two candles

- a pen
- a whale
- three elves
- a baseball bat and ball

©1997 by The Center for Applied Research in Education

Activity 3
PICTURE CARDS

Aim:

Can we make picture cards to learn new words?

Performance Objectives—Students will be able to:

- learn new vocabulary.
- use strategies to unlock the meaning of unfamiliar words.
- put new words in a sentence.

Performance Objectives for the Special Child:

- work cooperatively in a group
- make picture cards into word families

Materials Needed:

- PICTURE CARDS Activity Sheet
- 3" × 5" index cards
- glue
- safety scissors
- dictionary
- markers
- *The Ox-Cart Man* by Donald Hall, Viking: New York, 1979 or some other descriptive book
- copies of the illustrations from the book you choose

Motivation:

Tell children they will be making their own picture cards today.

Do Now:

List or draw any ways you can think of to learn the meaning of words.

Development:

1. Read the book you chose to the class. Discuss it.

2. Ask the children to name any words for which they did not know the meaning. (In *The Ox-Cart Man*, this might be loom, shawl, weave, spinning wheel, shear, linen, flax, birch broom, honeycombs, sap, goose feathers, shingles, maple sugar, cart, yoke, harness, embroidery, wax, wintergreen, kettle, and whittle.)

3. Review the "Do Now." Ask children how they would go about learning the meaning of words they don't know. List any suggestions they may have, like looking it up in a dictionary, asking an adult, and so on.

4. Tell children they will be learning a new way to unlock the meaning of new words today.

5. Group students into several groups.

6. Pass out the PICTURE CARDS Activity Sheets, index cards, markers, Xeroxes of pictures from the book, glue, and scissors.

7. Ask students to study the copies of the pictures in the book. See if they can find any picture clues to find the meanings of the words in the book they don't know.

8. Read the directions from the Activity Sheet. Have students glue the index cards to the blanks on the Activity Sheet. When they dry, have them cut them out.

9. Next have children glue the picture clue to the blank side and write the word on the other.

10. For words they cannot find illustrations for, have them check the dictionary and draw their own pictures.

11. Have each group show their flash cards and report on the word meanings they have found. Have each group use the new word in a sentence.

Individual Project for the Special Child:

- Have the special child work in a group. Have the group make word family cards. They could group words from the story, for example, *flax* and *wax*, or make up a word family, such as *yoke* and *joke*.

Summary:

1. What new words did you learn in your group?
2. How did you learn the meaning of these words?
3. Can you use these words in sentences?

Summary for the Special Child:

1. Which group did you work in?
2. What word families did you come up with?

Homework:

Make up a story or draw a picture, using the new words you learned.

Activity 3
PICTURE CARDS

Below are outline blanks that will fit on index cards. Glue the blanks to index cards and after they dry, cut them out. Then write the new word you've learned on the front and draw or glue the picture of the word on the back.

My new word is

_____.

My new word is

_____.

Activity 4
BOUNDLESS SOUNDS

Aim:

Can we identify sounds around us?

Performance Objectives—Students will be able to:

- identify common sounds.
- distinguish between sounds.
- identify rhyming words.

Performance Objectives for the Special Child:

- pick out some rhyming words from rhymes read aloud
- create other words from the same word families

Materials Needed:

- CHIMING RHYMING Activity Sheet
- crayons
- sleigh bells
- alarm clock
- telephone
- door-bell
- drum
- book of rhymes, like *The Mother Goose Treasury* by Raymond Briggs, Dell Publishing: New York, 1980, or *Happy Hippopotami* by B. Martin, Harcourt Brace Jovanovich: San Diego, 1991

Motivation:

Tell students they will be listening to common sounds today.

Do Now:

List or draw in your notebook some of your favorite sounds.

Development:

1. Review the "Do Now." List the children's favorite sounds on the board.

2. Tell the children to close their eyes. Then sound for them the five objects: door-bell, alarm clock, sleigh bells, drum, and telephone. Ask the children to identify the sounds.

3. Have the children open their eyes and sound the five objects again.

4. Have two student volunteers come to the front. Have one close his or her eyes while the other one picks one of the five objects to sound. Have the other child identify the sound.

5. Rotate the two volunteers until all the children have a chance to sound and guess a sound.

6. Choose a rhyming book, such as *The Mother Goose Treasury*. Read some rhymes aloud to the children.

7. As you finish each rhyme, ask students to identify the rhyming words. List the rhyming words on the chalkboard as the children name them.

8. Pass out the CHIMING RHYMING Activity Sheets to each child with crayons.

9. Read the directions aloud. Ask the children to match up the rhymes.

10. Have student volunteers share their Activity Sheets. Check for accuracy.

Individual Project for the Special Child:

• Have the special child choose several rhyming words from the rhymes read aloud. Then have him or her make word families from those rhyming words.

Summary:

1. Can you tell me what these sounds are?

2. Can you tell me how they are different?

3. Can you identify the rhyming words from this rhyme I'm reading?

Summary for the Special Child:

1. Can you pick out the rhyming words from this rhyme?

2. Can you show me the word families you made from the rhyming words?

Homework:

List as many rhyming words as you can think of.

Activity 4
CHIMING RHYMING

Below are listed many words. Match up the words that rhyme. Draw a line between them with your crayons.

dub   wool

man   gown

town   clean

full   tub

lean   can

Activity 5
ALPHABET FUN

Aim:
Can we identify the letters of the alphabet?

Performance Objectives—Students will be able to:
- identify the letters of the alphabet.
- learn a song about the alphabet.
- write the letters of the alphabet.

Performance Objectives for the Special Child:
- trace the letters of the alphabet in the sand
- read the letters from what he or she traced

Materials Needed:
- ALPHABET FUN Activity Sheet
- crayons
- sand
- a tray
- a book with the alphabet, such as *City Seen From A to Z* by Rachel Isadora, Mulberry Books: New York, 1992, or *Alphabet Bandits: An ABC Book* by Marcia Leonard, Troll Associates: Mahwah, NJ, 1990

Motivation:
Tell students they will be hearing a story about the alphabet today.

Do Now:
Write in your notebook as many letters of the alphabet as you can remember.

Development:
1. Review the "Do Now." List on the chalkboard the letters of the alphabet the students can name. Then fill in the missing ones.
2. Tell students they will learn a song about the alphabet today. Sing for them the alphabet song, on the Activity Sheet.

3. Pass out the ALPHABET FUN Activity Sheet and crayons. Have the children sing along with you.
4. Next, tell children you will be reading an alphabet book to them. Have them listen for each letter of the alphabet.
5. Read aloud *City Seen From A to Z* or *Alphabet Bandits,* or another alphabet book of your choice.
6. Have the children identify the letters as you go through the book.
7. Next, read the instructions on the Activity Sheet aloud.
8. Have children write each letter of the alphabet.
9. Have student volunteers share their Activity Sheets. Check for accuracy.

Individual Project for the Special Child:

- Give the special child some sand and a tray. Have the child trace the letters of the alphabet in the sand, then have him or her read the letters back to you.

Summary:

1. Can you read me the letters of the alphabet?
2. Can you sing the alphabet song?
3. Can you write the letters of the alphabet?

Summary for the Special Child:

1. Can you show me the letters you traced in the sand?
2. Can you read to me the letters you traced in the sand?

Homework:

Pick five letters of the alphabet and list or draw things at home that start with those letters.

Name _____

Activity 5
ALPHABET FUN

ABCDEFG, HIJKLMNOP, QRSTUV, WXY and Z. Now I know my ABC's. Next time, won't you sing with me?

Each of the pictures below starts with a different letter of the alphabet. List the letter below each picture:

_____   _____   _____   _____   _____

_____   _____   _____   _____   _____

_____   _____   _____   _____   _____

Activity 5
ALPHABET FUN, *continued*

_____ _____ _____ _____

_____ _____ _____ _____

_____ _____ _____

Activity 6
A FAMILY OF WORDS

Aim:
Can we create a word family from the words in a story?

Performance Objectives—Students will be able to:
- recognize rhyming words.
- create a word family from the words in a story.
- decode simple consonant-vowel-consonant words in a story.

Performance Objectives for the Special Child:
- identify the consonants at the beginning of a word in a word family
- find those consonants in other words from the story

Materials Needed:
- WORD FAMILIES Activity Sheet
- crayons
- *Horton Hatches the Egg* by Dr. Seuss, Random House: New York, 1940, or another Dr. Seuss book

Motivation:
Tell children they will be making their own word families today.

Do Now:
List or draw any rhyming words you can think of in your notebook.

Development:
1. Discuss what a rhyming word is—the like sounds at the ends of words.
2. Review the "Do Now." List any rhyming words the children come up with on the chalkboard.
3. Tell children that they will be hearing a story with rhyming words. Tell them that these rhyming words can be grouped into "word families." These word families can be easily read by just learning the sound of the first letter.

4. Ask children to listen for word families in the story. Tell them to raise their hands as they hear the word families. As you read and the children identify the word families, list them on the board.

5. Read *Horton Hatches the Egg*. List the word families on the board as children identify them.

6. Have the class read the word families aloud with you following the story.

7. Pass out the WORD FAMILIES Activity Sheet and crayons.

8. Read the directions aloud to the students. Have them match up the word families. Then have them add appropriate words to the families or make new families.

9. After students are finished, ask them to come to the front and share their Activity Sheets with the class. Have them take turns reading the word families aloud. Check for accuracy.

Individual Project for the Special Child:

- Give the special child the book you just read. Ask him or her to look through the book to identify some of the word families listed on the chalkboard. Ask the child to read the first letter of each word and find another word in the story that starts with that letter.

Summary:

1. What are words like *cat* and *hat* called?

2. Can you name some of the word families from your WORD FAMILIES Activity Sheet?

3. Can you read some of the words from your WORD FAMILIES Activity Sheet?

Summary for the Special Child:

1. Can you read the first letters of the words you found from the story?

2. Can you read the words you found in the story that begin with the same letter?

Homework:

Think of a word family. Make a list of words that belong in your word family.

Name _____

Activity 6

WORD FAMILIES

Look at the words below. Draw a line in the same color connecting those words that belong in the same word family:

sleet

hat

tree

fleet

cat

bee

feet

mat

glee

bat

see

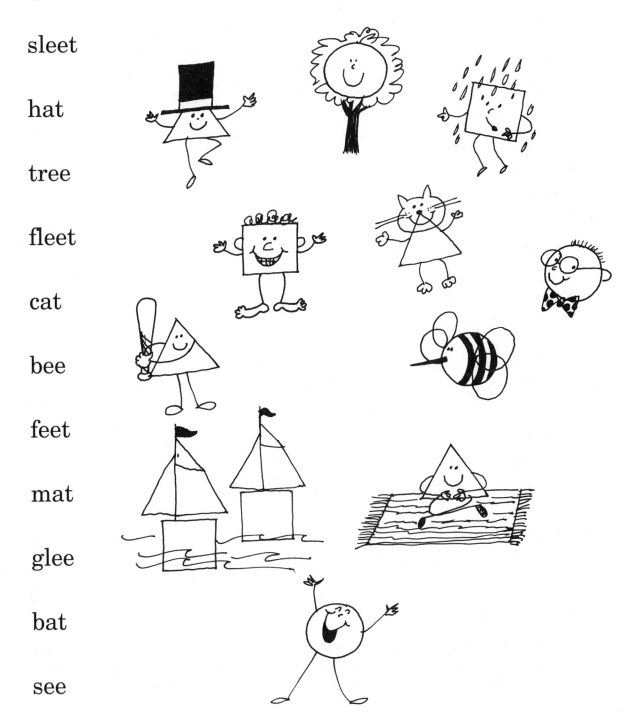

95

Activity 7

DAY AND NIGHT IN POETRY

Aim:

Can we learn about the pattern of the day from a story?

Performance Objectives—Students will be able to:

- recognize that there are different parts to the day—morning, afternoon, and evening.
- understand that each part of the day can be enjoyed for its uniqueness.
- develop skills of comparison.

Performance Objectives for the Special Child:

- work cooperatively with a group
- distinguish how the time of day affects his or her activities

Materials Needed:

- TIME OF DAY Activity Sheet
- crayons
- book to read aloud to the class that shows the pattern of a day, for example, *Big Red Barn* by Margaret Wise Brown, Harper & Row: New York, 1989, or *Coconut Kind of Day: Island Poems*, by Lynn Joseph, Lothrop, Lee & Shepard: New York, 1990

Motivation:

Tell students they will hear poems today about the day.

Do Now:

Write a list of activities that you do at different points in the day or draw pictures about it in your notebook.

Development:

1. Read the selection aloud to the class. In *Big Red Barn*, the rhymed text tells about the different animals that live in the big red barn by night and play in the great green field all day. The story begins as the sun rises and ends when darkness falls over the barnyard.

2. In *Coconut Kind of Day*, the poem "Morning Songs" is contrasted with "Night Songs," in describing life in the Caribbean.

3. Compare and contrast night and day in the selections read. Make columns on the board and list details from the story about each time of day.

4. Review the "Do Now." Write the activities of the children under the "day" and "night" columns.

5. Compare and contrast activities in the day and night. Discuss how the time of day affects the activities we do.

6. Discuss the characteristics of the different times of day with the class: day—sunlight; night—darkness, and so on. Share illustrations from the poems with the class.

7. Pass out the TIME OF DAY Activity Sheets and crayons. Read the directions aloud to the class.

8. Have the class draw a line between the activity and the time of day. Then color in the sheet.

9. Ask student volunteers to share their Activity Sheets. Check for accuracy.

Individual Project for the Special Child:

- Form a group with the special child and two or three other children. Have the group discuss different activities they engage in at different times of the day and why they do each activity at that time.

Summary:

1. Can you tell me what the different times of day are?
2. Can you tell me what those times of day are like?
3. How are they different?
4. How are they similar?

Summary for the Special Child:

1. Can you show me the children you worked with?
2. Can the group report to the class on the activities you discussed?

Homework:

Write or draw a log of the family's activities from morning until night.

Activity 7

TIME OF DAY

Below are pictures of things we do at different times during the day. Draw a line between the picture and the sentence that describes it. Then color in the pictures. Then write "morning," "afternoon," or "night" under the picture.

Reading a story before bed.

Eating a snack.

Getting dressed for school.

Getting on the bus for school.

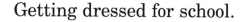

Activity 8
THIRTEEN MOONS

Aim:

Can we learn about the calendar from a story?

Performance Objectives—Students will be able to:

- learn about the twelve months of the year.
- name the twelve months of the year.
- make a picture to go with each month of the year.

Performance Objectives for the Special Child:

- create a word family from *moon*
- create picture cards to go with each word in the family

Materials Needed:

- STORY IN MONTHS Activity Sheet
- crayons
- 3" × 5" index cards
- *Thirteen Moons on a Turtle's Back* by Joseph Bruchac and Jonathan London, Philomel Books: New York, 1992, *A New Coat for Anna* by Harriet Ziefert, Alfred A. Knopf: New York, 1986, or another book that shows the cycle of the year.

Motivation:

Tell children they will be hearing a story today that will tell them about the months of the year.

Do Now:

List in your notebook as many months of the year as you can name.

Development:

1. Review the "Do Now." List on the chalkboard as many months as the children name. Make twelve columns.
2. Fill in the remaining months. Talk about what kind of weather you might be having during each month.

3. Tell students they will be reading a story that will show them the changes that occur during the year.

4. Read aloud *Thirteen Moons a on Turtle's Back* or *A New Coat for Anna*.

5. As you read each Native American legend about the moon in *Thirteen Moons*, list it under the month the children thinks it falls under. Explain that there are thirteen moons because a moon's cycle occurs within a little less than one month. As you read *A New Coat for Anna*, place each part of the year's production of the coat under one month.

6. Discuss the book and be sure to share the illustrations as you read aloud. Have the children note any seasonal changes in the illustrations.

7. Pass out the STORY IN MONTHS Activity Sheet and the crayons.

8. Read the directions aloud. Have children draw a picture for each of the twelve months in the square labeled for that month.

9. Have student volunteers share their pictures with the class. Check to make sure the drawings are appropriate.

10. Make a bulletin board entitled "A Story in Months." Put the book jacket from the book you read in the center. Hang the children's illustrated Activity Sheets on the bulletin board.

Individual Project for the Special Child:

• Give the special child 3″ x 5″ index cards. Have him or her create a word family from *moon*, putting each word on an index card. A word family for *moon* could include a phonogram like *spoon*, or a rhyming word like *June*. Then have the special child make a picture on the reverse side to illustrate the word.

Summary:

1. What are the twelve months of the year?

2. Can you tell me about each month?

3. Can you show me the pictures that go with the twelve months of the year?

Summary for the Special Child:

1. Can you show me the index cards with your word family for *moon*?

2. Can you now show me the pictures that go with each?

Homework:

Think about how the story we read in class today shows respect for the earth. Write or draw a picture about it.

Name _____

Activity 8
STORY IN MONTHS

Draw a picture under each month that shows what is happening at that time of year.

January	February	March	April

May	June	July	August

September	October	November	December

Activity 9
DRAMATIZATION OF A STORY

Aim:

Can we act out a story?

Performance Objectives—Students will be able to:

- recognize rhyme in a story.
- identify characters in a story.
- act out a part from a rhyming story.

Performance Objectives for the Special Child:

- create a story
- develop appreciation for the performance of others

Materials Needed:

- DRAMA Activity Sheet
- crayons
- clothing and hats for costumes (ask parents to send in old clothes)
- read-aloud books in rhyme, for example, *The Sneetches* by Dr. Seuss, Random House: New York, 1961, or *The Just Right Mother Goose* by Arnold Lobel, Random House: New York, 1989

Motivation:

Tell children they will be acting out a story today.

Do Now:

Write or draw in your notebook a story you remember that has rhyme.

Development:

1. Review the "Do Now." Discuss with students that a rhyme is something that has similar sounds.
2. Tell students that they will have the opportunity to act out a story today.
3. Read aloud the rhyming story you chose. "Old King Cole" or "Baa, Baa, Black Sheep" from *Mother Goose* is particularly good for this, but any rhyming story will do. Read several to the class.

4. Discuss who the people are in the story. Explain to the class that these are "characters."

5. Divide the class into groups. Pass out the DRAMA Activity Sheet and crayons.

6. Read directions aloud. First have children write or draw from one of the stories you read.

7. Then give a rhyming book to each group and some old clothing and hats.

8. Tell children to choose a rhyme to act out, then to make notes on the DRAMA Activity Sheet.

9. Have children choose the characters they want to be along with costumes from the old clothes.

10. Have each group act out their rhyme while the class acts as an audience.

Individual Project for the Special Child:

- Choose some clothing from the old clothes available. Make up a story about a character who would wear those clothes. Watch the performances of the other groups.

Summary:

1. What is a rhyme?
2. What is a character?
3. Can you show me how you acted out your character?

Summary for the Special Child:

1. Can you show me the story you made up?
2. Can you tell me which stories you liked that the children acted out?

Homework:

Write a description or draw a picture about one of the characters in the rhyming story you heard today.

Activity 9
DRAMA

Listen to the story that's read. Below, draw a picture or write notes that tell about the story:

Now, choose a character to act out. Write or draw your notes below on how you will act it out:

Activity 10
SINGING A SONG

Aim:

Can we learn a song?

Performance Objectives—Students will be able to:

- recognize the story in a song.
- learn about a culture through a song.
- learn a song.

Performance Objectives for the Special Child:

- recall some lines in a song
- recall details in a song

Materials Needed:

- SINGING A SONG Activity Sheet
- crayons
- *When I Was Young in the Mountains*, by Cynthia Rylant, E. P. Dutton: New York, 1987, or some other book about the mountains.

Motivation:

Tell children they will be reading and learning a song today.

Do Now:

List or draw in your notebook any songs you know by heart.

Development:

1. Review the "Do Now." List on the chalkboard the songs the children name.
2. Tell children they will be reading and learning a song today.
3. If the children did not name "She'll Be Comin' Round the Mountain," add it to the list.
4. Read aloud the book you chose like *When I Was Young in the Mountains* to the class.
5. Pass out the SINGING A SONG Activity Sheets and crayons.

6. Have children group into pairs and recite the verses together.

7. Sing the song from the verses on the Activity Sheet with the class.

8. Have the children color in the Activity Sheet.

9. Discuss the song. List any details the children remember from the song on the board. Have them draw lines between the descriptions and the pictures from the song.

10. Discuss with the class what the mountains are like. Name any clues from the book that talk about life in the mountains, such as *When I Was Young in the Mountains*.

11. Have student volunteers share their Activity Sheets with the class.

Individual Project for the Special Child:

- Give the child the SINGING A SONG Activity Sheet to read. Have the child read the Activity Sheet silently to himself or herself.

Summary:

1. Can you tell me about the story in the song we sang?

2. Can you tell me about the place in the song we learned?

3. Can you sing the song we sang in class?

Summary for the Special Child:

1. Can you recall some of the song we learned?

2. Can you tell me some of the things that are happening in the song?

Homework:

Go home and interview people in your family about their favorite songs. Write a story about it or draw a picture.

Activity 10
SINGING A SONG

Comin' Round the Mountain

She'll be comin' round the mountain when she comes.
She'll be comin' round the mountain when she comes.
She'll be comin' round the mountain, she'll be comin' round the mountain,
She'll be comin' round the mountain when she comes.

She'll be ridin' six white horses when she comes,
She'll be ridin' six white horses when she comes,
She'll be ridin' six white horses, she'll be ridin' six white horses,
She'll be ridin' six white horses when she comes.

She'll be wearin' pink pajamas when she comes,
She'll be wearin' pink pajamas when she comes,
She'll be wearin' pink pajamas, she'll be wearin' pink pajamas,
She'll be wearin' pink pajamas when she comes.

Oh, we'll all go out to meet her when she comes.
Oh, we'll all go out to meet her when she comes.
Oh, we'll all go out to meet her, and we'll be glad to see her,
Oh, we'll all go out to meet her when she comes.

Oh, we'll kill the old red rooster when she comes.
Oh, we'll kill the old red rooster when she comes.
Oh, we'll kill the old red rooster, 'cause he don't crow like he useter.
Oh, we'll kill the old red rooster when she comes.

Oh, we'll all have chicken and dumplin's when she comes.
Oh, we'll all have chicken and dumplin's when she comes.
Oh, we'll all have chicken and dumplin's, cause we all have chickens to dump in,
Oh, we'll all have chicken and dumplin's when she comes.

She'll be comin' round the mountain when she comes.
She'll be comin' round the mountain when she comes.
She'll be comin' round the mountain, blowin' steam off like a fountain,
She'll be comin' round the mountain when she comes.

©1997 by The Center for Applied Research in Education

Activity 10
SINGING A SONG

Below are listed some words from the song. Draw a line from the words to the picture it matches and color in the pictures:

six white horses

go out to meet her

old red rooster

chicken and dumplin's

Activity 11
BORDER ORDER

Aim:

Can we recall a story in sequence?

Performance Objectives—Students will be able to:

- compare family members in a story with their own families.
- recall literal details in a story.
- sequence a story.

Performance Objectives for the Special Child:

- compare and sort objects
- label and classify objects

Materials Needed:

- BORDER ORDER Activity Sheet
- jar of coins
- crayons
- safety scissors
- 3" × 5" index cards
- glue
- book about families with sequencing, for example, *A Chair for My Mother* by Vera B. Williams, Mulberry Books: New York, 1988, or *Peter's Chair* by Ezra Jack Keats, Harper & Row: New York, 1967

Motivation:

Tell children they will be reading stories about families today.

Do Now:

Have you or your family ever saved up to buy something? Draw or write about this item.

Development:

1. Review the "Do Now." List on the board the items the children name.

2. Tell children that you will be reading a story about a chair and a family today.

3. Read aloud to the class *A Chair for My Mother* or *Peter's Chair*.

4. Ask the children to identify the family members in the story. Then ask the children if they have the same family members in their families or if they have different family members. For example, in *A Chair for My Mother*, there is a grandmother, a mother, and a daughter. Ask the children if they have a grandmother in their family.

5. Then write 1 to 4 on the chalkboard. Ask children to recall what happened in the story. Then put the details in order.

6. Pass out the BORDER ORDER Activity Sheets, crayons, index cards, glue, and scissors.

7. Read the directions aloud to the children. Ask the children to fill in the story boxes.

8. Ask the children to cut out the story boxes and glue them to the index cards.

9. Then ask the children to place the story boxes in order.

10. Ask student volunteers to share their story cards with the class. Check for accuracy.

Individual Project for the Special Child:

- Ask the special child to take a jar of coins, like the one the family used in *A Chair for My Mother*. Ask the special child to sort the coins in the jar into nickels, dimes, quarters, and pennies. Then ask him or her to label the coins.

Summary:

1. How are the family members in the story like yours?

2. How are they different?

3. Can you tell me some of the things that happened in the story?

4. Can you put those things in order?

Summary for the Special Child:

1. Can you show me the coins that you sorted?

2. Can you tell me what they are called?

Homework:

What is your favorite chair at home? Draw a picture of it or cut a picture out of a magazine that looks like it.

Activity 11

BORDER ORDER

Below are four story boxes. In each one, draw something that happened in the story. Cut out the story boxes and glue them onto index cards. Then put the story boxes in order:

Activity 12
CREATE A BIOGRAPHY

Aim:

Can we create our own biography?

Performance Objectives—Students will be able to:

- identify a biography as a story about someone's life.
- recall details from someone's life in order.
- create a biography.

Performance Objectives for the Special Child:

- identify parts of a book, for example, title, author, and illustrator
- copy title, author, and illustrator

Materials Needed:

- MY BIO Activity Sheet
- crayons
- safety scissors
- stapler
- a biography, such as *Young Frederick Douglass: Fight for Freedom,* by Laurence Santrey, Troll Associates: Mahwah, NJ, 1983

Motivation:

Tell children they will be creating a biography today.

Do Now:

Draw or list in your notebook any famous people you can think of.

Development:

1. Review the "Do Now." List the famous people that the children name on the chalkboard.
2. Discuss with children that a biography is the story of a person's life. An autobiography is a the story of the life of the person writing the story.
3. Read the biography you have chosen, for example, *Young Frederick Douglass.*

4. List the numbers one to five on the board and have students give the sequence of the major events in the story.

5. Pass out the MY BIO Activity Sheets, crayons, and scissors. Tell students they will be creating their own biographies today.

6. Read the directions aloud. Read the sentence in each story box. Tell children to complete the Activity Sheets.

7. Have the children cut out the title page and the five story boxes on the Activity Sheet.

8. Have the children put their story boxes in order.

9. Help the children staple their biographies together.

10. Have student volunteers share their biographies with the class.

Individual Project for the Special Child:

- Give the special child the biography you just read. Have him or her copy in a notebook the title, author, and illustrator of the book.

Summary:

1. What is a biography?
2. Can you tell me what happened in order in the story?
3. Can you show me the biography you made?

Summary for the Special Child:

1. What is the title, author, and illustrator of a book?
2. Can you tell me the title, author, and illustrator of the book we read?

Homework:

Draw a picture or write about the biography we read in class today.

Activity 12
MY BIO

Below are six story squares. Fill them in with pictures, cut them out, and put them in order. Then make a book. <u>Don't forget to put your name on the first page.</u>:

My name is _____ **and this is** **my biography.**	When I was a baby, I looked like this:	Then I got teeth and hair, and looked like this:
Then I learned to walk and talk and looked like this:	Then I had a babysitter. Here I am with a babysitter:	Here I am today in my class:

Activity 13
MAKING POETRY

Aim:

Can we write a poem?

Performance Objectives—Students will be able to:

- identify a poem as a form of writing in verse that expresses imaginative thought.
- write five lines in sequence.
- write a cinquain.

Performance Objectives for the Special Child:

- create a word family from a word in a poem
- write a poem using the word family

Materials Needed:

- MAKING POETRY Activity Sheet
- crayons
- poetry books, for example, *A Little Book of Poems and Prayers* by Joan Walsh Anglund, Simon and Schuster: New York, 1989, *Goodnight Moon* by Margaret Wise Brown, HarperCollins, New York, 1991, or *Rhymes and Stories* by Burton Marks, Troll Books: Mahwah, NJ, 1992

Motivation:

Tell children they will be writing their own poetry today.

Do Now:

List or draw in your notebook some of your favorite things.

Development:

1. Review the "Do Now." List on the chalkboard some of the children's favorite things.
2. Tell the children to think about some of their favorite things as you read a poem.
3. Read a book about a child's favorite things, like *Goodnight Moon*, which tells about a child's favorite nighttime things.

4. Discuss the poem that you read. Define a poem with the class as a form of writing in verse that expresses imaginative thought.

5. Tell children that today they will be writing their own poems about a favorite thing.

6. Tell children they will be writing a special five-line poem called a *cinquain* today.

7. Pass out the MAKING POETRY Activity Sheet and crayons.

8. Read the cinquain on the MAKING POETRY Activity Sheet aloud. Then write it on the chalkboard.

9. Discuss and write the form of the cinquain:

   First line: One-Word Title
   Second Line: Two-Word Description
   Third Line: Three Words of Action
   Fourth Line: Four Words of Feelings
   Fifth Line: One-Word Summary

10. Read the directions aloud from the MAKING POETRY Activity Sheet. Have children write their own cinquains.

11. Have student volunteers share their cinquains with the class.

Individual Project for the Special Child:

- Help the special child choose a word to build a word family with, for example, *moon*. Next, have the special child build a word family. Then have the special child write a poem using the words in the word family.

Summary:

1. What is a poem?
2. Can you write five lines in sequence?
3. May I see the poem you wrote?

Summary for the Special Child:

1. Can you show me the word family you made?
2. Can you share your poem with the class?

Homework:

Write down five pairs of rhyming words, for example, *moon* and *June*.

Name _____

Activity 13
MAKING POETRY

Nighttime
No Light
Pillowfights With Sister
Cuddling My Teddy Bear
Sleepy

Below, write a cinquain about one of your favorite things. Then draw a picture about it.

Line One: One-Word Title _____

Line Two: Two-Word Description _____

Line Three: Three Words of Action _____

Line Four: Four Words of Feelings _____

Line Five: One-Word Summary _____

Draw a picture below to go with your poem.

Activity 14
COUNTRY LIVING

Aim:

Can we read a book about the country?

Performance Objectives—Students will be able to:

- recall literal details from a story.
- learn details about a different culture.
- write or draw a story about their own memories.

Performance Objectives for the Special Child:

- listen attentively to a read-aloud story
- write a postcard to the author, telling her what he or she liked about the story

Materials Needed:

- WHEN I WAS LITTLE Activity Sheet
- crayons
- postcard
- *When I Was Young in the Mountains* by Cynthia Rylant, E.P. Dutton: New York, 1982, *Owl Moon* by Jane Yolen, Philomel Books: New York, 1987, or some other book about a childhood memory in the country

Motivation:

Tell students they will be hearing a story about the country today.

Do Now:

Write or draw a picture about something you did with your family.

Development:

1. Review the "Do Now." Have volunteers share with the class their pictures or stories about a shared family experience.
2. Tell children they will be hearing a story written by an author about her memories from childhood of family life in the country. *When I Was Young in the Mountains* is the author's memory of her life in Appalachia with her grandparents. *Owl Moon* is a description of life in winter on a farm.

3. Read either story aloud to the class. Ask the class to consider if there is anything in the book that reminds the children of an incident that happened to them.

4. When you finish the story, ask students to retell any incidents the author describes about her childhood in Appalachia or winter on the farm. List these on the chalkboard.

5. Pass out the WHEN I WAS LITTLE Activity Sheet and crayons.

6. Read directions aloud. Ask students to draw or write about memories they have of things that happened in their lives with their families. Assist nonwriters in writing their sentences. Review what a sentence is, if necessary.

7. Have student volunteers share their Activity Sheets.

8. Create a bulletin board based on the book you have chosen, *When I Was Young in the Mountains* or *Owl Moon*. Hang the children's WHEN I WAS LITTLE Activity Sheets on the chalkboard, surrounding the title. Hang up the bookjacket on the bulletin board, if available.

Individual Project for the Special Child:

• Place the special child close to you while reading aloud the story. (This is particularly effective with the special child who has trouble focusing.) Give the special child a postcard to the author and ask him or her to write or draw to the author the parts of the book he or she liked. Help the special child address the postcard to the author through the publisher (listed in the front matter of the book).

Summary:

1. Can you recall the animals the main character named in the book we read?

2. Can you identify anything that was different about the life of the main character in the story compared with your own?

3. Can you show me the WHEN I WAS LITTLE Activity Sheet you did about your own memories?

Summary for the Special Child:

1. Did you listen closely to the story I read?

2. Can you show me the postcard you wrote or the picture you drew of what you liked about the story?

Homework:

Go home and ask the adults you live with to give you a memory from their childhoods. Write or draw a description of the memory.

Name _____

Activity 14
WHEN I WAS LITTLE

You have memories, just like the character in the story that was just read. Listed below are some sentence beginnings that say, "When I was little I _____." List memories you have in sentence form below. Then draw a picture to go with the memory:

When I was little I _____.

When I was little I _____.

When I was little I _____.

When I get older, I want to _____.

Activity 15
SAND CASTLES

Aim:
Can we learn about a different place in a story?

Performance Objectives—Students will be able to:
- recall details from a story.
- learn about a different place from a story.
- make a sand castle and the sensory table.

Performance Objectives for the Special Child:
- make the alphabet in the sand
- read back the letters made in the sand

Materials Needed:
- CASTLES IN THE SAND Activity Sheet
- crayons
- container of sand
- container for water
- shallow cardboard boxes
- a book about a place, such as *One Morning in Maine* by Robert McCloskey, Puffin Books: New York, 1976

Motivation:
Tell students they will build their own sand castles today.

Do Now:
Draw or write in your notebook about a place you visited.

Development:
1. Review the "Do Now." Have the children discuss places they have visited.
2. Tell children you will be reading a story about a new place. Read aloud *One Morning in Maine*, or another book about a place.

3. Discuss the book—what happens at the beginning of the story, the middle, and the ending.

4. Discuss the beach scene. Talk about the sand and the water.

5. Pass out CASTLES IN THE SAND Activity Sheet and crayons.

6. Read directions aloud. Have children fill in details from the story.

7. Have volunteers share their details from their Activity Sheets. Check for accuracy.

8. Have the children come over to the sensory table. Put the sand on it. Have children add water for consistency. Have them pour and mix it. Then have them build sand castles.

9. Have children exhibit their sand castles to the class.

Individual Project for the Special Child:

• Fill the bottom of a shallow box with sand. Add a little water for consistency. Have the special child make the alphabet in the sand. Then have him or her read it back to you.

Summary:

1. Can you tell me some of the details that you put on your CASTLES IN THE SAND Activity Sheet?

2. Can you tell me what you learned about Maine (or the place in the story you read)?

3. Can you show me the sand castle you built?

Summary for the Special Child:

1. Can you show me the alphabet you made in the sand?

2. Can you read the letters you made back to me?

Homework:

Go home and ask your parent or guardian about where he or she grew up. Draw a picture about it or write a story.

Name _____

Activity 15
CASTLES IN THE SAND

Below are squares for you to fill in details from the story. Tell what you learned about the new place in the story. Complete the sentences below with writing, or pictures, or both.

The place in the story

was _____

One of the things I learned about it

was _____

Another thing I learned about it

was _____

The thing I liked about it

was _____

Activity 16
DESERT EYE

Aim:

Can we identify cause and effect in a story?

Performance Objectives—Students will be able to:

- understand what the climate is like in the desert.
- identify animals and plants that live in the desert.
- identify cause and effect in a story.

Performance Objectives for the Special Child:

- look independently at pictures in a story
- interpret information from pictures

Materials Needed:

- DESERT LIFE Activity Sheet
- crayons
- a book about the desert, such as *A Day in the Desert* by the first-grade students at Robert Taylor Elementary School in Henderson, Nevada, Willowisp Press: St. Petersburg, FL, 1994

Motivation:

Tell students they will be learning about life in the desert today.

Do Now:

Write or draw in your notebook anything you know about the desert.

Development:

1. Review the "Do Now." List on the board any facts the children can name about the desert.

2. Discuss with the children the climate of the desert—that it is hot in the day and cold at night, and that special creatures, who can take extreme changes in temperature, live in the desert.

3. List on the chalkboard some cause-and-effect questions about the animals and plants that live in the desert, based on what you are about to read. Here are some examples:

   - Why does the cactus do well in the desert?
   - What protects the lizard from the hot sun?
   - Where does the roadrunner get his water?
   - Why does the desert tortoise walk slowly?

4. Read the questions aloud to the children. Tell them you will then read a book aloud that will give them answers to those questions. Have them listen carefully and look at the pictures.

5. Read aloud the book you have chosen on the desert, such as *A Day in the Desert*. Show the illustrations to the children as you go along.

6. Read the cause-and-effect questions from the chalkboard again and have volunteers give the answers.

7. Next, have children name the plants and animals that were named in the book. List them on the chalkboard.

8. Pass out the DESERT LIFE Activity Sheet and crayons.

9. Read the directions aloud. Have the children match the word with the drawing of the plant or animal.

10. After the students finish their Activity Sheets, have volunteers come to the front and share them. Check for accuracy.

Individual Project for the Special Child:

- Give the special child the book you read about the desert. Ask the child to look at the pictures and see if there is any other information he or she can add to the information on the chalkboard about the plants or animals that were found in the pictures.

Summary:

1. What is it like in the desert?
2. Can you name some of the plants and animals that live in the desert?
3. Why does the cactus do well in the desert?
4. What protects the lizard from the hot sun?
5. Why does the desert tortoise walk slowly?

Summary for the Special Child:

1. Can you show me the pictures that you looked at in the book?
2. Can you tell me what additional information you found in those pictures?

Homework:

How do you think life is different where you live from life in the desert? Draw a picture of it or write a story about it.

Activity 16
DESERT LIFE

Below are listed the names of desert animals and plants. There is a drawing of each one as well. Draw a line between the name of the animal or plant and the drawing of it. Then color each one in.

jack rabbit

desert tortoise

cactus

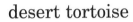

sagebrush

rattlesnake

kangaroo rat

roadrunner

Joshua tree

Activity 17
NUMBERS IN LITERATURE

Aim:

Can you find numbers in literature?

Performance Objectives—Students will be able to:

- recognize that numbers are a part of literature.
- identify numbers in a story.
- sequence events in a story.

Performance Objectives for the Special Child:

- identify what number is central to the story
- make a word family from one of the words in the story

Materials Needed:

- NUMBERS IN LITERATURE Activity Sheet
- crayons
- a folk tale to read aloud with numbers, such as *The Three Billy Goats Gruff*, retold by Robert Bender, Henry Holt and Company: New York, 1973, *Always Room for One More* by Sorche Nic Leodhas, Holt, Rinehart and Winston: New York, 1965, *Seven in One Blow* by Freire Wright, Random House: New York, 1978, or *The Three Little Pigs*, Random House: New York, 1994.

Motivation:

Tell children they will be hearing a story with numbers in it today.

Do Now:

List any stories you can think of with numbers in them (many folk tales have numbers; for example, *The Three Little Pigs*.)

Development:

1. Review the "Do Now." List as many stories with numbers that the children can think of on the chalkboard.

2. Tell children that many nursery rhymes and folk tales have numbers in them. Tell them that today they will be reading a folk tale with numbers in it that they should listen for.

3. Read the folk tale aloud to the class.

4. Discuss the folk tale with the class. In the case of the Scandinavian folk tale *The Three Billy Goats Gruff*, there are different numbers at different points in the story. For example, there are different numbers of goats at different sides of the bridge at different points in the story. Make note of this and illustrate number sentences to go with those points. Ask children to tell *when* the goats were *where* in sequence in the story.

5. In the case of *Always Room for One More*, based on a Scottish song, there are twelve people in the MacLachlan house. Every passing traveler is welcome to stay, until the house bursts at the seams and everyone tumbles out. Undaunted, the MacLachlan's rebuild the house twice as large. Discuss the concept of "twice as much" and "a dozen" and illustrate in number sentences on the chalkboard. Ask children to sequence the twelve people in the house and then the number as each traveler comes to stay in sequence.

6. Pass out the NUMBERS IN LITERATURE Activity Sheet and crayons.

7. Read the directions aloud. Have the children draw lines between the sentence and the picture.

8. Then ask children to draw an illustration from a folk tale with a number on their Activity Sheets.

9. Ask student volunteers to come to the front and share their Activity Sheets. Check for accuracy.

10. Collect the Activity Sheets and put them in a folder in the Mathematics Center, with some blanks for future use.

Individual Project for the Special Child:

• Ask the special child to identify the number central to the story you have read— *Three Billy Goats Gruff* (three) or *Always Room for One More* (twelve). Then have them create a word family from one of the words in the story, for example, *goat, moat, float, oat, throat.*

Summary:

1. Where do we often find numbers?

2. Can you tell me what numbers we found in the story we read?

3. Can you tell me in what order the numbers came up in the story?

Summary for the Special Child:

1. What was the important number in the story we read?
2. Show me the word family you made from a word in the story.

Homework:

Draw a picture, or make a story with one more character than the story we read, for example, Four Billy Goats Gruff.

Activity 17

NUMBERS IN LITERATURE

Below are several pictures and several sentences. Draw a line between the sentence and the matching picture, then color in the pictures. Last, on the back of this page draw a picture of a story with numbers that you remember. Label it.

<u>The Three Billy Goats Gruff</u>

<u>Always Room for One More</u>

<u>Seven in One Blow</u>

<u>The Three Little Pigs</u>

SECTION 3

Mathematics

MATHEMATICS

The interactive lessons and corresponding Activity Sheets in Section 3 teach basic mathematics to the most reluctant special child.

Both individual skills and cooperative learning techniques are encouraged, with emphasis on hands-on manipulatives—a must for the special child. The manipulatives used in the activities are not expensive manufactured products, difficult enough to get in these days of shrinking budgets, but easily found everyday items, such as paper clips, buttons, crepe paper, oaktag, and screws.

Important concepts and computation methods basic to the primary curriculum are covered, including shapes, patterns, sets, time and calendar concepts, money, measurement, graphing, numeration, addition, and problem solving.

Activity 1
CENTER CHARTS

Aim:

How do we decide who uses a learning center?

Performance Objectives—Students will be able to:

- use counting in daily activities.
- develop vocabulary related to mathematics, for example, more than, less than, first, last.
- identify sets.

Performance Objectives for the Special Child:

- make an independent choice
- read the centers from the board

Materials Needed:

- CENTER CHART Activity Sheet
- index cards
- oaktag strips
- markers
- safety scissors
- pictures to go with each learning center
- tape

Motivation:

Tell students they will be learning how to choose their own learning centers today. (This is an excellent activity for the beginning of the year.)

Do Now:

List or draw in your notebooks the types of learning centers you would like to participate in.

Development:

1. Review the "Do Now." List on the board the types of learning centers the children would like to have.

2. Guide them in making selections. Eliminate impractical ones and suggest omitted ones, like art, mathematics, housekeeping, and so on.

3. Suggest that the number of children should be limited. Decide with the class how many students that should be at one time.

4. Next, get a chart for each center. Write the name of each center in big letters at the top. Choose a picture to go with the center, for example, a palette and brushes for art, or have the children draw a picture, so the centers are recognizable for nonreaders.

5. Next, attach oaktag strips with tape to each center corresponding to the number of children, say five, that the class has decided should be maximum at one time in a center. Make sure the strips are large enough to hold the index cards.

6. Pass out one index card and markers for each child. Have the children print their names on the cards. Help nonwriters print theirs.

7. Next, demonstrate how to place a name card in a center space. Then have a student volunteer demonstrate it.

8. Pass out CENTER CHART Activity Sheets. Have children print their names on the center charts.

9. Tell children that when they choose a center to use, they must place the name card in the oaktag strip. If there are no spaces, they must choose another center.

10. Next, children must fill in on their CENTER CHART Activity Sheets what center they used and the date they used it on.

11. Have children store their name cards and CENTER CHART Activity Sheets in their desks when centers are not in use.

Individual Project for the Special Child:

- Have the special child choose a center to work at. Have the child place his or her index card in the center chart and note the choice on the CENTER CHART Activity Sheet. Have him or her read aloud every choice on the board.

Summary:

1. How many children are there in the art center (or any other center in use)?
2. Are there more children in the art center than before or fewer children?
3. How many learning centers are there in the class?

Summary for the Special Child:

1. What center would you like to use today?
2. Can you read to me the names of the centers from the board?

Homework:

Draw or list all the rooms in your home. Make a picture for each room and add up the number.

Name _____

Activity 1
CENTER CHART

Draw or write the center that you used and the date that you used it.

CENTER	DATE USED

Activity 2
TIMELY CLOCKS

Aim:

What is a clock?

Performance Objectives—Students will be able to:

- recognize that a clock can help us tell time.
- tell time by the hour.
- identify the hour as the number preceding the colon on a digital clock.

Performance Objectives for the Special Child:

- distinguish between a digital clock and a clock with hands
- tell time on a digital clock

Materials Needed:

- HOURS Activity Sheets
- chalk
- white cardboard
- markers
- crepe paper
- digital clock
- clock with hands

Motivation:

Tell students they will be making a human clock today.

Do Now:

Write in your notebook the times you get up, leave for school, get to school, leave school, eat dinner, and go to bed.

Development:

1. Display the clocks for the class. Recite the nursery rhyme "Hickory, Dickory, Dock." When the clock strikes one, demonstrate one o'clock on the display clocks.

2. Review the "Do Now." As children tell you what time they do things, display the times on the clock.

3. Explain that on the hour on the clock with hands, the small hand shows the hour, while the large hand is on 12. On the digital clock, explain that the hour is shown before the colon and the numbers behind the colon are 00.

4. Tell students today they will be going outside to the yard to make a human clock.

5. Take the class out to the yard. Draw a large circle on the ground. Ask for twelve student volunteers. Give each a piece of white cardboard numbered from 1 to 12.

6. Ask for two more student volunteers. Give each a different-color stream of crepe paper, one slightly longer than the other.

7. Recite "Hickory, Dickory, Dock." Have the children with the numbers get around the circle in the right places. Ask the children with the crepe paper to display one o'clock by putting the longer piece on the 12 and the shorter piece on the one.

8. Have student volunteers, or small groups, create new verses to "Hickory, Dickory, Dock" with new times, for example:

> Hickory, Dickory, Dock.
> The mouse ran up the clock.
> The clock struck four.
> The mouse ran out the door.
> Hickory, Dickory, Dock.

9. As someone finishes a new verse, have the human clock display the time.

10. Return to the classroom. Pass out the HOURS Activity Sheets and markers.

11. Ask students to complete the Activity Sheets. Read through the instructions aloud together.

12. After students complete the Activity Sheets, have volunteers show the right answers on the display clocks in the front of the room.

Individual Project for the Special Child:

- Ask the special child to draw a picture of a digital clock. Then have him or her draw the same time on a clock with hands. Have the child write the time on both clocks on the bottom of the HOURS Activity Sheet.

Summary:

1. What helps us to tell time?

2. What time is it when the little hand is on the 1 and the big hand on the 12 (display on a clock)?

3. Where is the hour number displayed on a digital clock?

Summary for the Special Child:

1. Which is a digital clock and which is a clock with hands? (Display both and have the special child show you which is which.)
2. Can you tell me what time it is on the digital clock?

Homework:

Record what time you eat dinner and what time you go to bed by drawing two clock faces and the times indicated.

Activity 2

HOURS

Match the clocks by drawing a line from the clock with hands to the digital clock that displays the same time.

1.

2.

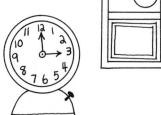

3.

4.

5.

Activity 3
WHAT DAY IS IT?

Aim:

What day is it?

Performance Objectives—Students will be able to:

- recognize the days of the week.
- identify the months of the year.
- recognize that there are approximately thirty days in a month.

Performance Objectives for the Special Child:

- identify the month his or her birthday falls in
- identify the day his or her birthday falls on

Materials Needed:

- MY MONTHLY CALENDAR Activity Sheets
- three large blank monthly calendars (You can use MY MONTHLY CALENDAR Activity Sheet if you don't have three blank calendars available.)
- three sets of index cards, numbered 1 to 31, the same size as the squares for the days on the calendar
- tape
- markers

Motivation:

Tell students they will be playing a calendar game today.

Do Now:

List in your notebooks any significant dates you can think of.

Development:

1. Review the "Do Now." List the dates on the chalkboard that the children give you. Put the months in order.
2. Name one significant date for each month and list the twelve months on the board in sequence.

3. Now name the seven days in the week and list them in order.

4. Explain that each month has approximately thirty days—although some have more and some have less.

5. Count from 1 to 31 with the children. Ask different children what comes before 15 or what comes after 23 to test if they understand the sequencing.

6. When you think the class is ready, divide them into three groups.

7. Give each group a set of index cards from 1 to 31. Have each child in the group take random numbers. Give each group tape.

8. Tape the three monthly calendars to the front of the room. Line up each group toward the back with their numbers.

9. Have the children take turns taping their numbers in sequence to the appropriate squares on their calendar.

10. The first team to have all the numbers on the calendar filled wins.

11. Pass out MY MONTHLY CALENDAR Activity Sheets. Read the instructions. Pass out the markers. Have students list all the numbers in the present month in the calendar, label the month, and list any important dates—for example, a birthday—that they can think of.

12. Have volunteers share their calendars and important dates with the class.

Individual Project for the Special Child:

- Have the special child draw himself or herself at a party and have the child label the month and date his or her birthday falls on.

Summary:

1. What are the days of the week?

2. What are the months of the year?

3. Approximately how many days are there in a month?

Summary for the Special Child:

1. What month is your birthday in?

2. What day is your birthday on?

Homework:

Record all of your family's birthdays.

Name _____

MY MONTHLY CALENDAR

Label the month we are in. Put the correct number in each box. Note any special days in the month for you with notes or drawings.

Month: _____

Sunday	Monday	Tuesday	Wednesday	Thursday	Friday	Saturday

Activity 4
GRAPHS

Aim:
What is a graph?

Performance Objectives—Students will be able to:
- recognize a graph.
- read a graph and understand the information presented.
- plot a simple graph.

Performance Objectives for the Special Child:
- understand that a graph provides valuable information
- compare information on a graph

Materials Needed:
- GRAPHIC GRAPH Activity Sheet—two copies for each child
- markers
- blue and red chalk
- two blank graphs (You can Xerox the graph on the Activity Sheet.)

Motivation:
Tell students they will be playing a team game with a graph today.

Do Now:
Write or draw in your notebook what you think a graph can be used for.

Development:
1. Display a blank copy of a graph. Elicit information from the class, such as their favorite colors, and plot it on the graph.
2. Ask students what they think graphs are used for. List the uses on the board.
3. Explain how graphs are set up. Show the coordinates of your graph to students. Explain that a graph is a drawing that shows a relationship between changing things.

4. Pass out the GRAPHIC GRAPH Activity Sheets and markers. Tell students they will be doing a graph of:

   - the number of students in the class.
   - the number of girls in the class.
   - the number of boys in the class.

5. Draw a graph on the chalkboard. List the numbers on one side and students—boys and girls—on the other.

6. Ask volunteers to come up and plot the coordinates on the graph.

7. Now ask students to plot another number of their choice on the graph, for example, the number of classes in the school or the number of students in the next grade.

8. Next, display a blank grid on the chalkboard. Write Red Team on the left side, Blue Team on the bottom, and Finish on top and on the right side. Write numbers from 0 to 6 on the left and bottom.

9. Divide the class into two teams. Give the red team a red chalk and the blue team a blue chalk. Have the lead child in the Red Team call a coordinate, for example, 0,3. Have the next child plot it with chalk on the graph. Repeat the process with the Blue Team.

10. Explain to the children that the object is to get to Finish, so the team should choose their coordinates to go in that direction. The first team to reach Finish wins.

Individual Project for the Special Child:

- Give the special child the graph you used at the beginning of the lesson. Ask the child to explain to you the information on the graph. Ask the child to compare the information on the graph with the information she or he just put on the GRAPHIC GRAPH Activity Sheet. How are they different? How are they similar?

Summary:

1. What is a graph?
2. Can you plot this graph? (Give students a blank graph and coordinates to graph.)
3. Can you read back the information from the graph you just plotted?

Summary for the Special Child:

1. What does a graph provide you with?
2. Look at these two charts. How are they different? How are they similar?

Homework:

Send the second GRAPHIC GRAPH Activity Sheet home for students to plot the birthdays of everyone in their household.

Name _____

Activity 4
GRAPHIC GRAPH

Activity 5
MEASURE FOR MEASURE

Aim:
What are some of the ways to measure?

Performance Objectives—Students will be able to:
- recognize that there are different units of measurement.
- identify such units of measuring length and width as meters and centimeters and inches and yards.
- measure some objects with some nonstandard units of measurement.

Performance Objectives for the Special Child:
- identify that a ruler can be used to measure length and width
- distinguish between a metric ruler and an inch ruler

Materials Needed:
- MEASURE FOR MEASURE Activity Sheet
- paper clips
- straws cut into thirds
- a 12-inch ruler
- a metric ruler
- roll of yarn cut into equal lengths
- safety scissors
- chalk

Motivation:
Tell students they will be measuring everyday things today.

Do Now:
Draw or list in your notebook anything you would like to measure.

Development:
1. Review the "Do Now." List on the board the things the children would like to measure.

2. Elicit from the class how they think you would measure things. Tell them that any common object can be a unit of measurement.

3. Display the metric ruler and 12-inch ruler. Tell students they are different units of measurement that are commonly used to measure width and length. Explain that some of these measurements are centimeters, meters, inches, and yards,

4. Choose something from the children's list to measure, for example, a pencil. Mark the chalkboard "Units of Measurement." Make five columns.

5. Next have a volunteer measure the pencil with the 12-inch ruler. Mark it on the chalkboard in the first column.

6. Next, have a volunteer measure the pencil with the metric ruler. Mark this in the second column.

7. Have a volunteer measure the pencil in paper clips. Mark it in the third column.

8. Have a volunteer measure the pencil in straw lengths. Mark it in the fourth column.

9. Have a volunteer measure the pencil in yarn lengths. Enter this in the fifth column.

10. Tell students they will be doing their own measuring today. Pass out the MEASURE FOR MEASURE Activity Sheets.

11. Divide the class into three groups. Give one group the paper clips, one group the yarn lengths, and the third group the straw lengths.

12. Have each group choose five objects to measure. Make some suggestions, such as fingers, desktops, favorite books, and so forth.

13. Have each group measure the objects with their unit of measurement and note it on the Activity Sheets.

14. After the class finishes, have them switch units of measurement and remeasure the same five objects. Note it on the Activity Sheets.

15. After the class finishes the second measurement, have them switch a third time and note the measurements on their Activity Sheets.

16. After all the students have had the opportunity to do the three measurements of the same objects, have them compare to see if they got similar results.

Individual Project for the Special Child:

• Give the special child the 12-inch ruler and the metric ruler. Ask him or her to choose one object and measure it with both rulers. Then ask the special child to draw the object and label the two measurements.

Summary:

1. Are there different units of measurement?

2. What are some of the standard units of measurement?

3. What are some of the ways you could measure something if you didn't have a ruler?

Summary for the Special Child:

1. What is a ruler used for?

2. Look at these two rulers. Can you tell me which is the metric and which measures inches?

Homework:

Find some objects at home to measure and measure them with nonstandard units of measurement.

Name _____

Activity 5
MEASURE FOR MEASURE

Find five objects to measure. Then use three nonstandard units of measurement to measure each:

Yarn	Paper Clips	Straws
1.		
2.		
3.		
4.		
5.		

Draw the objects here that you measured:

Activity 6
MEASURING WITH A RULER

Aim:

How do we measure with a ruler?

Performance Objectives—Students will be able to:

- recognize that length and width can be measured with a ruler.
- identify inches and yards, and centimeters and meters, as standard units of measurement for length and width.
- identify the relationship between inches and centimeters, and feet and meters.

Performance Objectives for the Special Child:

- measure one object in both centimeters and inches
- compare different units of measurement

Materials Needed:

- MEASURING WITH A RULER Activity Sheet
- centimeter ruler
- inch ruler
- yardstick
- metric ruler
- pencil
- book
- sheet of paper

Motivation:

Tell students they will be measuring common objects with rulers today.

Do Now:

Look around and see how many things around you look the same length. List or draw them in your notebook.

Development:

1. Review the "Do Now." List on the chalkboard any objects students think are the same size.

2. Display the metric ruler and the inch ruler. Explain that one is a centimeter ruler and one is an inch ruler and both are standard units of measurement for length and width.

3. Write the following measurements on the board:

    1 inch = 2.54 centimeters

    12 inches = 1 foot

    1 foot = .305 meter

    100 cm = 1 meter

4. Now take some of the objects you want to measure, such as the pencil, book, and sheet of paper, and measure them with the inch ruler. Write the object and the measurement on the board.

5. Make a second column. Measure the same objects with the metric ruler and list it next to the object in the second column.

6. Pass out the MEASURING WITH A RULER Activity Sheets and the metric and inch rulers in pairs.

7. Ask students to pick two objects they thought were the same length, then measure them both in meters and inches and list them on their Activity Sheets. Elicit from the class whether they were the same length or not.

8. Now ask students to choose three more objects, measure them in meters and inches, and note this on their Activity Sheets.

9. Have students share what they chose to measure. Compare metric lengths and inches.

10. Put the Activity Sheets in a folder marked "Mathematics Resource Center" and store them in the Mathematics Learning Center.

Individual Project for the Special Child:

- Ask the special child to choose an object to measure with both a centimeter and inch ruler. Have him or her draw the object to scale and label the metric and inch measurement.

Summary:

1. How do you measure length and width?

2. What are the standard units of measurement for length and width?

3. Can you take this object (show them a pencil) and estimate its length in inches and meters?

Summary for the Special Child:

1. (Give the special child a pencil and a centimeter and inch ruler.) Can you measure the pencil with both rulers?

2. (Then give him or her a yardstick and a metric ruler.) Can you measure the length of yarn with the length of the pencil?

Homework:

Find an object that is approximately six inches (or .15 meters) at home and bring it to school to share.

Activity 6

MEASURING WITH A RULER

The following are some measurements
for length and width:

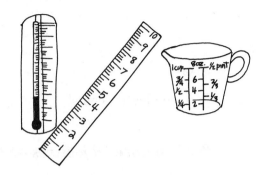

1 inch = 2.45 centimeters

12 inches = 1 foot

1 foot = .305 meters

100 centimeters = 1 meter

Choose five objects and measure them in inches and centimeters.

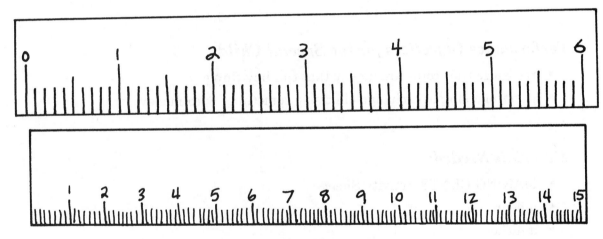

	Column 1: Inches	Column 2: Meters
Object 1		
Object 2		
Object 3		
Object 4		
Object 5		

Activity 7
MAKING CENTS

Aim:

Can we identify coins?

Performance Objectives—Students will be able to:

- identify a penny, nickel, dime, and quarter.
- understand that a penny is one cent, a nickel is five cents, a dime is ten cents, and a quarter is twenty-five cents.
- associate the written word with the coin it matches.

Performance Objectives for the Special Child:

- recognize that coins are money that can buy things
- perform a simple exchange of buying something with money

Materials Needed:

- MAKING CENTS Activity Sheet
- a penny
- a nickel
- a dime
- a quarter
- cutouts of the four coins from the MAKING CENTS Activity Sheet
- blank sentence strips on which you write the name of each coin two times
- markers

Motivation:

Tell students they will be playing a game about coins today.

Do Now:

Make a list or draw what you would like to buy with coins.

Development:

1. Display the four coins. Ask students if they know what the coins are called.

2. Show students the coins and then write their names on the board.

3. Ask students if they know what the coins are worth. Ask volunteers to name the coin value and write it next to the name on the board.

4. Review the "Do Now." Write the things students would like to buy on the board, for example, candy.

5. Next, ask volunteers to identify how much each item costs. Write the amount on the board next to the item.

6. Ask volunteers to tell you which coins would be needed to buy each item. Write the coins on the board.

7. Next, show two sets of coins from the MAKING CENTS Activity Sheet. Compare each to its actual coin for the class.

8. Pass out the MAKING CENTS Activity Sheets. Have students mark in the columns how much each coin is worth and have them draw what the coin looks like.

9. Ask volunteers to come to the front and share their MAKING CENTS Activity Sheets.

10. Tell students they will be playing a coin game.

11. Draw two circles on the board. Put a set of sentence strips with the coin names below each circle.

12. Divide the class into two teams. Show the class a coin. A team member from each team then must come to the front of the room and put the correct coin name in the circle. A wrong answer gets one point for the team.

13. The team with the fewest points wins.

Individual Project for the Special Child:

- Ask the special child to draw something he or she would like to buy. Then ask the child to draw the money he or she thinks it would take to buy it.

- Ask another child to join the special child and role-play "shopkeeper." Have the special child buy a pencil from the shopkeeper with the correct amount of coins.

Summary:

1. What are these coins called? (Show the four coins.)

2. What are these coins worth? (Show the four coins.)

3. What are the words that go with the coins? (Show the four coins and the four sentence strip words.)

Summary for the Special Child:

1. Show the child a pencil. How would you buy a pencil? Can you show me how many coins it would take to buy a thirty-five-cent pencil? (Show coins and have the special child show you which make thirty-five cents.)

2. Can you be a shopkeeper and sell a student a pencil? How many coins do you need to collect?

Homework:

Imagine you want to buy a pen for thirty cents, a comb for fifteen cents, and a candy for five cents. Draw or write in your notebook which coins you would need to make the purchases.

Name _____

Activity 7
MAKING CENTS

In the first column, marked Cent Value, put in the number value of the coin. In the second column, marked Coin, draw what the coin looks like:

	Cent Value	**Coin**
penny		
nickel		
dime		
quarter		

Activity 8
CHANGING DOLLARS

Aim:

Can we identify dollars?

Performance Objectives—Students will be able to:

- identify a one-dollar, five-dollar, ten-dollar, and twenty-dollar bill.
- identify the value of each dollar bill.
- recognize that dollars and coins are the basic unit of measurement of our currency.

Performance Objectives for the Special Child:

- recognize the dollar as a basic unit of currency that can buy things
- associate the written amount with the actual dollar currency

Materials Needed:

- CHANGING DOLLARS Activity Sheet
- bucket of dollar bills copied from the DOLLAR BILLS Activity Sheet
- magazines
- index cards
- glue
- safety scissors
- genuine dollar bills in one, five, ten, and twenty denominations.

Motivation:

Tell students they will be attending an auction in class today.

Do Now:

If you were to attend an auction, what kinds of things do you think you would like to buy? Draw or list them in your notebook.

Development:

1. Elicit from the class what they think an auction is. Explain that an auction is a place where things are sold to the person who offers or bids the most money. Tell the class they will hold an in-house auction.

2. Review the "Do Now." Write on the chalkboard the things students would like to buy at an auction.

3. Pass out the index cards, magazines, safety scissors, and glue. Tell students to find pictures of the things they would like to buy at an auction in the magazines, or come up with some new objects. Have them glue down the pictures on the index cards after cutting them out of the magazines. Collect the cards.

4. Display the dollar bills for students. Write the names down on the board. Write the number value of each next to the name. Explain that together with coins, these dollars make up the basis of the American monetary system and are used to purchase things.

5. Display the money copied from the Activity Sheet to the class. Display the copied money next to the appropriate real dollar so the children can associate them.

6. Divide the play money equally among the class. Have a student volunteer be auctioneer. He or she will pick an index card with an auction item and start the auction. Children will take their play money and bid on the item. The auctioneer will give the card to the highest bidder and give the child the card after he or she has collected the play money. Children should bid only in dollar denominations.

7. Rotate the auctioneer until all the index card items have been sold.

8. Pass out the CHANGING DOLLARS Activity Sheets. Explain that for each item, students must draw in the appropriate dollar bill to make the purchase.

9. Have volunteers share their Activity Sheets with the class at the end.

Individual Project for the Special Child:

- Have the special child choose one auction item from the index cards before the auction begins. Have the child draw the item on the sheet and what she or he thinks the item will go for in dollar amount. Put the item into the auction and have the child compare the sale price with the price he or she put down on the sheet. Have the child show the dollar amount in dollars.

Summary:

1. (Display a one-, five-, ten-, and twenty-dollar bill.) Can you identify these?

2. How much is each dollar bill worth?

3. What is the basis for American currency?

Summary for the Special Child:

1. (Hold up one of the index card auction items.) Can you tell me what you would use to buy this?

2. Can you write the amount you think the item is worth and show me that amount in dollars?

Homework:

Give yourself a budget of five dollars. Take one of the auction items and buy it for your home. Draw a picture of the item and how many dollars you think it would cost. Draw the dollar bills on your picture.

Activity 8
CHANGING DOLLARS

Rachel Rhino goes to the furniture store. She must purchase four pieces of furniture at the prices listed. Draw the correct number of dollar bills for each purchase and mark their dollar value:

Draw the dollars needed here:

DOLLAR BILLS

Reproduce these dollar bills and use them for your money activities:

Activity 9
SHOPPING FOR A PARTY

Aim:

How do we shop on a budget?

Performance Objectives—Students will be able to:

- plan a shopping list.
- price the things on a shopping list.
- exchange money.

Performance Objectives for the Special Child:

- understand the relationship between the price of an item and the money value required to buy it
- identify the coin value of one dollar

Materials Needed:

- SHOPPING LIST Activity Sheet
- markers
- supermarket coupons
- a bucket of money with dollars and coins

Motivation:

Ask children if they would like to have a party. Tell students they will be planning the items they will need and shopping at the supermarket today. (This trip may also be used for Activity 10 in Section 5, Social Studies, "My Supermarket," p. 285.)

Do Now:

If you were to plan a party for the class, what would you get for it? Draw or list the things in your notebook.

Development:

1. Tell students the class will be having a Halloween party. Tell students they will be planning the party and making a shopping trip to your local supermarket to buy things for the party. (The party can celebrate any holiday you choose.)
2. Give the class a budget for the party. (You can collect a fee per child or take it from a class fund arranged at the beginning of the year.)

3. Review the "Do Now." List on the board the items students want to get for the party.

4. Pass out the supermarket coupons. See if students can match up the items they chose with the items in the coupons.

5. List the prices next to the items. Estimate a cost for the items the children can't find in the coupons.

6. Add all the items up with the class. See if the items are within the budget you gave the class. Have the class add or eliminate items to fit the budget.

7. Have the class make note of the final party items list.

8. Take the class to the supermarket. Have them go through the list and find the items. Compare the items to the coupons to get discounts. Make any adjustment children want in items—as long as it fits the budget.

9. Bring the items to the checkout. Have the class watch the clerk ring up the items. Have a volunteer give the budgeted money and check the change. Have the class help pack the items.

10. Bring the party items and the class back to the classroom. Pass out the SHOP-PING LIST Activity Sheet and the markers. Tell students that after they finish their Activity Sheets they will have a party.

11. Have students share their Activity Sheets and compare their answers.

12. Have a great class party!

Individual Project for the Special Child:

• Ask the special child to choose one item that is under a dollar he or she would like to buy at the supermarket. Ask the special child to bring a dollar for the trip. Have the special child purchase it and check his or her own change for accuracy.

Summary:

1. What is a shopping list?

2. How would you price things on a shopping list?

3. How would you purchase the items on a shopping list?

Summary for the Special Child:

1. Pretend that you want an item in the supermarket. How would you go about getting it?

2. Can you show me how much change is needed to make up a dollar?

Homework:

Plan a shopping list for a birthday party for someone at home. Try to price or estimate the items and add up how much they would cost.

Name _____

SHOPPING LIST

Rachel Rhino goes to the supermarket. She must get all
the items on the list and she has $10. Help Rachel by
adding up all the items on her list.

Paper Towels	$1.50 ea.		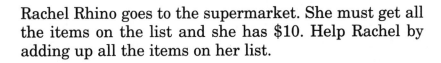
Two Bottles Juice	$1.00 ea.		
One Package Donuts	$1.00 ea.		
One Package Paper Plates	2.00 ea.		
One Package Cups	$1.50 ea.		
One Package raisins	$1.00 ea.		

Total _____   Change left from $10.00 _____

Activity 10
WHAT SHAPE ARE YOU IN?

Aim:

Can we identify shapes?

Performance Objectives—Students will be able to:

- recognize a circle, square, rectangle, and triangle.
- sort and classify shapes.
- recognize that objects have attributes.

Performance Objectives for the Special Child:

- match a shape with the written word for it
- sort shapes and written words

Materials Needed:

- SHAPES Activity Sheet
- crayons
- objects from class trip to the park
- cutouts in the shape of a triangle, square, rectangle, and circle
- sentence strips (Prepare label names for triangle, square, rectangle, and circle.)

Motivation:

Tell students they will be taking a walk in the park to identify shapes today.

Do Now:

Silently identify as many shapes as you can find in the classroom. Draw them in your notebooks.

Development:

1. Review the "Do Now." Ask students to name the shapes they find in the class-room. Write the object and the shape it represents on the board, for example, desk— rectangle.
2. Display the shapes to the class. Display the sentence strip labels with each. Name each one aloud and ask volunteers to name them. Discuss the fact that objects have attributes; for example, a triangle is made of three sides.

3. Tell students they will be taking a walk to the park today to identify shapes in the park.

4. Pass out SHAPES Activity Sheets and crayons. Ask children to note on their Activity Sheets the shapes they see and where they see them in the classroom.

5. Take children for a walk. Have them identify the shapes they see on their Activity Sheets. Include anything they see on the way to and from the park on the Activity Sheets.

6. Discuss what students see as they make notes on their Activity Sheets. If they identify a shape in something they can pick up, such as a circle in an acorn, encourage them to bring it back to the classroom.

7. Bring the class back to the classroom. Have volunteers share the objects they brought back and the shape they see in the object.

8. Have volunteers share their SHAPES Activity Sheets and display their drawings.

9. Make a bulletin board called "What Shape Are You In?" Put the four cutout shapes in the center. Hang the SHAPES Activity Sheets around them.

Individual Project for the Special Child:

- Give the child the shape cutouts. Ask him or her to match the sentence labels with the shapes.

Summary:

1. What is a circle, a triangle, a square, a rectangle? (Show cutout shapes and have them select the appropriate shape.)

2. Can you sort these shapes and classify them by name? (Give them the shape cutouts to sort.)

3. Do objects have special qualities?

Summary for the Special Child:

1. Can you sort the words and shapes?

2. Can you match the label with the shape? (Give the special child the cutouts and sentence strip labels.)

Homework:

Go home and locate shapes in common household objects, for example, a rectangle in a cereal box. Bring in an item to share.

Name _____

SHAPES

Draw pictures of the objects you see that resemble these shapes:

Draw the picture in the shape column that fits:

CIRCLE	TRIANGLE	RECTANGLE	SQUARE
◯	△	▭	▢

Activity 11

REPEATING PATTERNS

Aim:

What is a pattern?

Performance Objectives—Students will be able to:

- recognize that a pattern is the way in which shapes, colors, or lines are arranged in some order or design.
- make a repeating pattern.
- discriminate shapes and colors.

Performance Objectives for the Special Child:

- identify colors
- identify shapes

Materials Needed:

- REPEATING PATTERNS Activity Sheet
- 3" × 5" blue index cards
- 3" × 5" orange index cards
- 3" × 5" white index cards
- safety scissors
- markers

Motivation:

Tell students they will be making their own repeating patterns today.

Do Now:

List or draw in your notebooks as many colors and shapes as you can imagine.

Development:

1. Review the "Do Now." Ask students to name all the colors and shapes they can think of.
2. List the shapes and colors that the students name on the chalkboard.
3. Elicit from the class a definition for a pattern. Guide them into saying that a pattern is the way in which shapes, colors, or lines are arranged in some order or design.

4. Discuss with the class that *repeating* means *doing something again*.

5. Demonstrate some repeating patterns with the index cards. (Prior to the lesson cut out, or have students cut out, circles, squares, and triangles from each color group of index cards.) Make a color pattern and a shape pattern.

6. Tell students they will be making their own repeating patterns today.

7. Call volunteers to the front to arrange repeating patterns from the index card shapes. Encourage students to make both color and shape patterns.

8. Pass out REPEATING PATTERN Activity Sheets and markers.

9. Review directions aloud with students.

10. Demonstrate drawing a color pattern on the board. Demonstrate drawing a shape pattern.

11. Tell students they can copy the pattern from the board on their Activity Sheets or create their own.

12. Have volunteers share their Activity Sheets with the class and display their patterns.

13. Make a bulletin board called "The Repeating Patterns Express." Make a repeating train from the index card squares in the center and hang the children's REPEATING PATTERNS Activity Sheets on the bulletin board around it.

Individual Project for the Special Child:

- Have the special child draw and color in triangles, circles, and squares. Have him or her label colors and shapes.

Summary:

1. What is a pattern?

2. Can you make a repeating pattern from these shapes? (Show index card shapes.)

3. Can you pick out a white triangle and a blue circle from these cards? (Show index card shapes.)

Summary for the Special Child:

1. What color is this index card? (Show index card shapes.)

2. What shape is this index card?

Homework:

Find a repeating pattern in your home, for example, a row of windows or a repeating pattern of shelves on a bookcase. Draw it and label it.

Name _____

Activity 11
REPEATING PATTERNS

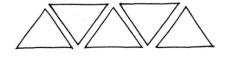 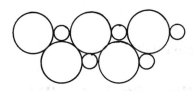 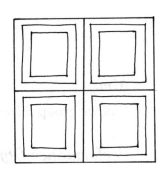

Draw a repeating pattern of shapes here:

Draw a repeating pattern of colors here:

Draw any repeating pattern you want here:

Activity 12
GIRAFFE GROUPING

Aim:

Can we group things into sets?

Performance Objectives—Students will be able to:

- sort objects by color.
- sort objects by attribute.
- count from one to five.

Performance Objectives for the Special Child:

- recognize that numbers have order
- select some objects for a set

Materials Needed:

- GIRAFFE GROUPING Activity Sheet
- a nail
- a bobby pin
- a straight pin
- six boxes with compartments
- six bags containing an assortment of small objects in different sizes, including paper clips, screws, pencils, pens, crayons
- markers
- safety scissors

Motivation:

Tell students they will get to play a game with sets today.

Do Now:

Look silently around the room. List or draw in your notebook any groups of things you see that have similar characteristics.

Development:

1. Show the nail, the bobby pin, the straight pin. Ask students if they see what the three things have in common.

2. Elicit from the group that all three objects are long and straight.

3. Explain to students that a set is a group of objects with common characteristics.

4. Review the "Do Now." List the groups of things students note on the board. List the common characteristics that students find. Explain that this is a set.

5. Divide the class into six groups. Give each group a box and a set of objects. Tell the groups to sort objects into sets of five, or sort them according to their common characteristics, for example, all the screws, all the pencils.

6. Have a representative of each group come up and share the sets they have created.

7. Pass out GIRAFFE GROUPING Activity Sheets and crayons.

8. Have children select three colors. Ask students to color the giraffes in each row one of the three colors.

9. Pass out the scissors. Ask students to cut up the squares after they finish coloring.

10. Choose one group member in each group to pick an attribute, for example, a giraffe with a hat. The other children have to come up with an appropriate square with the same attribute. Have children play the game until all the group members have a chance to pick an attribute.

Individual Project for the Special Child:

- Ask the special child to draw a set from the object box that was sorted. Ask him or her to number the objects.

Summary:

1. Can you sort these squares by color? (Give them the squares from the GIRAFFE GROUPING Activity Sheet.)

2. Can you sort these objects by attribute? (Give them objects from the object box.)

3. Can you count these objects? (Show them five objects.)

Summary for the Special Child:

1. Can you show me the object you made into a set?

2. Can you count the objects I show you in order?

Homework:

Find a set of objects at home. Draw or list them on your homework paper. Label the common characteristics.

GIRAFFE GROUPING

Color the giraffes in each row a different color. Then cut out each square.

Activity 13
MY NUMBERS

Aim:

Why are numbers important to us?

Performance Objectives—Students will be able to:

- recognize that numbers are important in our everyday lives.
- read and compare information on a graph.
- count the number of letters in their names.

Performance Objectives for the Special Child:

- recall his or her address
- recall his or her phone number

Materials Needed:

- MY NUMBERS CHART Activity Sheet
- graph paper (See Activity Sheets under Activity 4, Graphs, page 145.)
- markers

Motivation:

Tell students they will be learning about numbers that are important in their everyday lives today.

Do Now:

Think of as many numbers as you can that are important in your everyday life, for example, age, phone number, address. List them in your notebook.

Development:

1. Review the "Do Now." List categories of numbers that children think are important—phone number, address, age, number of family members.
2. Add any statistics students may have left out, for example, shoe size or height. Discuss why these numbers are important.
3. Ask children to write their names. Then ask them to count the number of letters in their names.

4. Demonstrate one child's name in the class, for example, Amy, 3.

5. Display the graph paper. Write numbers 2 to 10 on the top square of the chart.

6. Have each child come up individually and write his or her name in the number box corresponding to the number of letters in his or her name. "Amy" would be in box 3.

7. Ask children to compare numbers. For example, ask them to tell you how many children in the class have three-letter names, compared with the number that have four-letter names.

8. Pass out the MY NUMBERS CHART Activity Sheets and markers.

9. Read through the directions aloud. Tell children that if they don't know any of their important numbers, such as address or height, you'll come around individually and help children find the information.

10. Have students complete the Activity Sheets. When they are finished, have them share their numbers with the rest of the class.

Individual Project for the Special Child:

- Ask the special child to draw his or her house, putting the house number in the front and labeling the street on which it is located. Also ask the child to draw a telephone in the house and list his or her telephone number on it.

Summary:

1. Why are numbers important in our everyday lives?

2. How many children in the class have the same number of letters in their names as you? (Show the graph.)

3. How many letters are in your first name?

Summary for the Special Child:

1. What is your address?

2. What is your phone number?

Homework:

Make a graph of the number of letters of everyone's name in your household.

Name _____

Activity 13
MY NUMBERS CHART

1. Fill in the blanks:

   My name is _____

   My name has _____ letters.

   I am _____ years old.

   Draw the right number of candles on your birthday cake:

2. Draw a picture of your house:

   My address is _____

   _____

3. Draw your phone number on the telephone:

   My phone number is _____

4. Draw a picture of your family, including yourself:

   I have _____ people in my family.

5. I am _____ feet _____ inches tall.

6. My shoe size is _____.

Activity 14
NUMBERS ALL AROUND US

Aim:

Where do we find numbers?

Performance Objectives—Students will be able to:

- recognize that numbers can be found in many places, including our neighborhood.
- recognize that numbers facilitate identification and organization.
- identify *random* versus *ordered* numerals.

Performance Objectives for the Special Child:

- record numbers accurately
- read back recorded numbers on request

Materials Needed:

- NUMBERS ALL AROUND US Activity Sheet
- pictures of buildings, signs, and license plates with numbers
- markers

Motivation:

Tell students they will be taking a neighborhood walk to locate numbers today.

Do Now:

Look around the room, silently identify any numbers you can find in the room, and list the numbers in your notebooks.

Development:

1. Review the "Do Now." List any numbers the children have found in the room on the board.
2. Distinguish between random and ordered numbers. Explain that an ordered number would be in a sequence, such as the numbers on lockers, whereas the numbers on automobile license plates would be out of sequence and random. Discuss the importance of each kind of number for identification; for example, students know which locker is theirs by the number.

3. Tell students they will be taking a neighborhood walk to look for numbers.

4. Display the pictures of numbers on buildings, signs, and vehicles. Ask students to pick out the numbers in the pictures.

5. Pass out the NUMBERS ALL AROUND US Activity Sheets and markers.

6. Read through the instructions and categories of buildings, signs, and vehicles with students. Ask them to note the numbers they see on their walk on their Activity Sheets.

7. Take the class out for the neighborhood walk. Remind children to write down the numbers they see, and the sequence they see them in.

8. Have children point out numbers they see as they mark them down.

9. Bring the children back to the classroom.

10. Have volunteers share the numbers they wrote on their Activity Sheets.

11. Collect the Activity Sheets and put them in a folder in the Math Learning Center.

Individual Project for the Special Child:

- During the neighborhood walk, ask the special child to find five numbers on buildings and to draw the buildings with the numbers on them. Check the numbers for accuracy.

Summary:

1. Where are numbers found in the neighborhood?

2. What do we use numbers for?

3. What is the difference between a number that is not in order and a number that is?

Summary for the Special Child:

1. Can you copy down these numbers? (Show the special child some numbers to copy.)

2. Can you read to me the numbers you copied down?

Homework:

List some of the numbers you find at home. Draw pictures of the things the numbers are on and draw the numbers on them.

Activity 14
NUMBERS ALL AROUND US

Write down all the numbers you can find in the following categories:

Buildings	Signs	Vehicles	Other
10	42 Pearl St.	SCHOOL 12	12

Activity 15
ORDINAL NUMBERS

Aim:

Can you order place from first to fifth?

Performance Objectives—Students will be able to:

- recognize place order in numbers.
- identify place from first to fifth.
- order place from first to fifth.

Performance Objectives for the Special Child:

- count from one to five
- write numbers from one to five

Materials Needed:

- FROM FIRST TO LAST Activity Sheet
- index cards
- markers

Motivation:

Tell students they will be learning a song about their fingers today.

Do Now:

Draw a line of animals. Number them, from first to last.

Development:

1. Teach students the song "Where Is Thumbkin?" holding up each of your five fingers as you name the finger. Here are the words (to the tune of "Frère Jacques"):

   > Where is thumbkin,
   > Where is thumbkin?
   > Here I am.
   > Here I am.
   > How are you this morning?

> Very well, I thank you,
> Run away, run away.

Repeat four more times, substituting for thumb, in sequence, pointer, Tom Tall, ring finger, and pinky.

2. Tell students that thumbkin is first, pointer is second, Tom Tall is third, ring finger is fourth, and pinky is fifth.

3. Hold up one index card with each finger, which says first, second, third, fourth, and fifth. (Prepare index cards in advance.)

4. Review the "Do Now." Have students share their drawings and check to see that they numbered their animals in sequence.

5. Have five student volunteers come to the front. Have them stand in a row. Have another volunteer come to the front and hand each child the appropriate index card for the child's place.

6. Pass out the FROM FIRST TO LAST Activity Sheets and the markers. Read the directions aloud with students.

7. Have students follow the directions and make the appropriate drawings.

8. Have volunteers share their drawings with the class. Check to see that they followed directions correctly.

9. Make a bulletin board labeled "From First to Last." Make a train of the index cards from first to last, linking them with marker. Hang the students' Activity Sheets on the bulletin board.

Individual Project for the Special Child:

- Give the child five index cards. Ask him or her to label them "one" to "five" and put them in order.

Summary:

1. Is there order in numbers?

2. Can you pick out the second puppy? (Show the FROM FIRST TO LAST Activity Sheet.)

3. Can you order these index cards from first to fifth?

Summary for the Special Child:

1. Can you count the number of puppies on the sheet? (Show the FROM FIRST TO LAST Activity Sheet)

2. Can you label the puppies on the sheet with the correct numbers?

Homework:

Write your name. Then write what the third letter of your name is.

Activity 15

FROM FIRST TO LAST

On the fourth dog, draw a tie.

On the first dog, draw socks.

On the second dog, draw shoes.

On the fifth dog, draw a hat.

On the third dog, draw a shirt.

1

2

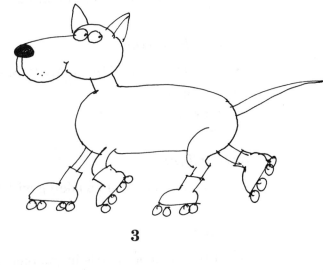

3

4

5

Activity 16
ADDING IT ALL UP

Aim:

Can we understand addition?

Performance Objectives—Students will be able to:

- recognize that addition is the act of putting two or more sets together.
- identify that the answer to an addition problem is a sum.
- add one-digit numbers from one to nine.

Performance Objectives for the Special Child:

- add one-digit numbers from one to five
- make different set combinations

Materials Needed:

- ADDITION ANIMAL Activity Sheet
- box of buttons
- crayons

Motivation:

Tell students they will be adding with buttons today.

Do Now:

Count the number of girls in the room and the number of boys. Mark it in your notebook.

Development:

1. Review the "Do Now." Ask the children to name the number of girls and the number of boys.
2. Write the numbers one under the other on the board. Add an addition sign and a line underneath.
3. Take out the buttons. Display the same number of buttons as boys in the class. Display the same number of buttons as girls in the class.
4. Have a volunteer come up and count the number of buttons in total.

5. Write the answer to the problem that the volunteer gives you under the addition problem on the board.

6. Explain to students that addition is the act of putting together two or more sets (for example, the number of boys and girls in the room).

7. Explain that the sum is the answer to an addition problem.

8. Divide the class into groups of two. Give student groups nine buttons each.

9. Ask students to take turns using the buttons and recording.

10. Have one student create an addition problem with two sets of buttons, for example, two and three.

11. Have the recorder note the addition problem in his or her notebook. Have the student with the buttons find the sum of the problem.

12. Have students repeat, switching roles.

13. Pass out ADDITION ANIMAL Activity Sheets. Read instructions aloud to students. Ask students to write the sums in pencil and color in the picture with their own crayons.

14. Have student volunteers come to the front of the room and share their sums and animal.

Individual Project for the Special Child:

- Give the special child five buttons. Ask him or her to make different set combinations, for example, two and three. Ask the child to write down the sets and add them to find the sums.

Summary:

1. What is addition?

2. What is a sum?

3. Can you look at these two sets of buttons and give me the sum? (Use nine buttons in different combinations.)

Summary for the Special Child:

1. Can you show me the different combinations you made from the two sets of buttons?

2. Can you look at these two sets of buttons and give me the sum? (Use five buttons in different combinations.)

Homework:

Go home and find a group of nine small objects and make up some addition problems from two sets. Note them, and their sums, on your homework.

Activity 16
ADDITION ANIMAL

Find the sums of the addition problems. Find the color the sum matches. Color the spaces with the correct color and find the animal.

1	3	1	3	3	3	1
+ 2	+ 6	+ 8	+ 4	+ 3	+ 5	+ 7

2	2	4	2	5	2	3
+ 5	+ 2	+ 1	+ 7	+ 4	+ 3	+ 1

3 = blue
4 = green
5 = black
6 = yellow
7 = brown
8 = orange
9 = red

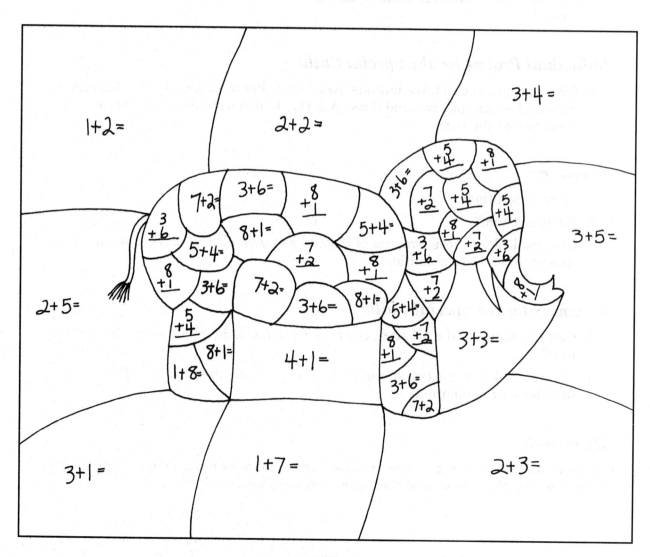

©1997 by The Center for Applied Research in Education

Activity 17
PROBLEM-SOLVING MYSTERY

Aim:
How do we solve a verbal problem?

Performance Objectives—Students will be able to:
- work cooperatively in groups on a mathematics problem.
- identify a mathematics problem in verbal form.
- solve a simple verbal problem.

Performance Objectives for the Special Child:
- recognize that problems can be in numeral or verbal form
- solve a verbal subtraction problem in number form

Materials Needed:
- PROBLEM SOLVING Activity Sheet
- index cards
- markers

Motivation:
Tell students they will be playing a number mystery game today.

Do Now:
Find the mystery number. The number is less than nine and greater than one. List your guesses in your notebooks.

Development:
1. Review the "Do Now." Explain to students that this problem is an example of a verbal problem and that all mathematics problems are not written in number form.
2. Ask a student volunteer to give his or her guesses. List the guesses on the board. Possibilities are from two to eight. Give them the mystery number.
3. Explain to students that in order to solve a verbal problem, they should consider all the possibilities before they take a guess. Also explain the concepts of *less than* and *more than*.

4. Tell students they will be solving a verbal number mystery today.

5. Divide the class into groups. Give each group two index cards and markers.

6. Ask each group to choose a number from one to nine and write it on one index card.

7. Next, have each group come up with one clue to identify the number they have chosen, for example, the number of hats you can see in the room is the number on the card. Have them write the clue on the second card. (Help nonwriters.)

8. Have the groups exchange clue cards. Each group has to guess the number, based on the clue.

9. After each group has guessed, have them exchange clue cards with another group, until all groups have had a chance to guess each mystery number.

10. Pass out PROBLEM SOLVING Activity Sheets. Read them aloud with the class. Have them work on the problems in their groups.

11. Have one group member report the answers.

12. Place the Activity Sheets in a folder in the Mathematics Resource Center.

Individual Project for the Special Child:

- Tell the child that you have a special problem for him or her. He or she brings four apples to school and gives three away to other students. How many does he or she have left? Write the problem and answer in number form.

Summary:

1. Can we work in groups?

2. Is this problem in verbal or number form? (Show students a problem from the PROBLEM SOLVING Activity Sheet.)

3. Can you solve this problem? (Show students a problem from the Activity Sheet.)

Summary for the Special Child:

1. Are both of these mathematical problems? (Show student the PROBLEM SOLVING Activity Sheet and a traditional number problem.)

2. Can you write this problem in number form and solve it?

Homework:

The mystery number is greater than 4 and less than 6. What is it?

Name _____

Activity 17
PROBLEM SOLVING

Solve the problems below by writing the correct number in each space:

1. I am less than 9 and more than 7 _____

2. I am more than 5 and less than 7 _____

3. I am more than 1 and less than 3 _____

4. I am less than 4 and more than 2 _____

5. I am less than 8 and more than 6 _____

6. I am more than 4 and less than 6 _____

7. I am less than 3 and more than 1 _____

Bonus: Maria forgot her locker number. Can you help her find it? It is more than 7 and less than 9.

What is the number? _____

SECTION 4

Science

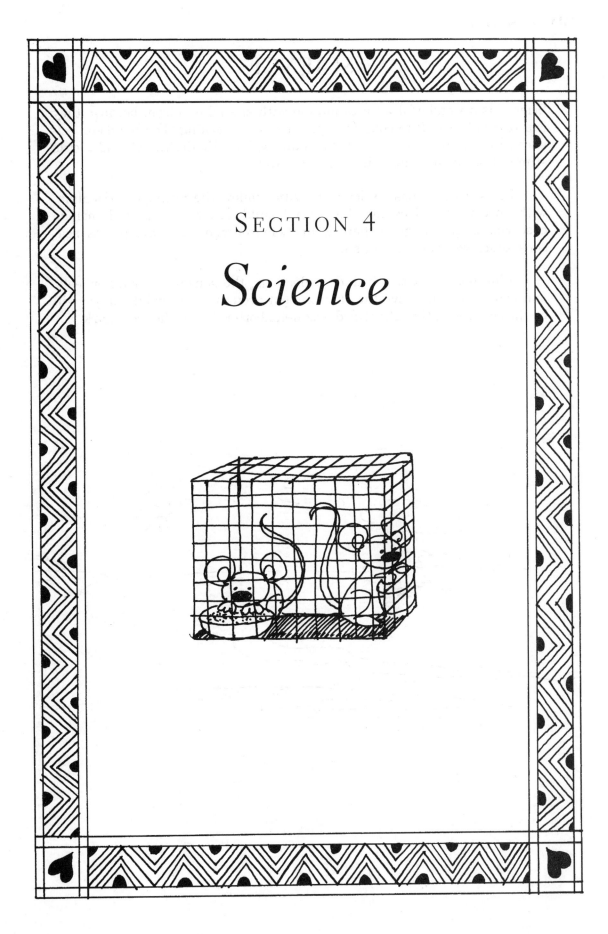

SCIENCE

Science is a wonderful area to pursue with special children, because they can respond so well to concrete approaches to learning. The hands-on science activities in this section have auditory, kinesthetic, visual, and tactile stimuli that all students will respond to well.

The seventeen basic science activities follow the primary curriculum, with special objectives for the special child. Activities covered include observing living things in their natural environment, animals, plants, seasons, time, weather, magnetism.

Additional activities include collections, the senses, growing, wheels, and how we can improve the environment around us. Your laboratory will be the classroom, the schoolyard, the neighborhood, and the local park.

Activity 1
MY NATURE JOURNAL

Aim:

What is a living thing?

Performance Objectives—Students will be able to:

- observe living things in their natural environment.
- realize that the natural world has essential resources.
- recognize that the natural world fulfills human needs, both physical and aesthetic.

Performance Objectives for the Special Child:

- recognize the difference between living and nonliving things
- recall facts from a class trip

Materials Needed:

- LIVING THINGS Activity Sheet
- construction paper
- drawing pencils
- nature magazines with pictures of plants and animals
- safety scissors
- paste

Motivation:

Tell students they will be taking a walk to the park today.

Do Now:

(Pass out nature magazines and scissors.) Choose a picture of a plant or animal to share and cut it out. (Pair the special child with another one to help cut out the picture.)

Development:

1. Review the "Do Now." Have each child share the plant or animal he or she chose, including the special child. If a child picks out something nonliving, like a rock, explain the difference between living and nonliving things.

2. Tell students they will have the opportunity to go to the park today and make their own "Nature Journal."

3. Pass out construction paper, paste, and drawing pencils.

4. Have students fold the construction paper in half for a journal.

5. Have students paste the pictures they chose onto the front of their diaries and have them print their names on the front.

6. Pass out the LIVING THINGS Activity Sheet. Tell students they will be answering the following questions on their Activity Sheets. These will later be included in their journals..

> What is my plant?
> What does it look like?
> What does my animal look like?
> How does it live?
> What is my animal doing?
> How do plants and animals interact?
> How do we interact with plants and animals?

7. Pair students and walk them to the park. Have them observe and record their observations by writing or drawing. Remind students that animals don't have to be big, but can be very small, like insects or worms.

8. Back in the classroom, allow all of the children to share their journals and observations. Paste them inside the construction paper.

9. Discuss how the plants and animals interact and how they depend on one another to live.

10. Elicit from the students that we too need the environment's natural resources to live and eat.

11. Hang the children's journals, including the special child's, on the bulletin board. Call it "My Nature Journal."

Individual Project for the Special Child:

Ask him or her to compile a book of living versus nonliving things. Have the child draw the things chosen.

Summary:

1. What are living things?
2. What in the natural world is essential to us?
3. What do we need the natural world for?

Summary for the Special Child:

1. What is the difference between living and nonliving things?
2. Can we remember some of the things we discussed on the trip?

Homework:

Choose a living thing in your home to talk about in school tomorrow, for example, a household pet or a plant.

Name _____

Activity 1
LIVING THINGS

Below, draw or write answers to the questions asked:

What is my plant? _____

What does my plant look like? _____

What does my animal look like? _____

How does it live? _____

What is my animal doing? _____

How do plants and animals interact? _____

Here are some of the ways in which I use plants and animals: _____

Activity 2
WHERE ANIMALS LIVE

Aim:

Where do animals live?

Performance Objectives—Students will be able to:

- understand that many different kinds of animals exist, including insects, worms, and so on.
- recognize that animals live in many different places.
- distinguish by sight between certain animals and where they live.

Performance Objectives for the Special Child:

- make a book about his or her animals
- label the animals in the book

Materials Needed:

- ANIMAL HOMES Activity Sheet
- nature magazines showing animals living in various places—a fish in water, a bird in a tree
- construction paper
- string
- crayons
- wool
- safety scissors

Motivation:

Tell students they will be collecting pictures of animals' homes.

Do Now:

Have students draw pictures of as many animals as they can think of and where they live.

Development:

1. Pass out the ANIMAL HOMES Activity Sheet.

2. Review the "Do Now." Make two columns on the board and identify them, as on the ANIMAL HOMES Activity Sheet—as "What We Saw" and "It's Habitat."

3. List the animals the children identify and where they live. Explain that a habitat is an animal's home.

4. Explain that animals don't include only the big ones like mammals, but also small ones like insects and worms.

5. Get children to form groups. Place reliable children with the special child.

6. Pass out the nature magazines. Ask children to pick out one animal shown where it lives.

7. Have each child either draw or write the animal and where it lives, on his or her ANIMAL HOMES Activity Sheet.

8. Have one child from each group share the animal and its habitat with the class.

9. Tell students they will be taking a walk to the park today. On the walk, each pair will first observe any animals they see and where they live, and record it on their Activity Sheets.

10. Pass out construction paper, string, wool, scissors, and crayons.

11. Instruct students to use the materials you're passing out to make their own animal home.

12. Demonstrate how to make a bird's nest by weaving some of the materials together. Tell students they can also make a nest, or any other animal home they wish.

13. Make a bulletin board called "Animal Homes" and display ANIMAL HOMES Activity Sheets. Display animal homes the students created.

Individual Project for the Special Child:

- Supply the special child with construction paper, safety scissors, tape, and a nature magazine. Have the child cut out pictures of animals. Paste them on construction paper and label them. Then combine the whole thing into a book called "My Animals."

Summary:

1. Are there many different kinds of animals?

2. Where do animals live?

3. What different animals have you observed?

Summary for the Special Child:

1. What animals are in your book?
2. Can you show me their names?

Homework:

Describe a pet you have at home. If you don't have a pet, imagine you have one. Tell where your pet likes to sleep.

Name _____

ANIMAL HOMES

List below the animals you saw and where you saw them:

WHAT WE SAW | ITS HABITAT

Activity 3
WHAT ANIMALS NEED TO LIVE

Aim:

What do animals need to live?

Performance Objectives—Students will be able to:

- recognize that animals need things from their environment to survive.
- realize that animals need food and water to live.
- understand that animals in captivity need care from their caretakers.

Performance Objectives for the Special Child:

- draw a picture of the mice in the experiment
- recall facts about the mice

Materials Needed:

- WHAT ANIMALS NEED TO LIVE Activity Sheet
- two white mice (can be gotten at most pet shops relatively inexpensively)
- cage
- pine chips
- seeds and nuts
- water bottle and water
- food dish
- pencils

Motivation:

Tell students they will be doing their own experiment to see what animals need.

Do Now:

Draw a picture of your household pet, real or imaginary. Put next to it what you think the pet needs to survive.

Development:

1. Review the "Do Now." List the pets the children come up with on the board. Have children share their pets with the class.

2. Write on the board, "Food and Water."

3. Tell students they will be doing an experiment to see which of these things animals need to survive.

4. Help students set up the experiment. Choose certain students, including the special child, to participate.

5. The first child should get the cage and pine chips. He or she should put about an inch of pine chips on the bottom of the cage.

6. Another child should get the water bottle and fill it with water. Then he or she should put the water bottle in the cage where it can be reached by the mice.

7. Have another child place seeds and nuts in the food dish.

8. Have another child place the food dish at the bottom of the cage.

9. Place the mice carefully in the cage. Remind students that all animals need to be handled carefully.

10. Place the cage away from the light, but in full view of students for observation.

11. Hand out WHAT ANIMALS NEED TO LIVE Activity Sheets and pencils. Have students make predictions as to what they think will happen.

12. Have them observe what the cage looks like. They can draw a picture, write, or both.

13. Assign children, including the special child, to feed and water the mice.

14. After a week, have students do another observation.

15. Students should record their observations and draw conclusions with notes and drawings.

16. Discuss that all living things need water and food to live. Also discuss how, when we take animals out of their natural environment, we need to provide these things for them.

17. Have student volunteers share their Activity Sheets, particularly their conclusions.

Individual Project for the Special Child:

- Draw a picture showing the mice. Then draw anything you've learned about the mice from watching them.

Summary:

1. Do animals need things from their environment to survive?

2. What are the elements that animals need to live?

3. What do we have to supply to animals when we bring them into our home or classroom from outside?

Summary for the Special Child:

1. Can you show me the picture you drew?
2. Can you tell me what you learned about mice?

Homework:

Describe, in words or pictures, what you observed about the mice in the classroom this week. Use your WHAT ANIMALS NEED TO LIVE Activity Sheet as a reference.

Activity 3
WHAT ANIMALS NEED TO LIVE

Describe what the mice look like in the cage today. Draw or write your notes:

A week later, what does the inside of the cage look like?

What I found:

What I think:

Check "yes" or "no"—do animals need food and water to live?

	Yes	No
Water		
Food		

Activity 4
PLANT SURVIVAL

Aim:

What do plants need to survive?

Performance Objectives—Students will be able to:

- recognize that plants need certain conditions to grow.
- understand that plants need air, water, and sun to survive.
- recognize the difference between living and nonliving things.

Performance Objectives for the Special Child:

- draw a picture of a plant
- include in the drawing all the things a plant needs to survive

Vocabulary:

roots—the branching part of the plant that grows down into the ground, absorbs
water, stores food, and keeps the plant in place

stem—the main, supporting part of the plant

leaves—the thin, flat, green parts attached to a stem

Materials Needed:

- PLANTING Activity Sheet
- seedlings of a green plant for each student
- potting soil
- pots with plates
- a watering can

Motivation:

Tell students, including the special child, that they will get to plant their own plants
and observe firsthand how living things survive.

Do Now:

How many different kinds of plants can you name or draw in your notebook?

Development:

1. Review the "Do Now" and list all the plants on the board that students name.
2. Name the green plant that children will be planting.
3. Ask students what they think is the best way to pot a new seedling.
4. List the procedure, step by step, on the board. Pass out PLANTING Activity Sheets. Have children record the procedure.
5. Pass out pots and soil to each student.
6. Have each student plant a seedling.
7. Have each student water his or her plant with the watering can and record it on the PLANTING Activity Sheet.
8. Have each child place his or her plant on the windowsill, where the plant will receive light during school hours. Record on Activity Sheet.
9. Elicit from students that plants need water, sun, and air to survive. List the three things on the board.
10. Elicit from students that nonliving things, such as rocks, do not need these things to survive.
11. Make a bulletin board of the Activity Sheets called "Plant Survival."

Individual Project for the Special Child:

- Draw a picture of a plant. Show all the things in the picture that the plant needs to live.

Summary:

1. What conditions do plants need to grow?
2. What are the things that plants need to survive?
3. What is the difference between living and nonliving things?

Summary for the Special Child:

1. Can you show me your drawing of the plant?
2. Can you show me the things in the drawing the plant needs to survive?

Homework:

Describe in writing or draw as many plants as you can find in your home or on the way to and from school.

Name _____

Activity 4
PLANTING

Fill in or draw the information below:

I got a pot for my plant on _____

I got soil for my plant on _____

I planted my plant on _____

I watered my plant on _____

I put my plant on the windowsill on _____

Plants need the following to survive:

		Yes	No
Water			
Sun			
Air			

Activity 5
TREE ADOPTION

Aim:

Do living things adapt to the seasons?

Performance Objectives—Students will be able to:

- recognize how a tree changes with the seasons.
- recognize how living things adapt to seasonal changes.
- recognize the four seasons: winter, spring, summer, and fall.

Performance Objectives for the Special Child:

- draw pictures of self in the different seasons
- label the four seasons in the pictures

Materials Needed:

- FOUR SEASONS Activity Sheet
- scenic pictures of the four seasons, showing tree changes for each
- nature pictures of some of the changes animals go through in winter, for example, fur changes
- drawing paper and pencils
- camera (preferably Polaroid) and film
- poster board

Motivation:

Tell students they will take a walk in the schoolyard today to adopt their own tree.

Do Now:

Write or draw about your summer vacation. Indicate how you know summer vacation has passed.

Development:

1. Review the "Do Now." Have children share their work on summer vacation. Elicit how they know summer is over.
2. Show scenic pictures of the different seasons. Elicit from students what season each picture represents.

3. Display the pictures with appropriate labels for winter, spring, summer, or fall.

4. Ask students if they have observed any changes in animals during seasonal changes, for example, fur changes or hibernation practices. Display appropriate pictures.

5. Explain to students that all living things adapt to seasonal changes. Explain that humans, animals, and plants are all living things.

6. Ask students if they have observed any changes in the trees during seasonal changes. Elicit from the class that trees change with the seasons.

7. During the height of the fall colors, take the class on a neighborhood walk. Tell students, including the special child, that the class will be adopting a nearby tree.

8. Take them to a tree in the schoolyard or close by. Have the class observe it. Have the children circle it and describe how it looks. Pass out the FOUR SEASONS Activity Sheets and pencils. Ask students to sketch the tree under "Fall."

9. Choose a leaf from the tree to bring back to the classroom. Take a picture of the tree.

10. Back in the classroom, pass out drawing paper and have children draw the tree the way they remember it, referring to their drawings on their Activity Sheets.

11. Make a chart in four parts from the poster board. Mark the first part "Fall" and glue the leaf and the picture on it. Make a bulletin board entitled "The Seasons" and display the "Seasons" chart and the drawings, including the special child's. Save the Activity Sheets for the other seasons.

12. After the leaves have fallen and the cold weather has come, have the class revisit the adopted tree. Repeat the procedure, including getting something from the tree, for example, peeling bark, and having the children draw the tree under "Winter."

13. Repeat the procedure in Spring. Get something from the tree for the "Seasons" chart, for example, a bud and display some of the children's drawings.

14. Finally, make a last visit to the adopted tree before school breaks for summer. Get another leaf for the chart and display children's drawings.

15. Review the four seasons with the class. Elicit that all living things, including trees, humans, and animals, adapt to the seasons.

Individual Project for the Special Child:

- Draw a picture of yourself in all four seasons. Show appropriate clothing in each drawing. Label the seasons.

Summary:

1. How does a tree change with the seasons?

2. How do living things adapt to seasonal changes?

3. What are the four seasons?

Summary for the Special Child:

1. Can you show me the pictures of you and the four seasons?
2. Can you tell me which seasons they are?

Homework:

Describe in words or pictures different things your family does to adapt to the seasons, for example, putting up storm windows or buying winter coats.

Activity 5
FOUR SEASONS

Below are the four seasons. Draw the tree and how it looks in each season:

FALL	WINTER
SPRING	SUMMER

Activity 6
TIMELY EVENTS

Aim:

Does an event take time to occur?

Performance Objectives—Students will be able to:
- recognize that an event takes time to occur.
- identify that one property of an event is determined by time.
- distinguish that different common events take different amounts of time.

Performance Objective for the Special Child:
- create a time chart of daily events
- write down the times that things occur

Materials Needed:
- TIMELY EVENTS Activity Sheet
- a clock
- a candle in a holder
- water
- cassette player and tape of short songs
- paper cups—enough for each child
- sugar cubes

Motivation:

Tell students they will be doing experiments today to determine the time of common events.

Do Now:

Try to estimate how long it takes you to get ready for school in the morning.

Development:
1. Review the "Do Now." See how long each child estimates, including the special child. Write the times on the board.
2. Compare the times that children give. Discuss the differences.

3. Elicit that different events take different amounts of time. Explain that one of the properties of an event is determined by time.

4. Tell students you will be doing different experiments to determine the time of events.

5. Pass out the TIMELY EVENTS Activity Sheet. Tell students to record each experiment and the time it takes.

6. Display the clock. Review telling time with students. The special child, or other children who have not learned to tell time to the minute, may round to the half hour.

7. Display the candle. Light it and have the class time it until it burns down. Caution children to keep away from the flame. Record it on Activity Sheets.

8. Play a short song on the cassette tape for children. Have students time the song until it finishes on their Activity Sheets.

9. Pass out cups. Have students fill them with water. Give each child a sugar cube to dissolve in water and record the time on Activity Sheets.

10. Have students compare Activity Sheets and compare the timing of events.

Individual Project for the Special Child:

- Have special student time some of his or her daily activities in school and record them, for example putting on or off coat, putting books in desk.

Summary:

1. What takes time to occur?
2. What is one property of an event determined by?
3. Do different events take different amounts of time?

Summary for the Special Child:

1. Can you show me your time chart?
2. Can you tell me what times your activities take place?

Homework:

Record a household routine at home, for example eating dinner, on your Activity Sheet.

Name _____

Activity 6
TIMELY EVENTS

List below the time it takes for each item to occur. At the end, compare the times.

Event	Time It Took	Comparison
Candle Burning		
Song Playing		
Sugar Melting		

I timed the following at home _____

_____

and it took this much time _____

216

©1997 by The Center for Applied Research in Education

Activity 7
MY ENVIRONMENT AND ME

Aim:

What is the environment?

Performance Objectives—Students will be able to:

- realize that we perceive the environment through our senses.
- name the five senses.
- identify the environment as everything that surrounds us.

Performance Objectives for the Special Child:

- develop an increased awareness of the environment
- identify items in the daily environment

Materials Needed:

- MY FIVE SENSES Activity Sheet
- drawing paper
- crayons
- big sheet of paper for a mural (a roll of newsprint is good for this)
- jar of honey

Motivation:

Tell students they will develop a class mural about the environment.

Do Now:

Decide how our senses tell us about our environment. Draw or write about it.

Development:

1. Review the "Do Now." Discuss with students how their five senses will help them learn about the environment.
2. Review the five senses: hearing, seeing, tasting, touching, and smelling. Discuss that the environment is everything that surrounds us indoors or out.
3. Tell students they will be taking a walk to the schoolyard. Give each child, including the special child, the MY FIVE SENSES Activity Sheet.

4. As you leave the building, have children observe the building environment.

5. Gather children in a circle in the schoolyard. Have students close their eyes and report on what they hear individually. When they open their eyes, have them record what they heard under "the ear" on the Activity Sheet. Have students record something for each of the five senses on the Activity Sheet as you go through the lesson.

6. Gather children around a honey jar. Have children close their eyes again.

7. Have children keep eyes closed and smell the honey.

8. Next, have children feel the honey.

9. Next, have children taste the sweet honey.

10. Have children open their eyes and pass out drawing paper and crayons. Have children draw something from the environment.

11. Return the children to the classroom. Have each child paste his or her drawing on the mural paper.

12. Make a bulletin board of the mural. Call it "My Environment."

Individual Project for Special Child:

Give the child drawing paper and crayons. Ask the child to draw and label as many things in his or her environment as possible.

Summary:

1. How do we perceive the environment?

2. What are our five senses?

3. What is the environment?

Summary for the Special Child:

1. Can you show me your drawing of the environment?

2. Can you tell me what is in this drawing?

Homework:

List or draw items in the home environment.

Name _____

List or draw below the things you use for each sense:

_____

HEARING

_____

FEELING

_____

SMELLING

_____

TASTING

_____

SEEING

Activity 8
WEATHER OR NOT

Aim:

Can weather be predicted?

Performance Objectives—Students will be able to:

- understand that weather is forecasted or predicted daily.
- identify various weather conditions.
- recognize energy sources in the environment.

Performance Objectives for the Special Child:

- locate information on the weather in a newspaper
- report it to the class

Vocabulary:

> *forecast*—to tell what will or may happen
> *prediction*—the act of telling beforehand
> *accurate*—making few or no errors
> *weather*—the condition of the air at one time and place
> *sleet*—partly frozen rain
> *hail*—small pieces of ice that fall like rain
> *solar*—from the sun

Materials Needed:

- DAILY WEATHER WATCH Activity Sheet
- herbal tea bags
- large jar
- water
- newspaper weather forecast for the day
- paper cups

Motivation:

Tell students they will be using "solar energy" to make tea today.

Do Now:

Describe what kind of weather is your favorite and why.

Development:

1. Review the "Do Now." Most children will describe warm, sunny weather as their favorites. Discuss the weather differences between sun, rain, snow, wind, hail, sleet, and so on. Put a column on the board for each weather condition identified. List characteristics of each under the column, for example sunny—light, rainy—dark.

2. Ask students how they know how to dress for the weather that day. Elicit that a weather forecast can be heard or seen from the radio, television, or newspaper.

3. Bring in a newspaper forecast of the weather for that day. Read it aloud to the class. Discuss the prediction and whether the class thinks it's accurate or not.

4. Pass out DAILY WEATHER WATCH Activity Sheets. Tell students to record the prediction for the day and whether it is accurate or not.

5. Explain to students that weather conditions may be a source of energy. Solar energy comes from the sun.

6. Tell students they will be making herbal tea with solar energy today. (Make sure you choose a bright, sunny day to do this.)

7. Fill a large jar with water. Place tea bags in and close the lid.

8. Put the jar on the windowsill and point it out throughout the day as it darkens.

9. In the afternoon, take the jar off the windowsill and pass out paper cups. Give tea to each child.

10. Bring in the weather forecast each day for a week. Have children record the predictions on their Activity Sheets. By the end of the day, evaluate the accuracy of the prediction.

11. At the end of the week, discuss each day's weather and the accuracy of the predictions. Compare weather day by day. Plot it on a graph on the board. Find out if the class sees a pattern of weather.

Individual Project for the Special Child:

- Give the child a newspaper and have him or her look up the weather forecast for the next day in the newspaper. Have the special child report it to the class. The following day, have the child report on the accuracy of the newspaper forecast for the following day.

Summary:

1. What is predicted daily?

2. What are the different weather conditions?

3. Where can we find energy sources?

Summary for the Special Child:

1. Did you locate the weather forecast in the newspaper?
2. Can you tell the class what it is?

Homework:

Bring the Activity Sheet home and get a weather forecast at home for the following day by listening to the evening news on television or radio or clipping the weather forecast from the newspaper.

Activity 8
DAILY WEATHER WATCH

List or draw your weather guess in the columns below for the next day's weather. Then follow up the next day to see if you were right or not.

Date	Forecast	Was My Guess Right?

What pattern I see in the weather _____

Activity 9
COLLECTIONS

Aim:

What is a collection?

Performance Objectives—Students will be able to:

- define a collection as a variety of objects that have a property in common.
- distinguish that there are many ways to organize an object based on the object's properties.
- identify that a group is composed of more than one thing.

Performance Objectives for the Special Child:

- identify pictures of collections
- make a book of collections

Materials Needed:

- COLLECTIONS GAME Activity Sheet
- picture magazines
- safety scissors
- construction paper
- coins—pennies, nickels, dimes, and quarters
- paste
- white and colored chalk
- marbles
- buttons
- paper clips
- erasers
- color markers
- crayons
- math manipulatives in different shapes and colors

Motivation:

Tell students they will be playing a game with different collections today.

Do Now:

Describe by word or drawing any group you can identify in the room.

Development:

1. Review the "Do Now." List the groups that students can identify on the chalkboard.

2. Show pictures of groups from the magazine. For each one, discuss what property the group has in common.

3. Elicit from students that a group is more than one thing, and that a collection is a variety of objects that have a property in common.

4. Explain that there are many ways to organize a collection of objects based on the properties of an object—size, shape, color, and so on.

5. Pass out picture magazines. Have each student pick a group picture. If the collection does not have a property in common, explain why to the class.

6. Tell students they will now play a game about collections.

7. Divide students into groups of four. Pass out groups of objects in different sizes or denominations to each group of four students. Pick one child in each group to be the recorder and give that child a COLLECTIONS GAME Activity Sheet.

8. Have children in each group of four take turns making a collection from the groups of objects passed out. A point is earned for each correct group identified. The child with the most points in each group wins. The recorder in each group should announce the winner after tallying the COLLECTIONS GAME Activity Sheet. Replay, having different children in the group as recorders.

Individual Project for the Special Child:

- Give the child construction paper, safety scissors, paste, and picture magazines. Have the child identify pictures of collections, cut them out, and paste them in his or her construction paper book. Label it "My Collections," with the child's name.

Summary:

1. What is a collection?

2. Are there many ways to organize a collection?

3. Of what is a group composed?

Summary for the Special Child:

1. Can you show me the pictures of collections you found?

2. Can you show me your book of collections?

Homework:

Go home and identify as many collections as you can around the house.

Activity 9
COLLECTIONS GAME

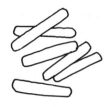

The recorder for this game should write down the name of each player. Each player takes five turns making a collection from the groups of things. A point is earned for each correct group identified. The recorder should tally the point after the five rounds and announce the winner.

Player	Points Earned					Tally
Player 1						
Player 2						
Player 3						
Player 4						

The winner is _____

Activity 10
GROWING

Aim:

How do we grow?

Performance Objectives—Students will be able to:

- recognize that people become taller and heavier as they grow.
- understand that children resemble their families.
- realize that while we all have common characteristics as we grow, we also have our own unique traits.

Performance Objectives for the Special Child:

- draw self now
- draw self as an adult

Materials Needed:

- BABY AND ME Activity Sheet
- students' baby pictures (or pictures from baby magazines)
- crayons
- roll of newsprint
- safety scissors
- pencils

Motivation:

Tell students they will be making paper outlines of themselves today.

Do Now:

Think about your family characteristics. Describe or draw some of them.

Development:

1. Prepare a poster board collection of the children's baby pictures.
2. Review the "Do Now." Have children share their family characteristics, for example, black hair, brown eyes. Write these different characteristics on the board.

3. Display the baby picture poster. If a child did not bring in a baby picture, have that child choose a baby from the baby magazine who he or she thinks resembles him or her and use it in the poster.

4. Examine the baby pictures and have children compare and contrast how they look now to their baby pictures then.

5. Elicit from students that they have grown taller and heavier since they were babies. Also elicit that they have developed many skills such as talking, walking, and running.

6. Now elicit from students how they have not changed. Have the special child participate. Elicit that such things as eye color and skin color do not change. We inherit these characteristics from our families. Discuss the ways in which students will always resemble their families.

7. Do a chart on the board of characteristics that have changed and characteristics that have not.

8. Explain that while all people will grow taller and heavier, some characteristics are unique to people and make them different from everyone else.

9. Pass out BABY AND ME Activity Sheets and crayons. Have students make a drawing of themselves as babies and now. Have them use such details as hair, facial features, clothing.

10. Divide class into pairs. Pass out rolls of paper, pencils, and scissors.

11. Have one child lie down while the other child traces him or her on the paper with a pencil. Then have students cut out the outline. Repeat with the partner.

12. Have volunteers share their outlines.

Individual Project for the Special Child:

• Give the special child two cutouts and crayons. Ask the child to draw on one figure what he or she looks like now and on the other what the child thinks he or she will look like as an adult.

Summary:

1. How do people change as they grow?
2. How do people resemble their families?
3. What unique traits do some people have?

Summary for the Special Child:

1. Can you show me your drawing of yourself now?
2. Can you show me your drawing of yourself as an adult?

Homework:

Go home and talk to your families. See what unique traits your family has. Share them with the class tomorrow.

Activity 10
BABY AND ME

Below are two outlines. Draw yourself as a baby. Draw yourself now. Show how you've changed.

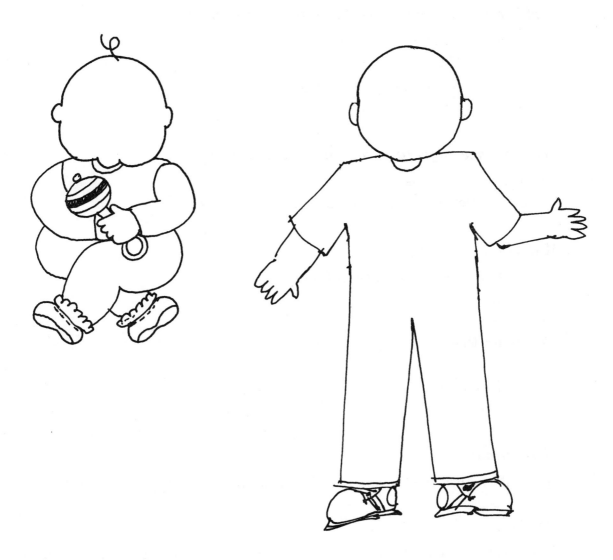

Activity 11
HEARING

Aim:

How do we identify the sounds around us?

Performance Objectives—Students will be able to:

- recognize that there are different sounds around us.
- comprehend that we hear sounds with our ears.
- identify different sounds in the everyday environment.
- identify hearing as one of the five senses.

Performance Objectives for the Special Child:

- distinguish sounds
- draw objects that the child thinks he or she hears

Materials Needed:

- HEARING SOUNDS Activity Sheet
- drum
- shaker
- minute timer
- bell
- toy telephone
- crayons

Motivation:

Tell students they will be experimenting with the sounds of different objects today.

Do Now:

Close your eyes and listen carefully for sounds. Can you identify mentally what the sounds are coming from? Open your eyes and draw or list them in your notebooks.

Development:

1. Review the "Do Now" and ask students to share the sounds they heard.

2. Make two columns on the board—one for the description of the sound and one for the object the student thinks the sound is coming from.

3. Elicit from the class that we hear sounds with our ears. Identify hearing as one of the five senses, the other four being sight, taste, touch, and smell.

4. Have the children form a circle.

5. Display the drum, shaker, minute timer, bell, and toy telephone. Pass out HEARING SOUNDS Activity Sheets and crayons. Read directions aloud.

6. Demonstrate the sound of each object.

7. Ask students to identify each object.

8. Display name labels for each object next to the object.

9. Ask students to close their eyes.

10. Choose one child to make a sound with one of the objects.

11. Choose another child to identify the object by the sound.

12. Repeat procedure with each object.

13. Have student volunteers share their Activity Sheets with the class. Check for accuracy.

Individual Project for the Special Child:

- Have the child close his or her eyes and listen for sounds. Then have the child draw and label the objects he or she hears.

Summary:

1. Are there different sounds around us?

2. What do we hear sounds with?

3. What are some of the sounds in our everyday environment?

4. What are the five senses?

Summary for the Special Child:

1. Can you describe the sounds you heard?

2. Can you show me the drawing of the objects you heard?

Homework:

Write down or draw objects in your household that have distinctive sounds.

Name _____

Activity 11
HEARING SOUNDS

List or draw the sound that you hear for each sound:

Sound 1

Sound 2

Sound 3

Sound 4

Sound 5

Activity 12
SMELL

Aim:

How do we use our noses to smell?

Performance Objectives—Students will be able to:

- recognize that we smell and identify objects with our noses.
- identify smell as one of the five senses.
- recognize that most animals are able to identify odors and tell them apart with their noses.

Performance Objectives for the Special Child:

- identify a smell
- draw a picture of the object that he or she smells and which group the object belongs in

Materials Needed:

- A WEALTH OF SMELLS Activity Sheet
- a bouquet of flowers
- four empty film cartridges
- cotton ball soaked in after-bath lotion and the bottle
- cotton ball soaked in some lavender extract and the bottle of extract
- cotton ball soaked in sour milk and the container of milk
- cotton ball soaked in a crushed onion and an onion
- crayons

Motivation:

Show students the bouquet of flowers and tell them they will have a chance to smell them, in addition to some other interesting things today.

Do Now:

Think of as many things as you can with distinctive smells. Draw them or list them in your notebooks.

Development:

1. Review the "Do Now." List on the board the things students have named with distinctive odors.

2. Display the bouquet of flowers. Pull out a few individual flowers and pass them around the class. Ask students, including the special child, to smell the flowers.

3. Ask students to imagine it's a beautiful spring day. The flowers are in bloom and the sun is shining brightly. Tell students to imagine what they smell while they take a deep breath of fresh air.

4. Explain that the sense of smell is in their noses, and that most animals smell with their noses.

5. Explain that the nose enables us to identify odors and tell them apart. The sense of smell is one of the five senses. The other four are sight, hearing, taste, and touch.

6. Tell students that they are about to do an experiment in which they will use their noses and their sense of smell to identify certain odors.

7. Take the four film cartridges and label them 1, 2, 3, and 4.

8. Put one cotton ball in each cartridge.

9. Divide the class into four groups. Distribute A WEALTH OF SMELLS Activity Sheet and crayons. Distribute a cartridge to each group.

10. Read directions aloud. Have the entire group record the number of the cartridges and list 1, 2, 3, and 4 in the column. Then, under "What Was Smelled," have the group record what they think they smelled.

11. After each group records on their Activity Sheets what they think the smell is, have the groups switch cartridges and repeat the procedure until all groups have smelled all cups.

12. Have each group present their findings to the class and discuss. Display the Activity Sheets in the classroom.

13. After the class has presented its finding, put the object in front of the appropriate cartridge—the onion in front of the cup with the onion odor, and so on.

Individual Project for the Special Child:

- Have the child identify smells in the school, for example, from the cafeteria or the schoolyard. Have the child draw pictures of the things he or she smells, and label them.

Summary:

1. What do we use to smell and identify odors?

2. What are the five senses?

3. What do most animals use to smell and identify odors?

Summary for the Special Child:

1. Can you show me the drawing of the things you smelled?
2. Can you identify one thing for me?

Homework:

List or draw as many animals as you can think of who use their noses to smell and identify odors.

Activity 12

A WEALTH OF SMELLS

Draw what you think is in each cartridge. Then label it.

CARTRIDGE	SMELL
CARTRIDGE 1	
CARTRIDGE 2	
CARTRIDGE 3	
CARTRIDGE 4	

Activity 13
TOUCH

Aim:

How do we use our sense of touch?

Performance Objectives—Students will be able to:

- recognize that our skin has a sense of touch.
- identify the five senses as touch, smell, sight, hearing, and taste.
- identify four different textures—smooth, rough, soft, and hard.

Performance Objectives for the Special Child:

- draw an object from each of the four texture groups
- label the object and the texture group it belongs in

Materials Needed:

- TOUCH Activity Sheet
- chart made from poster board
- block of wood
- sandpaper
- glass snow globe
- piece of cotton
- black marker
- crayons

Motivation:

Tell students they will be feeling different textures today.

Do Now:

Describe in words or pictures different things you like to feel with your hands.

Development:

1. Prepare a poster board chart with four sections. Mark the sections, with the black marker, "Rough," "Smooth," "Hard," and "Soft."

2. Review the "Do Now." List the things on the board the children like to feel. See if they can describe the type of texture the object has.

3. Review the five senses: touch, hearing, sight, taste, and smell.

4. Elicit from the class that we use our sense of touch through our skin.

5. Display the block of wood, sandpaper, glass snow globe, and piece of fabric to the class.

6. Pass them around and have children feel them. Then have students describe the feeling of the object.

7. Elicit from the class that there are four textures: rough, smooth, hard, and soft.

8. Display the chart with the four textures. Have four students, including the special child, bring up one object and identify the right category. Write it on the chart.

9. Ask students to find objects that fit into the four texture categories from the different objects in the classroom.

10. After the search, allow students to share their objects with each other. Pass out TOUCH Activity Sheets and crayons. Read directions aloud.

11. Have each child, including the special child, list the objects they collected on their TOUCH Activity Sheets.

12. Student volunteers should share their Activity Sheets with the class.

Individual Project for the Special Child:

- Have the child draw one object from each of the texture groups, then label each object and the texture.

Summary:

1. Where does our sense of touch come from?

2. What are the five senses?

3. What are the four textures?

Summary for the Special Child:

1. Can you show me the drawing you made from each texture group?

2. Can you show me how you labeled each of the four objects?

Homework:

Find something at home that fits into one of the four categories. Bring it in to share.

Activity 13
TOUCH

List or draw below the objects you collected in the correct touch category:

Objects

Hard	Soft	Smooth	Rough

Activity 14
TASTE

Aim:

What is the tongue used for?

Performance Objectives—Students will be able to:

- realize that our sense of taste comes from our tongues.
- recognize taste as one of the five senses.
- identify five separate tastes: salty, sweet, sour, bitter, and spicy.

Performance Objectives for the Special Child:

- draw one food from each taste group
- label the taste groups

Materials Needed:

- TASTE Activity Sheet
- lemon
- hot pepper
- potato chips with salt
- bitter chocolate
- jelly beans
- crayons
- chart made from poster board
- glue

Motivation:

Tell students that as part of the experiment with taste, they will get to sample different foods.

Do Now:

List or draw in your notebooks your favorite food in one column. In a second column, try to identify the type of taste the food has.

Development:

1. Prepare a chart from poster board with the following categories heading five columns: salty, sweet, sour, bitter, and spicy.

2. Review the "Do Now." List on the board, in two columns, the students' favorite foods from the "Do Now." List the taste next to each food.

3. Elicit from the students that our tongues have the sense of taste, which helps to identify the food.

4. Review taste as one of the five senses. The other four are touch, sight, hearing, and smell.

5. Explain that there are five tastes: salty, bitter, sweet, sour, and spicy.

6. Divide the class into five groups. Assign one taste category to each. Assign the special child to one group.

7. Have each group sample their own food—potato chips to the "salty" group, lemons to the "sour" group, and so forth.

8. Have each of the groups switch foods and have them sample foods from a different group outside their taste group.

9. Continue two more times until all groups have tasted all tastes.

10. Distribute crayons and have each group cut out pictures of food from their original taste group, for example, pie for the "sweet" group.

11. Have one member of each group come to the front of the room. Have the student show the picture of the food from his or her taste group and describe the taste for each.

12. Glue the pictures of food to the poster board chart in the appropriate column.

13. Pass out the TASTE Activity Sheets and crayons. Read directions aloud. Have children list or draw foods in the correct columns.

14. Have student volunteers share with the class.

Individual Project for the Special Child:

- Have the child draw one food from each taste group, then label the food and the taste.

Summary:

1. What part of the body helps to identify taste?

2. What are the five senses?

3. What are the five tastes?

Summary for the Special Child:

1. Can you show me the picture of the foods you drew?
2. Can you tell me which taste category they each belong in?

Homework:

List or draw what you have for dinner. Identify each item by taste category.

Activity 14
TASTE

Below are listed five tastes: salty, sweet, sour, bitter, and spicy. List or draw a food for each category.

Salty	Sweet	Sour	Bitter	Spicy

Activity 15
SIGHT

Aim:

What do we use our eyes for?

Performance Objectives—Students will be able to:

- recognize that humans, and many animals, have two eyes to see.
- understand that sight is one of the five senses.
- recognize that sight enables us to determine color, shape, size, and distance.

Performance Objectives for the Special Child:

- draw an object emphasizing your sight
- identify the eyes as the source of sight

Vocabulary

> *vision*—the ability to sense light that enters the eyes and make fine judgments about the color of light and the directions the rays are coming from
> *sight*—the ability to see
> *distance*—the length of a path that joins two points
> *focus*—a point in an optical system where rays of light come together
> *peripheral*—located at the outermost part within a boundary

Materials Needed:

- THE EYES HAVE IT Activity Sheet
- a large picture of many small objects
- clay formed into two balls
- pencils

Motivation:

Tell students that today they will look at everyday objects in a totally new and interesting way.

Do Now:

List or draw in your notebooks all the objects you can observe in the classroom as you sit at your desks.

Development:

1. Review the "Do Now" with students. List all the objects students name on the board.

2. Hold up a pencil and ask students to describe it.

3. Elicit from students that our eyes provide us with a sense of sight, which enables us to see an object and determine its color, shape, size, and distance from us.

4. Review the other senses—touch, smell, hearing, and taste. Reinforce that sight is just one of the five senses.

5. Tell students they will be doing more experiments to learn about the sense of sight.

6. Hold up a picture. Choose one student to focus on one object in the picture. Ask the same student to identify some of the other objects in the same picture without moving his or her eyes. Call on other students, possibly the special child, to do the same.

7. Ask the whole class to focus on something on the opposite side of the classroom. Then ask them to try to see objects around their focus point without moving their eyes. Allow students to share reactions and draw conclusions.

8. Explain to students that although we think we have a wide picture of the world in front of us, we can focus only on one object at a time.

9. Clear a space in the classroom. Have a student take a small clay ball in each hand and look ahead. Have the student begin with arms slightly behind him or her, at shoulder level, then slowly bring the arms together.

10. Tell the student to stop moving his or her arms when the fingers come into view and drop the clay to mark the spot. Discuss everyone's observations.

11. Explain to students that although people cannot see behind them without turning around, they can see to their sides. Tell them this is *peripheral vision*.

12. Review that humans, and many animals, have two eyes to see.

13. Pass out THE EYES HAVE IT Activity Sheet and pencils. Read directions aloud and have students draw in eyes. Then have student volunteers share their Activity Sheets.

Individual Project for the Special Child:

- Have the child focus on one object in the room, then draw it in as much detail as possible. Have him or her label the sense that is used to see with.

Summary:

1. What do humans, and many animals, use their eyes to do?

2. What sense allows us to see?

3. What enables us to determine color, shape, size, and distance?

Summary for the Special Child:

1. Can you show me your drawing of an object?
2. Can you tell me what part of the body allows us to see?

Homework:

List, or draw, every animal you can think of with two eyes.

Name _____

Activity 15
THE EYES HAVE IT

Below are several animals. Draw the eyes on each one.

Activity 16
MAGNETS

Aim:

What is a magnet?

Performance Objectives—Students will be able to:

- identify a magnet by sight.
- define a magnet as a stone or piece of iron or steel that attracts or draws it to other pieces of metal.
- recognize that a magnet does not attract nonmetallic items like a plastic buttons or a paper cup.

Performance Objectives for the Special Child:

- pick up a paper clip with a magnet
- identify the magnet as a force that attracts metal

Materials Needed:

- MAGNETS Activity Sheet
- magnets
- paper clips
- pencils
- plastic buttons
- metal screws
- paper cups
- crayons

Motivation:

Tell students they will be doing their own experiments with magnets today.

Do Now:

Draw a picture of your refrigerator at home, with drawings or messages displayed—or imagine it if your refrigerator doesn't have messages on it.

Development:

1. Review the "Do Now." Have students share their drawings.

2. Ask students how they think those drawings or messages stay up. Elicit from students that magnets stick to the metal of the refrigerator and hold up objects.

3. Display a magnet. Explain that magnets attract metal and for this reason they stick to the refrigerator.

4. Demonstrate how a magnet can attract a paper clip and how a paper clip sticks to the magnet.

5. Pass out the magnets, paper clips, plastic buttons, metal screws, pencils, and paper cups to all the students.

6. Allow students time to do their own experiments with different materials.

7. Pass out MAGNETS Activity Sheets. Read directions aloud. Have students record their findings on the Activity Sheet.

8. Have student volunteers share their Activity Sheets with the class. Check for accuracy.

Individual Project for the Special Child:

- Have the child take a magnet and a paper clip, and experiment with how the magnet picks up metal.

Summary:

1. What is this (display the magnet)?
2. What is a magnet?
3. What is a compass?

Summary for the Special Child:

1. Can you show me what happens to the paper clip when the magnet is near it?
2. Can you tell me why this happens?

Homework:

Look around your house. Draw or list places where you think a magnet could be used.

Activity 16
MAGNETS

Below check the correct column that shows whether or not the magnet picked up the object:

Picked Up By Magnet	Not Picked Up

1. Paper Clip

2. Plastic Button

3. Paper Cup

4. Metal Screw

5. Pencil

Activity 17
WHEELS

Aim:

Can wheels help us?

Performance Objectives—Students will be able to:

- identify a wheel as round and solid.
- recognize that wheels can be very helpful.
- identify some common vehicles with wheels, for example, bicycles, cars, and trucks.

Performance Objectives for the Special Child:

- draw something with wheels
- label it

Materials Needed:

- WHEELS Activity Sheet
- blocks of wood
- large plastic buttons
- nails
- crayons
- model cars

Motivation:

Tell students they will do an experiment to see if wheels help us.

Do Now:

List or draw as many things as you can think of with wheels.

Development:

1. Prepare a block with wheels for each group of four in your class. Put a nail through four large buttons and put a wheel at each corner of the block. Also prepare a block without wheels for each group.
2. Review the "Do Now." List on the board as many vehicles as the students come up with. Elicit from students that a vehicle is a thing with wheels.

3. Show students the model cars. Have some volunteers push them across the floor. Ask students if they think they would get to go faster by car or on foot.

4. Most students will guess the car. If they don't, explain why the car would be faster.

5. Display the wood block cars and the wood blocks without wheels. Tell students they will be conducting an experiment to see which one moves more easily.

6. Divide students into groups of four and include the special student. Give each group a wood block with wheels and one without wheels. Tell them to experiment to see which one moves more easily.

7. Tell each group to have one member push a block without wheels across the floor and have the group observe how easily it moves.

8. Next, have another member of the group push a block with wheels across the floor. Observe how it moves.

9. Have students discuss their observations. Elicit from the group that the block with wheels moves more easily.

10. Ask students to identify as many vehicles as they can think of (for example, bicycles, cars, wheelchairs, and so on). List them on the board.

11. Pass out WHEELS Activity Sheets and crayons. Read directions aloud. Have students complete sheets and check them.

Individual Project for the Special Child:

- Ask the child to draw something with wheels and what it's used for (for example, a shopping cart with groceries).

Summary:

1. What is a wheel?
2. What are wheels used for?
3. What are some common things with wheels?

Summary for the Special Child:

1. Can you show me your drawing of a vehicle?
2. Can you tell me what it is used for?

Homework:

List or draw any vehicles you find in or around your home.

Activity 17
WHEELS

Below are a number of things that usually have wheels. Some do not. Draw wheels on the things that need wheels and color them in.

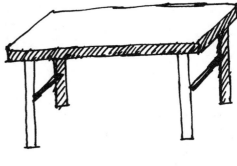

SECTION 5

Social Studies

SOCIAL STUDIES

Section 5 focuses on the child as a member of a family, a school, a community, and the world. The emphasis for the special child will be on himself or herself as an individual.

Social Studies is presented from a social, political, economic, geographic, and historic perspective. Common materials are turned into manipulatives for learning, and everyday community resources such as libraries, supermarkets, and pet stores become expanded classrooms for you and your class.

Social activities cover families, their uniqueness and of whom they are composed; friends and how to make them; and the school as community. Political activities help to identify local officials, how government functions, and how the government welcomes immigrants to the community. Economic activities stress the community as a resource and take students to local stores such as pet stores and supermarkets to explore how the community functions economically and who works in it.

Geographic activities include mapmaking of the local area and visits to local attractions to explore the students' communities and surrounding areas. Finally, historic activities include a trip to the local library to research local history; ethnic heritages, past and future; and the unique circumstances surrounding the founding of the community in which the school is located.

Activity 1
MY FAMILY AND ME

Aim:

What is a family?

Performance Objectives—Students will be able to:

- identify a family as a group of people living in the same household.
- recognize that families differ in their composition—parents, guardians, grandparents, siblings.
- recognize that they live in some family composition.

Performance Objective for the Special Child:

- identify the family that he or she lives in
- draw a picture of his/her own family with labels

Materials Needed:

- MY FAMILY AND ME Activity Sheet
- magazine pictures of people
- safety scissors
- photographs of each child's family
- paste

Motivation:

Tell students they will be creating MY FAMILY AND ME Activity Sheets today.

Do Now:

List or draw in your notebooks all the people in your families.

Development:

1. Review the "Do Now." Ask students to name the people in their families. List the family members on the board.
2. Discuss what a family is. Elicit from the class that a family is a group of people living in a household and varying in composition from one to another. Ask children to take out pictures of family members, including their own.

3. Pass out picture magazines and scissors. Ask students to cut out pictures that resemble their families and present them to the class.

4. Pass out MY FAMILY AND ME Activity Sheets and paste.

5. Ask children to paste the pictures of their family on their MY FAMILY AND ME Activity Sheets and to label each family member. (Children without pictures can use cutouts of people from magazines.)

6. Have students share their Activity Sheets with the class.

7. Place MY FAMILY AND ME Activity Sheets on bulletin board. Label it "My Family."

Individual Project for the Special Child:

- Ask the special child to draw his or her own family and label each family member.

Summary:

1. What is the group you live in called?
2. What is a family?
3. What makes up a family?

Summary for the Special Child:

1. Who are the members of your family?
2. What are they called?

Homework:

Ask your parents about their parents. Write or draw a story about them.

Name _____

Activity 1
MY FAMILY AND ME

Paste pictures of your family on this page. If you
don't have pictures, cut them out from a magazine
or newspaper. Label family members.

In my family there is:

Me

_____

_____

_____

_____

_____

Activity 2
MY FRIENDS AND ME

Aim:

What is a friend?

Performance Objectives—Students will be able to:

- comprehend that a friend is a person we know and like well.
- explore the idea that friendship consists of different and identifiable actions.
- recognize that everyone has different ideas about what constitutes friendly actions.

Performance Objective for the Special Child:

- identify one friend
- define the behaviors that make this person a friend

Materials Needed:

- FRIENDSHIP Activity Sheet
- sentence strips of friendly actions
- large chart paper
- tape
- markers

Motivation:

Tell students they will be hearing special stories about friendship.

Do Now:

Write a story or draw a picture about a friend who did something nice for you.

Development:

1. Review the "Do Now." Ask students to share their experiences with a friend with the class.
2. Discuss what a friend is. Elicit from the class that a friend is someone we know and like.
3. List on the board all the different characteristics children associate with friendship. Point out that people have different ideas about what a friend is.

4. Have student volunteers read their stories or talk about their drawings.

5. Discuss what characteristics the friends had in the stories.

6. Decide on two basic characteristics that friends have, such as helping and having fun.

7. Put up a "Friendship" chart on the bulletin board. List those two characteristics on the chart.

8. Pass out the prepared sentence strips and FRIENDSHIP Activity Sheets. Sentence strips should say things like "plays with you," "listens when you talk," and "helps you when you get hurt."

9. Ask volunteers to read their strips and classify the action according to whether it's helpful or fun.

10. Tape the sentence strip on the chart in its appropriate category. Have students note the sentence on their FRIENDSHIP Activity Sheets in the right category.

Individual Project for the Special Child:

- Ask the special child to draw his or her friend on a sheet of paper and label the friend.

Summary:

1. What is a friend?

2. What does friendship consist of?

3. Do different people have different ideas about what a friend is?

Summary for the Special Child:

1. Can you name a friend?

2. Can you tell me why he or she is your friend?

Homework:

Read a story at home about friends, with or without a parent, and think about what category the friends' actions belong in, to share the next day in class.

Name _____

Activity 2
FRIENDSHIP

HELPFUL   **FUN**

_____   _____
_____   _____
_____   _____
_____   _____
_____   _____
_____   _____
_____   _____
_____   _____
_____   _____
_____   _____
_____   _____
_____   _____
_____   _____

Activity 3
MY ETHNIC HERITAGE

Aim:

What is my ethnic heritage?

Performance Objectives—Students will be able to:

- recognize that people come from many different backgrounds.
- understand that they all have an ethnic heritage of their own.
- recognize that varied backgrounds enrich our cultural life.

Performance Objectives for the Special Child:

- identify his or her own ethnic background
- communicate his or her country of ethnic background through drawings or a story

Materials Needed:

- DIFFERENT BACKGROUNDS Activity Sheet
- objects brought in from home that reflect the students' ethnic backgrounds
- Ethnic Culture Chart
- markers
- folk tale that reflects a student's culture

Motivation:

Tell students they will be hearing an ethnic folk tale today.

Do Now:

Draw a picture of the object you brought from home in your notebook and describe it.

Development:

1. Review the "Do Now." Ask students to share some of their drawings and descriptions.
2. Discuss with the class what an ethnic background is. Talk about how people come from different places and take customs and traditions from those places.
3. Read a folk tale from one of the children's ethnic backgrounds.

4. Discuss what culture is represented in the story.

5. Make an Ethnic Culture Chart, with three columns. List the story title in one column, the cultural background in another, and the language of that culture in the third.

6. Ask a student volunteer to bring up the ethnic object brought from home. (This should be the homework assignment for the previous night.)

7. Have the student display the object and have the rest of the class guess the culture it's from (for example, a sombrero—from Mexico).

8. List the object in the first column (sombrero), the cultural background (Mexican) in the second, and the language spoken (Spanish) in the third.

9. Repeat the procedure with each child, including the special child.

10. Pass out the DIFFERENT BACKGROUNDS Activity Sheet and markers.

11. Have children work on their Activity Sheets, sharing their own ethnic backgrounds in box 4 with one another.

12. Create a bulletin board called "Our Ethnic Heritage." Put the Ethnic Culture Chart in the center and hang up the children's DIFFERENT BACKGROUNDS Activity Sheets.

Individual Project for the Special Child:

• Have the child bring in a travel brochure about the country of origin of his or her ancestors. The child can make a story about the country by cutting and pasting pictures.

Summary:

1. Do people come from different backgrounds?

2. What do we all share in common?

3. What adds to the richness of our cultural life?

Summary for the Special Child:

1. What is your ethnic background?

2. Can you tell me about your country of ethnic origin?

Homework:

Go home and interview a relative about your country of origin. Be prepared to share the interview with the class the next day.

Activity 3
DIFFERENT BACKGROUNDS

1. Color the Christmas tree.

2. Color the fifth candle of the menorah for the fifth night of Hanukkah.

3. Color the dragon for Lunar New Year.

4. Draw something that you use to celebrate a holiday. Label it.

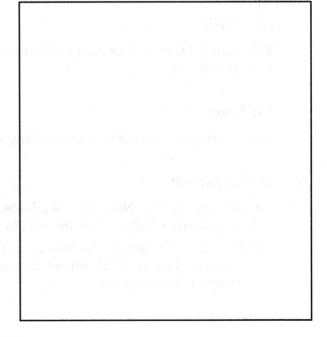

Activity 4
MY COMMUNITY'S HISTORY

Aim:

What is my community's history?

Performance Objectives—Students will be able to:

- recognize that the town or city the students live in existed before they came along, if not for their families, for others.
- learn some basic facts about the community's history.
- recognize that the local library can provide information on many things, including the community's history.

Performance Objectives for the Special Child:

- identify the name of the community he or she lives in
- draw a picture of his or her community

Materials Needed:

- MY COMMUNITY'S HISTORY Activity Sheet
- library books (from a class trip)
- markers

Motivation:

Tell students they will be making a trip to the library today to learn about their community's history.

Do Now:

List or draw in your notebooks anything you know about the community's history.

Development:

1. Review the "Do Now." Ask students to tell you anything they know about the community's history. List the events on the board with approximate dates.
2. Tell students they will be making a trip to the library to get books about the community's history. (Call ahead to the librarian to make books and periodicals available for students.)

3. Break the students up into four groups, according to periods of history, for example, the Revolutionary War, the Civil War, Emancipation of Slaves, the Great Depression.

4. Bring the class to the library, introduce them to the librarian, and break them into their historical groups.

5. Have each group gather information from the librarian on their period of history. Also, show the children the other parts of the library and explain that there is much more information available to them than just their community's history. Also, explain to children that library cards are available to people to take out books.

6. Return the class to the classroom.

7. Have students break into groups and look at the material they got from the library to find out information about their community in the era assigned. Help nonreaders, including the special student if applicable, to read relevant material.

8. Have each group choose a speaker to come to the front and tell what the group learned about their community in the assigned era.

9. List the four eras on the board and the relevant facts the group has found.

10. Pass out MY COMMUNITY'S HISTORY Activity Sheet and markers.

11. Have children write down the facts that you listed on the board with a drawing to accompany each one.

12. Make a bulletin board entitled "My Community's History" and hang up the children's MY COMMUNITY'S HISTORY Activity Sheets.

Individual Project for the Special Child:

- Ask the special child to draw a picture of his or her community and label it.

Summary:

1. Does your town or city have a history?
2. Can you tell me some things about your community's history?
3. What kind of information does your community library have?

Summary for the Special Child:

1. Where do you live?
2. Can you show me a picture of your community?

Homework:

Ask your parents what they know about the local community. Write or draw a story about what you learn.

Activity 4
MY COMMUNITY'S HISTORY

Our community is _____ .

These are the things that happened at different times here:

Era 1 _____	Era 2 _____
Era 3 _____	Era 4 _____

Activity 5
MY REPRESENTATIVES

Aim:
Who represents us in government?

Performance Objectives—Students will be able to:
- define a government as a group of people that manage a place.
- recognize titles of government office, for example, mayor or representative.
- identify the names of local government officials.

Performance Objectives for the Special Child:
- name the city in which he or she lives.
- name the mayor of the city in which he or she lives.

Materials Needed:
- MY REPRESENTATIVES Activity Sheet
- local newspapers
- safety scissors
- glue
- markers
- *Congressperson*, by Louis Sabin, Troll Associates: Mahwah, NJ, 1985

Motivation:
Tell students they will be using their own newspapers to learn about government today.

Do Now:
List in your notebook any government officials you can think of.

Development:
1. Review the "Do Now." Elicit from students the names of any government officials they can name. Make two columns, one with the title and one with the officials names.

2. Discuss what government is. Elicit from students that a government is a group of people that manage a place, such as a town, city, or country.

3. Discuss what representatives are. Elicit from the class that representatives are people who speak for us in government.

4. Divide the class into three groups. Assign each to be national, state, or local government.

5. Pass out newspapers and scissors. Ask each group to find pictures and articles about representatives from their government group. Help nonreaders, including the special child, find information. Make the book *Congressperson* available to the class.

6. Have each group report on the representatives they find. Have groups share pictures and articles they have found.

7. List on the board the representatives that the children find. Divide the names into state, national and local governments (for example, President: Clinton, under national).

8. Pass out the MY REPRESENTATIVES Activity Sheets and glue. Have children list the representatives on their Activity Sheets and either glue in newspaper photos or draw pictures of the representatives in the appropriate spaces.

9. Make a bulletin board called "My Representatives," and hang up children's Activity Sheets.

Individual Project for the Special Child:

- Ask the special child to find a picture or draw a picture of the mayor of his or her city and label it with the correct name.

Summary:

1. What is government?
2. What are "mayor," "senator," and "president" titles of?
3. Can you name some of your representatives?

Summary for the Special Child:

1. What is the city in which you live?
2. Who is your mayor?

Homework:

Go home and listen to the local news on radio or television. List the government representatives you hear mentioned.

Name _____

Activity 5
MY REPRESENTATIVES

Fill in each blank and draw or glue in the picture
of the person in the blank:

The President of the United States is _____.

My senator is _____.

My congressional representative is _____.

My state senator is _____.

My state assemblyperson is _____.

My mayor is _____.

My _____.

Activity 6
HELPING MY COMMUNITY

Aim:

How can people help in the community?

Performance Objectives—Students will be able to:

- recognize that a community is made up of people who depend on one another for goods and services.
- identify the people who help in the community—firefighters, police officers, librarians, and so on.
- identify some ways in which ordinary citizens can make the community a better place to live.

Performance Objectives for the Special Child:

- explain one way in which you could help the community
- explain one way in which someone could help in the community

Materials Needed:

- HELPING MY COMMUNITY Activity Sheet
- magazines
- safety scissors
- paste
- markers

Motivation:

Tell students they will be making posters to help the community today.

Do Now:

Ask students to list or draw in their notebooks people who help in the community.

Development:

1. Review the "Do Now." Have students name community helpers, such as fire-fighters and police officers, and list them on the board.

2. Discuss what a community helper is. Make the definition broad to include people like cafeteria workers and custodians in the schools and apartment buildings.

3. Discuss what a community is. Elicit that it is made up of people who depend on one another for goods and services.

4. Discuss the ways in which ordinary citizens can make the community a better place to live, for example, by conserving water, recycling, or driving carefully in a school zone.

5. Elicit from students the ways that people encourage good community actions, like radio campaigns, television commercials, and posters.

6. Pass out HELPING MY COMMUNITY Activity Sheets, scissors, magazines, markers, and glue.

7. Explain to students that they will be designing their own posters to encourage a community-minded action. Tell students they can use magazine pictures or draw their own pictures with their markers.

8. Do a sample poster with the children. For example, cut out a picture of a beautiful lake and paste it on your poster sheet. Label it "Conserve Water," with markers.

9. Tell students they can do something similar, or create their own community helping poster.

10. Display the posters in a special section of the school.

Individual Project for the Special Child:

- Ask the special child to draw a picture of himself or herself doing a community helping activity, such as recycling a can.

Summary:

1. What is a community made up of?
2. Who are the people in the community who are helpers?
3. How can ordinary citizens help in the community?

Summary for the Special Child:

1. Can you name one way in which you could help in the community?
2. Can you name one way in which anyone could help the community?

Homework:

Go home and discuss with your family how the family could help the community, for example, by recycling trash. Draw a picture or write a summary of it.

Activity 6
HELPING MY COMMUNITY

Here is how we could help the community:

Activity 7
WHERE MY COMMUNITY IS

Aim:

Where is my community?

Performance Objectives—Students will be able to:

- name their community.
- recognize the region in which it exists.
- recognize that a map helps us locate places.

Performance Objectives for the Special Child:

- identify his or her community on a map
- identify his or her region on a map

Materials needed:

- MY COMMUNITY MAP Activity Sheet
- maps of the state and country
- a map of the local community, including city and surrounding areas
- markers

Motivation:

Tell students they will be making a map of their community today.

Do Now:

List or draw in your notebook as many local landmarks as you can think of in the community.

Development:

1. Review the "Do Now." List the landmarks the students name on the chalkboard. Label them.
2. Display the map of the country. Show students where their home state lies on the map.
3. Display the map of the state. Show students where their community falls within the state.

4. Display the map of the community. Ask students to identify the landmarks listed on the board on the community map—their school, library, parks, monuments, and so forth.

5. Display MY COMMUNITY MAP Activity Sheet. Draw the outline of the community and place on the map the landmarks the students listed.

6. Pass out MY COMMUNITY MAP Activity Sheets and markers. Ask students to make maps of the community.

7. Tell students to put drawings where the landmarks go, for example, trees for the parks or a soldier for a war memorial. (If it is difficult for students to draw a map outline, do this in black marker for students before you make copies.)

8. Make a MY COMMUNITY MAP bulletin board. Hang student maps.

Individual Project for the Special Child:

• Give the special child maps of the country, state, and city. Ask him or her to identify his or her city and regional area on each.

Summary:

1. What is the name of your community?

2. In what region does your community lie?

3. How does a map help us?

Summary for the Special Child:

1. From this map, can you pick out your city?

2. From this map, can you pick out your region?

Homework:

Make a map of the route from your home to school.

MY COMMUNITY MAP

Draw a map of your community. Put important landmarks and buildings on the map. Label the streets.

Activity 8
MY COMMUNITY RESOURCES

Aim:

What are my community's resources?

Performance Objectives—Students will be able to:

- recognize that every community has resources to offer its citizens.
- identify specific resources within the community—library, post office, fire station.
- learn how to get some information within the community.

Performance Objectives for the Special Child:

- learn what community resources to call upon for an emergency
- learn what community resource to call on if you're having trouble with your homework

Materials Needed:

- DIRECTORY OF COMMUNITY SERVICES Activity Sheet
- markers
- a telephone

Motivation:

Tell students they will be learning about the many resources available to them in their community.

Do Now:

List or draw in your notebooks any community resources you can name.

Development:

1. Review the "Do Now." List on the board any community resources children name—fire station, library, and so on.
2. Discuss that their community holds much information and many services for solving problems.
3. Display a telephone in the front of the room. Ask a student to come to the front of the room and help role-play a problem situation.

4. The student can pretend he or she thinks that his or her little sister just swallowed some lead paint. Ask the class to help the student solve this problem.

5. Elicit from students that he or she could use the telephone to call for help. He or she could call an emergency number, such as 911, for help.

6. Have the student get on the telephone and role-play making a call to the emergency number for help.

7. Pass out DIRECTORY OF COMMUNITY SERVICES Activity Sheets and markers. (On your copy only, fill in the appropriate phone numbers before the class starts.)

8. Read through the directory of phone numbers and services with the children.

9. Ask students to read each situation and have them come up to the telephone and role-play calling the correct number to solve the problem.

10. Have students fill out their Activity Sheets with the correct phone number for each situation. Help the nonreaders locate the correct numbers.

Individual Project for the Special Child:

- Ask the special child to come to the front of the room and pretend that he is home alone with a caretaker who faints. Ask the child to role-play on the phone calling for help.

Summary:

1. What does every community have to offer?
2. What are some of the resources in this community?
3. How would you get information within this community?

Summary for the Special Child:

1. Whom would you call in an emergency?
2. Whom would you call if you were having trouble with your homework?

Homework:

Make or draw a list of community resources you or your family might use.

Name_____

DIRECTORY OF COMMUNITY SERVICES

AIDS Hotline

Ambulance

Meals on Wheels

American Society for Prevention
of Cruelty to Animals

Consumer Complaints

Fire

Food and Drug Administration

Hazardous Materials Complaints

Dial-a-Teacher or Community
School Board

National Parks Services

Pothole Complaints

Water

Drug and Alcohol Abuse Hotline

©1997 by The Center for Applied Research in Education

Activity 8
DIRECTORY OF COMMUNITY SERVICES, *continued*

After each situation listed below, list an agency and telephone number you could call for information:

1. Your elderly neighbor needs help in getting meals _____.

2. There is a child with AIDS in your class
   and you want to know more about it _____.

3. Your older brother may have a drug problem
   and you want to get advice _____.

4. A new cassette player you just bought broke
   and the store won't take it back or replace it _____.

5. You want to adopt a puppy _____.

6. You are stuck on your homework and
   there is no one available to assist you _____.

7. You get a kite for your birthday and need
   to find a park with a big meadow to fly it _____.

Activity 9
MY LIBRARY

Aim:

What is the library?

Performance Objectives—Students will be able to:

- recognize that the library is a source of many books, periodicals, computers, and other materials, with a wide variety of information.
- comprehend that the library's information is organized in different places.
- recognize that the librarian is the person who keeps the library organized and helps people locate things.

Performance Objectives for the Special Child:

- recognize that he or she can get a book from the local library
- check out a book from the library

Materials Needs:

- LIBRARY INFORMATION Activity Sheet
- library books—fiction and nonfiction
- crayons

Motivation:

Tell students they will be visiting the library today.

Do Now:

Have students list or draw the books they have read or had read to them lately. The previous day's homework should ask children to bring in a favorite book to share.

Development:

1. Discuss the difference between fiction and nonfiction. Label the books the children named as fiction or nonfiction.
2. Review the "Do Now." Ask students to tell you the books they have read lately. List them on the board.
3. Discuss how the library is run. Elicit from the class that a librarian is in charge of the library. Discuss that there are books, periodicals, computers, and other resources in the library.

4. Choose one student volunteer to be librarian and one to be a student seeking a book.

5. Role-play a student going into the library and seeking a book. Have the student find an appropriate book in the class library.

6. Pass out LIBRARY INFORMATION Activity Sheets and crayons.

7. Explain to the children that they must identify the librarian and locate one fiction and one nonfiction book. Also, children can choose one book to borrow from the library. All should be recorded on the chart.

8. Take the class to the library. (Arrange the trip with the librarian in advance.) Introduce the class to the librarian by name. Show them the librarian's name plate on his or her desk or door. Have the children record the name on their LIBRARY INFORMATION Activity Sheets. Ask the librarian the name and address of the library and have children record it.

9. Have the librarian show the children different sections in the library, including the computer area and books on cassette. Check this on their Activity Sheets and make notes.

10. Have the librarian show the class the children's section—fiction and nonfiction.

11. Have children pick one book from each section and record the title.

12. Have the students pick one book to take out of the library. Have them record the title on their Activity Sheets.

13. Have children share the books they got and the books they found in groups back in the classroom.

Individual Project for the Special Child:

- Have the special child borrow a book, with his or her own library card.

Summary:

1. What in the community is a big source of information?
2. How is the library organized?
3. What is a librarian?

Summary for the Special Child:

1. Where can you borrow a book?
2. Do you have the book you checked out of the library?

Homework:

Make a list or draw pictures of any books or magazines in your home. Bring one in to share in class tomorrow.

Activity 9

LIBRARY INFORMATION

Find each thing listed below in the library
and draw or write notes about them:

Library name _____

Library address _____

Librarian's name _____

Nonfiction book _____

Fiction book _____

Books on cassette _____

Computers found in the library _____

Software found on computers _____

Book I chose _____

Activity 10
MY SUPERMARKET

Aim:

What is a supermarket?

Performance Objectives—Students will be able to:

- recognize a supermarket as a community resource where people may buy food.
- perceive that a supermarket is divided into departments and categories—produce, frozen foods, dairy, and so forth.
- organize food into categories.

Performance Objectives for the Special Child:

- identify the supermarket as a place to buy food
- buy something at a supermarket

Materials Needed:

- FOOD CATEGORIES Activity Sheet
- supermarket coupon flyers
- newspaper supermarket flyers
- magazines
- safety scissors
- glue

Motivation:

Tell students that they will be preparing a food guide for the class resource center.

Do Now:

List or draw in your notebooks items that your families usually buy in their supermarket shopping.

Development:

1. Review the "Do Now." List on the board the items that the children name.
2. Ask the children to categorize the items—for example, dairy, produce, frozen foods.

3. Tell students they will be taking a trip to the local supermarket and making a food guide for the class resource center.

4. Pass out supermarket and newspaper discount coupons. Ask children to find coupons that match the food identified on the chalkboard.

5. Take the class to the local supermarket. Pass out FOOD CATEGORIES Activity Sheet and crayons. (Arrange the visit in advance.)

6. Introduce students to the supermarket manager. Have him or her point out the different sections in the supermarket and what items they might find there.

7. Bring children around to each section. Have children record each section and some food items that can be found there.

8. Bring children back to the classroom. Have them share the food items they located and what categories they belong in.

9. Pass out magazines, safety scissors, and glue.

10. Ask students to complete the FOOD CATEGORIES Activity Sheets by drawing pictures or cutting out pictures from newspaper circulars, supermarket coupon flyers, or magazines.

11. Have children share their Activity Sheets, then collect them. Place them in a folder marked "Food Guide," and place them in the class resource center.

Individual Project for the Special Child:

- Have the special child bring money from home and buy a food item for lunch while he or she is at the supermarket.

Summary:

1. What is a community resource where people may buy food?
2. How is a supermarket organized?
3. What are the different categories found in the supermarket?

Summary for the Special Child:

1. Where can you buy food?
2. What did you buy at the supermarket?

Homework:

Make up a shopping list for your family's weekly shopping.

Name _____

Activity 10
FOOD CATEGORIES

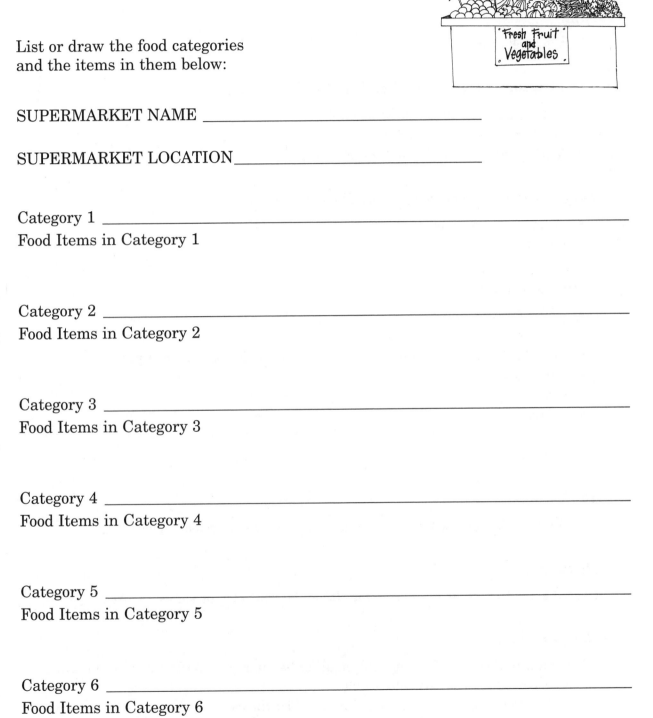

List or draw the food categories
and the items in them below:

SUPERMARKET NAME _____

SUPERMARKET LOCATION _____

Category 1 _____
Food Items in Category 1

Category 2 _____
Food Items in Category 2

Category 3 _____
Food Items in Category 3

Category 4 _____
Food Items in Category 4

Category 5 _____
Food Items in Category 5

Category 6 _____
Food Items in Category 6

Activity 11
MY PET STORE

Aim:

What is a pet store?

Performance Objectives—Students will be able to:

- understand how pets can be friends.
- identify ways to care for pets.
- learn about humane treatment of animals.

Performance Objectives for the Special Child:

- observe pet behavior
- describe what foods the class pet eats

Materials Needed:

- PETS Activity Sheet
- markers
- pictures of domestic animals, for example, bird, dog, cat, guinea pig
- hamster cage
- cedar chips
- exercise wheel
- hamster food
- water bottle

Motivation:

Tell children the class will be visiting a pet store today to select a class pet.

Do Now:

Describe a pet in words or by drawing. It can be your own or someone else's.

Development:

1. Review the "Do Now." Have children describe their pets. Write the different types on the board—dog, bird, and so on.
2. Ask students how they care for the pets. List the care requirements for each pet under the type of pet on the board. Emphasize that a pet needs care and consideration in the home.

3. Show students pictures of pets. See if they can identify them. Include a picture of a hamster. Elicit from the class that pets can be our friends.

4. Tell students that the class will be visiting a pet store today to pick out a class pet.

5. Pass out the PETS Activity Sheets and markers. Tell the children to identify four pets in the pet store and to list their care needs.

6. Bring the class to the pet store. (Prearrange the visit with the owner.)

7. Introduce the class to the store owner. Have the owner explain about the different pets in the store and their care needs. Have children make notes on their PETS Activity Sheets.

8. Have the owner show the children the hamsters, gerbils, and guinea pigs, and other possible pets. Have him or her explain that a hamster needs a cage, a wheel for exercise, cedar chips to sleep on, and food and water.

9. Have the owner demonstrate how to clean and care for the hamster.

10. Pick out a hamster and bring the pet and the class back to the classroom.

11. Set up the cage with the children. Demonstrate how to fill up the water bottle, set up the wheel, and put in the cedar chips and food. Then place the hamster in the cage. Have the class vote on a name for the hamster. Put a name label on the cage.

12. Have the children share their Activity Sheets with the class and discuss what they learned.

13. Collect the PETS Activity Sheets in a folder and place them in the class resource center.

Individual Project for the Special Child:

- Ask the special child to be the hamster monitor and feed the hamster and change its cage, if appropriate. Ask him or her to observe the hamster's behavior (for example, daytime sleeping).

Summary:

1. Can pets be our friends?
2. How do we care for pets?
3. How do we treat pets?

Summary for the Special Child:

1. How did the hamster behave?
2. What food did the hamster eat?

Homework:

Imagine you could own any pet from the pet store. Which one would you choose? Why?

Name _____

Activity 11
PETS

Select one pet for each square. Draw a picture and label it. List the care needs under each one.

Square 1: Pet _____

[drawing box]

Needs _____

_____

Square 2: Pet _____

[drawing box]

Needs _____

_____

Square 3: Pet _____

[drawing box]

Needs _____

_____

Square 4: Pet _____

[drawing box]

Needs _____

_____

Activity 12
WORKERS IN MY NEIGHBORHOOD

Aim:
What are some of the jobs in my neighborhood?

Performance Objectives—Students will be able to:
- recognize that it takes many people working to make a community run smoothly.
- understand that a worker is responsible for a specific task.
- discover the relationship between a supervisor and a worker.

Performance Objectives for the Special Child:
- identify one assigned classroom job
- describe how to do the job

Materials Needed:
- WORKERS IN MY NEIGHBORHOOD Activity Sheet
- popsicle sticks
- paper plates
- glue
- safety scissors
- markers
- construction paper

Motivation:
Tell students they will be making their own worker puppets today.

Do Now:
List any jobs you can think of within your school.

Development:
1. Review the "Do Now." List on the board any jobs the children identify in the school building, (for example, teacher, custodian, principal, and so on).
2. Elicit from the class if any jobs are supervisors of any other jobs; for example, a principal is a supervisor of a teacher.

3. Discuss with the class responsibilities of each job. List those next to the job.

4. Ask children to recall a recent visit to the supermarket. See if they can name any workers in the supermarket. List these on the board and responsibilities of each.

5. Ask children to recall a recent visit to the library. See if they can name any workers there. List these on the board and their responsibilities.

6. Ask children to identify jobs within the classroom, for example, chalkboard monitor, door monitor, messenger. List responsibilities for each.

7. Elicit from the class any other community workers they can recall—firefighters, crossing guards, postal carriers. List responsibilities for each.

8. Pass out WORKERS IN MY NEIGHBORHOOD Activity Sheets and markers.

9. Ask children to choose four community workers. They should draw pictures of them, label them, and list their responsibilities.

10. Have children share their Activity Sheets with the class.

11. Tell children they will be making community worker puppets today. Pass out paper plates, popsicle sticks, glue, construction paper, markers, and scissors.

12. Ask children to choose one community worker from their list and make a puppet of that worker. Have them draw the worker on the pie plate and have them make a hat from the construction paper, cut it out, and glue in on the pie plate.

13. Help the children glue the popsicle to the back of the pie plate.

14. Ask children to come up and role-play two workers interacting, for example, a teacher and principal, or a police officer and firefighter.

15. Collect all the Activity Sheets and put them in a folder in the class resource center.

Individual Project for the Special Child:

- Ask the special child to make a puppet of one classroom job. Ask the child, if appropriate, to do that job.

Summary:

1. What does a community need to run smoothly?
2. What is a worker responsible for?
3. What is the difference between a supervisor and a worker?

Summary for the Special Child.

1. What is one classroom job?
2. How do you do that job?

Homework:

Interview someone in your household about his or her job. Write it down or draw a picture about it. Share it with the class the next day.

Name _____

Activity 12
WORKERS IN MY NEIGHBORHOOD

Choose four community workers. Draw pictures of them, label them, and list their responsibilities.

Worker 1 _____

Responsibilities _____

_____

Worker 2 _____

Responsibilities _____

_____

Worker 3 _____

Responsibilities _____

_____

Worker 4 _____

Responsibilities _____

_____

©1997 by The Center for Applied Research in Education

Activity 13
WE COME FROM MANY PLACES

Aim:

What is an immigrant?

Performance Objectives—Students will be able to:

- define an immigrant as a person who comes to live in a country in which he or she was not born.
- recognize that most people in the community come from different countries, or that their parents or ancestors did.
- recognize that immigrants enrich the community in many ways.

Performance Objectives for the Special Child:

- identify someone in the community or class who comes from another country
- identify his or her country of origin

Materials Needed:

- IMMIGRANT INTERVIEW Activity Sheet
- an ethnic folk tale (choose one from the ethnic background of one of the children in the class)
- pictures of people from different cultures (Reflect the cultures of the classroom students.)
- markers

Motivation:

Tell students you will be reading a folk take from another culture today.

Do Now:

List or draw in your notebooks any ethnic cultural backgrounds you know of from the students in the classroom.

Development:

1. Review the "Do Now." Ask students to name the different ethnic groups they listed.
2. List the ethnic groups on the chalkboard. Add any that may have been omitted.

3. Tell students you will be reading a folk tale from one of the ethnic groups listed. Tell students the title and read the story.

4. Ask the students if they can identify the culture the folk tale is from. Ask students to identify clues from the story that tell about the culture, for example, dress, food, or customs.

5. Display pictures of people from different cultures. Discuss similarities and differences.

6. Discuss any ethnic groups within the community of the school. Include ethnic restaurants where special food is found.

7. Pair children off. Pass out markers and IMMIGRANT INTERVIEW Activity Sheets. Tell children to interview their partners about ethnic backgrounds. Go back to parents and grandparents if children were born in this country.

8. Read through the IMMIGRANT INTERVIEW Activity Sheets with the children. Help the nonreaders.

9. After the children finish their Activity Sheets, call them back and have student volunteers read their interviews.

10. Summarize the ethnic groups found in your community and how they have contributed to make it a better place to live. Have children take home their Activity Sheets for their homework assignments.

Individual Project for the Special Child:

• Ask the special child to find someone in the school—it can be a member of the school staff or student—who is from another culture. Have the child draw a picture of the immigrant in the country he or she came from.

Summary:

1. What is an immigrant?
2. Where do people in the community come from?
3. How do people from other countries enrich the community?

Summary for the Special Child:

• Can you name someone in school who is from another country and the country that person is from?

Homework:

Interview someone at home about his or her ethnic background. If no one at home is from another country, ask about ancestors.

Name _____

Activity 13
IMMIGRANT INTERVIEW

Interview someone about where he or she or his or her relatives come from. Answer the following questions in notes or drawings:

	Classmate	My Relatives
What country are you or your relatives from?		
What was it like there?		
Why did you come to the United States?		
What problems did you or your relatives face coming here?		
After you or they arrived, what did they or you like about America?		

Activity 14
AMERICAN IMMIGRATION

Aim:

What is American immigration?

Performance Objectives—Students will be able to:

- identify an American immigrant as someone who was born in another country but came to live in America.
- realize that immigrants had to go through a process at Ellis Island during the years 1891 to 1915.
- understand the process that occurred when an immigrant arrived in America.

Performance Objectives for the Special Child:

- identify one American immigrant
- identify his or her country of origin

Materials Needed:

- AMERICAN IMMIGRATION FLOW CHART Activity Sheet
- world globe or map
- markers
- materials from the Ellis Island Foundation, Inc. (address: 52 Vanderbilt Ave., New York, NY 10017.)

Motivation:

Tell students they will be hearing a talk by a real American immigrant today.

Do Now:

List or draw in your notebook any people you know who came to America from another country.

Development:

1. Review the "Do Now." List on the board the countries of origin of any immigrants the children can identify.
2. Display the world globe or map. Show students the different places on the map that you listed on the board.

3. Show students where the United States is. Then show them where the country of origin of the immigrant speaker is.

4. Tell students they will be hearing a talk by a real American immigrant. (Arrange the visit in advance, unless one of the children qualifies and is willing.) Introduce the immigrant and ask him or her to tell the class about coming to this country—why, what problems were encountered, and so on.

5. Allow the class to ask questions of the immigrant. Thank that person for speaking to the class.

6. Explain to the class that if this immigrant had entered the country between 1891 and 1915, he or she would have gone through Ellis Island in New York.

7. Display any materials collected from the museum. Pass the materials around for the children to see.

8. Explain to the students that they will be learning about the steps involved in the immigration process at Ellis Island. Pass out the AMERICAN IMMIGRATION FLOW CHART Activity Sheets and markers.

9. Go through the six steps involved in the process. Have children take notes and make drawings on the Activity Sheets. Put the steps on the board as you explain them.

10. Explain that step 1 involved storing the baggage you had with you from your native country.

11. Step 2 involved having a medical examination. If something was found to be wrong with the immigrant, he or she was sent for further examination.

12. Step 3 involved a legal inspection. Every immigrant was asked a long list of personal questions. There were many interpreters hired to speak with people who didn't speak English. About 20 percent of the immigrants were held for questioning by a board if it was suspected that they might become public charges, dependent on the government for basic needs.

13. Step 4 involved a stop at the social service area. Immigrant aid societies were placed here to help the immigrant locate relatives.

14. Step 5 involved money changing. The immigrants would take their money in their native currency and change it into American dollars.

15. Step 6 involved buying a ticket to whatever destination in America the immigrant wanted to go. From the New York room, the government ferry would take people to New York City, or the immigrant could buy a railroad ticket to the desired destination.

16. Have children share their Activity Sheets with one another. Ask student volunteers to role-play immigrants and immigration officials going through the six steps of the immigration process.

Individual Project for the Special Child:

- Ask the special child to draw the American immigrant while he or she is speaking. Ask the child to write the immigrant's name under the drawing and the immigrant's country of origin.

Summary:

1. Do you know what an American immigrant is?
2. From the years 1891 to 1915, where did American immigrants enter the country?
3. What occurred when they arrived at Ellis Island?

Summary for the Special Child:

1. Can you give me the name of one American immigrant?
2. Can you name the country he or she comes from?

Homework:

Write or draw a picture about the American immigrant you heard speak today and the country of origin.

Activity 14
AMERICAN IMMIGRATION FLOW CHART

At each step, make a drawing, and make notes on the drawing about what you know about it.

Step 1: Store Baggage

Step 2: Medical Examination

Step 3: Legal Inspection

Step 4: Social Service Area

Step 5: Money Changing

Step 6: Ticket Purchasing

Activity 15
BECOMING AN AMERICAN CITIZEN

Aim:

How do you become a citizen of the United States?

Performance Objectives—Students will be able to:

- identify a citizen as a person who was born in a country or who chooses to live in and become a member of a country.
- recognize that many people come from other countries and seek citizenship in the United States.
- name some of the basic requirements for becoming a United States citizen.

Performance Objectives for the Special Child:

- identify one immigrant from a foreign country
- identify one immigrant who became a citizen of this country

Materials Needed:

- BECOMING AN AMERICAN CITIZEN Activity Sheet
- world globe or map
- markers

Motivation:

Tell students they will be meeting a real naturalized citizen today.

Do Now:

List or draw in your notebooks all the different countries you know that different people come from.

Development:

1. Review the "Do Now." List all the different countries the students name.
2. Display the globe or world map to students. Have them identify the different countries on the globe or map by pointing them out.
3. Prearrange to have a naturalized citizen visit to talk with the class. Make sure the guest speaker's native country is included in the list and the discussion.

4. Discuss with children that a citizen is a person who is either born in a country or who chooses to live in and become a member of that country.

5. Pass out the BECOMING AN AMERICAN CITIZEN Activity Sheets and markers.

6. Tell children they will be meeting an immigrant today who became an American citizen.

7. Tell the students they will be hearing about the naturalization process, or the process to become an American citizen. Students should record on their Activity Sheets, in writing or drawing, the steps involved as they hear them from the guest speaker.

8. Introduce the guest speaker. Ask the guest speaker to talk about the reasons he or she sought U.S. citizenship.

9. Ask the guest speaker to explain the steps he or she went through in the naturalization process. Make sure the speaker covers the five steps on the Activity Sheet: living in the United States five years prior to application, showing a basic understanding of the U.S. political system, demonstrating a knowledge of English, demonstrating that in the last ten years he or she has not supported any political belief against the United States, and swearing an oath of loyalty to the United States.

10. Ask the guest speaker to finish up with what it means to him or her to be an American citizen now.

11. Thank the guest speaker. Review the five parts of the process with the class and write them on the board.

Individual Project for the Special Child:

- Ask the special child to draw the guest speaker as she or he speaks. Have the special child label the picture with the person's name and country of origin.

Summary:

1. What is a citizen?

2. Do people from other countries seek citizenship in the United States?

3. What are the steps involved in becoming a citizen?

Summary for the Special Child:

1. Can you name a person who came from another country?

2 Can you name a person from another country who became a citizen?

Homework:

Write a summary or draw a picture about the person you heard speak in class today.

Name _____

Activity 15
BECOMING AN
AMERICAN CITIZEN

Outline the five steps below in becoming
a United States citizen:

Step 1

Step 2

Step 3

Step 4

Step 5

Activity 16
MY HOLIDAYS

Aim:

What are the holidays we celebrate?

Performance Objectives—Students will be able to:

- define a holiday as a day on which most people do not go to work or school.
- recognize the holidays commonly celebrated.
- identify the time of the year the defined holidays occur.

Performance Objectives for the Special Child:

- identify one holiday commonly celebrated in the year
- draw a picture about your favorite holiday

Materials Needed:

- HOLIDAYS Activity Sheet
- a long strip of paper, for example, a roll of newsprint
- markers
- objects associated with holidays, for example, a flag for Independence Day, a pumpkin for Halloween

Motivation:

Tell students they will be making a holiday time line.

Do Now:

List or draw as many holidays as you can think of in your notebook.

Development:

1. Review the "Do Now." List on the board the holidays the children name. If children are from different cultures, list their holidays on the board also, even if they are not commonly known.
2. Ask children if they know when the holidays occur during the year. List these also on the board.
3. Display common holiday objects in front of the class. Ask them if they can associate the object with a holiday (for example, a plastic turkey for Thanksgiving).

4. Discuss with students what a holiday is—a day on which people celebrate or remember a special event and commonly do not go to work or school.

5. Divide the children into twelve groups. Assign each a month of the year.

6. Spread out the paper for the time line. Pass out the markers. Have each group put their month at the top of their section.

7. Have each group fill in the holidays that fall in their months. Make sure the children include Martin Luther King's Birthday, Washington's Birthday, New Year's Eve, Valentine's Day, Easter, Memorial Day, Independence Day, Halloween, Thanksgiving, Hanukkah, Kwanzaa, and Christmas. Have children draw things associated with the holidays they list.

8. Pass out HOLIDAYS Activity Sheets. Ask children to draw a line from the holiday to the picture associated with it.

9. Have volunteers share their Activity Sheets. Review the answers for accuracy.

Individual Project for the Special Child:

- Ask the special child to draw a picture about his or her favorite holiday and label it.

Summary:

1. What is a holiday?

2. What are the most commonly celebrated holidays?

3. When do these holidays occur?

Summary for the Special Child:

1. Can you name your favorite holiday?

2. Can you show me your drawing about your holiday?

Homework:

Choose one holiday. Write a paragraph about it or draw a picture.

Note: Answers to HOLIDAYS Activity Sheet: New Year's Eve goes with the noisemaker, Valentine's Day goes with the heart, Lunar New Year goes with the dragon, Independence Day goes with the American flag, Halloween goes with the jack-o-lantern, Thanksgiving goes with the turkey, Hanukkah goes with the menorah, Christmas goes with Santa Claus.

Activity 16
HOLIDAYS

Draw a line from the holiday in Column 1 to the picture that goes with the holiday in Column 2.

COLUMN 1   COLUMN 2

COLUMN 1	COLUMN 2
• Christmas	
• Halloween	
• Lunar New Year	
• Valentine's Day	
• Hanukkah	
• Independence Day	
• New Year's Day	
• Thanksgiving	

©1997 by The Center for Applied Research in Education

Activity 17
THANKSGIVING

Aim:

How do we celebrate a holiday?

Performance Objectives—Students will be able to:

- recognize that holidays are special times when people celebrate and do not work.
- identify Thanksgiving as a uniquely American holiday in which we count the things we are grateful for.
- recall some of the facts surrounding the first Thanksgiving.

Performance Objective for the Special Child:

- draw some things associated with Thanksgiving
- identify some of the traditions of Thanksgiving

Materials Needed:

- MY CORNUCOPIA Activity Sheet
- magazines
- paste
- safety scissors
- blank chart paper
- markers
- *Oh What a Thanksgiving* by Kevin Kroll, Scholastic, Inc.: New York, 1988

Motivation:

Tell students they will be hearing a story about the first Thanksgiving today.

Do Now:

Write or draw in your notebook anything you know about the holiday of Thanksgiving.

Development:

1. Review the "Do Now." Display the blank chart paper in the front of the room.
2. Write "Thanksgiving" at the top of the chart. Make an "experience chart" of the children's experiences at Thanksgiving by writing down what they have to say about it.

3. Have students read back the experience chart when you finish it.

4. Tell students they will be hearing a story about the first American Thanksgiving today. Read the story.

5. Recall the story of the pilgrims and the Indians with the children. Ask children what they think the pilgrims were grateful for that first Thanksgiving. Write their comments on the board.

6. Tell students they will be noting what they are grateful for on their MY CORNUCOPIA Activity Sheets. Explain what a cornucopia is and display an Activity Sheet.

7. Pass out MY CORNUCOPIA Activity Sheets, magazines, paste, scissors, and markers. Read through the instructions.

8. Ask children what they feel grateful about. Write these things on the board.

9. Tell children to find things they are grateful for in pictures in magazines or by making their own drawings and putting them on their Activity Sheets.

10. When finished, ask volunteers to come to the front and share their Activity Sheets.

11. Make a bulletin board entitled "Our Cornucopias" and display the students' Activity Sheets.

Individual Project for the Special Child:

- Ask the special child to make a drawing of anything he or she can think of that means Thanksgiving—a turkey or a pilgrim's hat, for example. Ask him or her to label the items.

Summary:

1. How do we celebrate holidays?
2. What is unique about Thanksgiving?
3. What is the history of Thanksgiving?

Summary for the Special Child:

- What are some of the things we associate with Thanksgiving?

Homework:

Write about or draw a picture about what you are grateful for in your family.

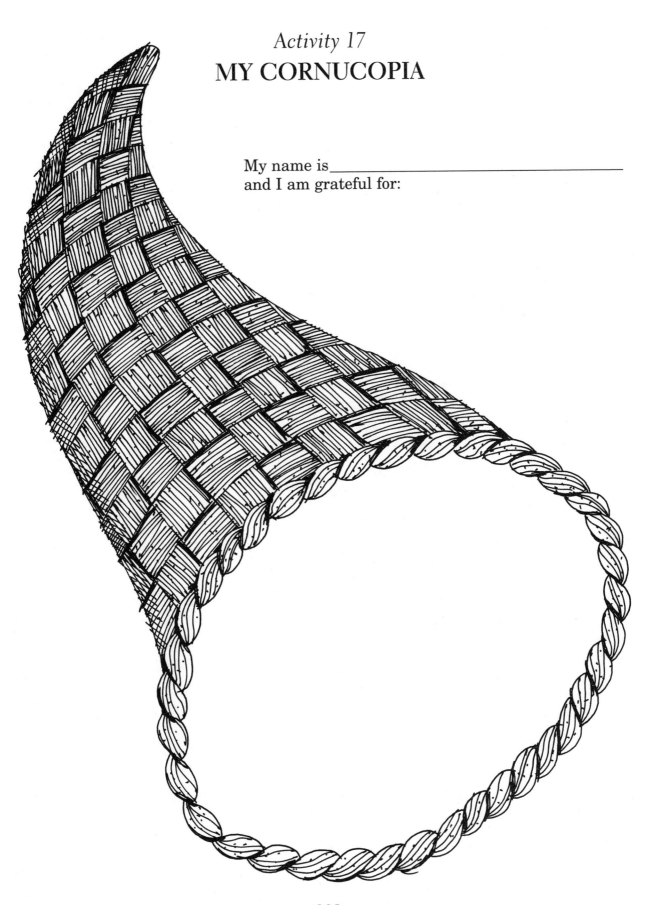

Activity 17
MY CORNUCOPIA

My name is_____
and I am grateful for:

SECTION 6
Arts

ARTS

The arts are particularly important for the special child. Special children often have a unique relationship to art and music. The arts provide a good opportunity for the special child to work with media through movement.

Special children should be included with the class whenever possible on art projects, although individual projects are available. The process of creation is much more important than the finished piece.

In this section, we will explore art, music, dance, and drama. Fine art is presented in many media, including collage, painting, construction, printmaking, puppetry, and bookmaking.

Music is explored through rhythm, movement, instrument making, and song. Dance is performed through music and pantomime, and drama is developed in role plays, oral readings, and choral readings.

Activity 1
SCHOOL ARTS

Aim:

How can we get familiar with our school?

Performance Objectives—Students will be able to:

- recreate what they see through art and construction.
- clarify things about the school through the creative process.
- work cooperatively in groups on a creative project.

Performance Objectives for the Special Child:

- develop positive feelings about his or her own artwork
- create a "talking picture" about the school

Materials Needed:

- OUR SCHOOL Activity Sheets
- blocks
- paint
- brushes
- scraps for collages
- watercolors
- drawing paper
- clay
- safety scissors
- glue
- markers
- crayons

Motivation:

Tell students they will be taking a class walk around the school today.

Do Now:

Draw or list in your notebook as many details as you can think of about the school.

Development:

1. Review the "Do Now." List as many details as the children can think of about the school.

2. Pass out the OUR SCHOOL Activity Sheets. Tell children they will be going for a walk around the school today and that they should note on their sheets as many details as they can observe about their school. They can list or draw them on their sheets.

3. Begin the walk outside the school. Have the children observe the school from the front, then walk around it to the back or the schoolyard. Enter again by the front door. Have children discuss and make notes on what they see as they go.

4. Next, go inside the school, floor by floor, and have children discuss and make notes on what they see as they go. Point out anything they might not be familiar with, such as the upper-grade classrooms.

5. Return the class to the classroom. Have volunteers display their sheets and discuss the details they noted.

6. Next, tell children they will be using different media to depict the school.

7. Discuss the different media available in the classroom with which they may work. If you have an Arts Center, you may go to it and display the different materials. If not, display the materials you brought for the project, including blocks, drawing paper, markers, paint, brushes, collage materials.

8. Have children divide themselves into groups and have each group choose a different medium to work with—blocks for one, collage materials for another, and so on.

9. Tell the groups to refer back to their OUR SCHOOL Activity Sheets for details and to create a representation of the school from the details they noted.

10. After the groups have finished, have one member of each group present the art project and discuss the details used.

Individual Project for the Special Child:

- Assign the special child and two or three other children to work together. Ask the group to create a "talking picture" from their OUR SCHOOL Activity Sheet. Give them paper and markers and have them draw the pictures they remember about the school. Then have them draw large bubbles next to the pictures to describe what they have drawn. Have the group present their "Talking Picture" to the class.

Summary:

1. What kind of materials did you use for your artwork to show what you learned about the school?

2. What things did you learn about the school on your walk?

3. Can you show me the project your group made about the school?

Summary for the Special Child:

1. Can you show me the "talking picture" your group did?
2. Can you tell me about the "talking picture" you did with your group?

Homework:

Go home and look at your house the way we looked at the school today. Create an art project out of whatever materials you can find around your house.

Activity 1
OUR SCHOOL

On this sheet, list or draw all the details about the school you can think of:

1. My school building looks like:

2. My schoolyard looks like:

3. My classroom looks like:

4. My school's general office looks like:

5. My custodian's room looks like:

6. The floors in my school look like:

7. My auditorium looks like:

8. My gymnasium looks like:

9. My cafeteria looks like:

10. Other things I have noticed about my school:

Activity 2
BRUSHWORK

Aim:

Can you experiment with brushes?

Performance Objectives—Students will be able to:

- define a brush as a tool with a handle and bristles.
- recognize that many different forms of brushes exist for many different reasons.
- paint a picture.

Performance Objectives for the Special Child:

- recognize that there are fine-art and work brushes
- identify a fine-art brush versus a work brush

Materials Needed:

- BRUSHWORK Activity Sheet
- various brushes, from fine-art sable brushes to cleaning brushes and toothbrushes
- bristles
- handles
- fasteners
- watercolors
- enough paintbrushes for the class
- easels
- pictures of watercolor paintings
- paper

Motivation:

Tell students they will be painting their own pictures today.

Do Now:

Draw or list as many different kinds of brushes as you can think of in your notebook.

Development:

1. Display pictures of watercolor paintings to the class. Tell the class they will be working on their own watercolors today.

2. Review the "Do Now." List on the board any brushes children come up with. Make three lists, one for "art," one for "house," and one for "work."

3. Display the brushes you brought in for the class. Ask for volunteers to come to the front and identify the brushes and classify them into one of the three categories.

4. Show the bristles, handles, and fasteners. Explain how each part goes into making a brush.

5. Pass out the BRUSHWORK Activity Sheets. Ask children to draw and label brushes for each category. Read directions aloud and assist nonwriters.

6. Ask volunteers to come to the front of the room and display the brushes they listed and the labels and categories.

7. Pass out paper, watercolors, and paintbrushes. Distribute easels. Model the proper use of the paints.

8. Children should put on their own smocks. (It's best if children bring smocks in prior to the lesson, preferably at the beginning of the year.)

9. Tell children to paint their own watercolors.

10. Ask volunteers to come to the front and show their work.

11. Clean up the materials. Then take the materials to a corner and set up an Arts Center.

Individual Project for the Special Child:

• Ask him or her to draw one fine-art brush and one work brush, and to label each.

Summary:

1. What is a brush?
2. Can you name some of the different kinds of brushes?
3. Can you show me the watercolor you painted?

Summary for the Special Child:

1. Can you name two different categories of brushes?
2. Can you show me one fine-art brush and one work brush from this collection of brushes?

Homework:

Go home and draw any brushes you can find in your house. Label them.

Name _____

Activity 2
BRUSHWORK

Draw as many brushes as you can think of in each column. Label them.

ART	HOUSE	WORK

Now draw your favorite brush below:

Activity 3
RURAL MURAL

Aim:

Can we use art to describe our experiences?

Performance Objectives—Students will be able to:

- create and appreciate a specific art form—a mural.
- work cooperatively to fulfill a common goal.
- learn about color, texture, and shape.

Performance Objectives for the Special Child:

- draw a picture story of a trip to the farm
- describe verbally things he or she has seen on a class trip

Materials Needed:

- RURAL MURAL Activity Sheet
- paper in a variety of sizes, colors, and textures
- markers
- paste
- fabric scraps
- triangle, square, circle, and rectangle
- crayons
- safety scissors
- markers
- roll of newsprint

Motivation:

Tell children they will be visiting a farm and working on a mural.

Do Now:

List or draw as many things as you can think of about a farm in your notebook.

Development:

1. Review the "Do Now." List any "farm facts" the children come up with on the chalkboard.

2. Tell children they will be visiting a farm on a class trip today.

3. Pass out RURAL MURAL Activity Sheets. Read directions aloud and ask them to draw or write about anything they observe about the farm on their trip. Tell children that after the trip, they will make a mural about their observations.

4. Take children to the farm. (Arrange this in advance. *Note:* Even city areas have farms close by. Check your local directory.)

5. Have children fill out their RURAL MURAL Activity Sheets during the visit.

6. Return to the classroom. Have children share their RURAL MURAL Activity Sheets.

7. Roll a big piece of newsprint onto a wall in the classroom and tape to the wall. Ask children to imagine what the mural will look like.

8. Ask children to suggest color, texture, and paper for the mural.

9. Ask children to check their RURAL MURAL Activity Sheets and decide what they want to use to describe their farm trip.

10. Make decisions about what to use. Make light chalk lines on the paper to outline areas to be pasted.

11. Guide the children in coming up and placing their items in the right areas.

12. Review the shapes of triangle, square, circle, and rectangle. Ask children to note the shapes they can see in the mural.

13. Display the mural.

Individual Project for the Special Child:

- Ask the special child to describe what he or she saw at the farm through a picture story.

Summary:

1. What is a mural?

2. Did you work on the mural the class made?

3. What color, texture, and shape did you contribute to the farm mural?

Summary for the Special Child:

1. Can you show me the picture story you made about the farm?

2. Can you describe the trip you took to the farm?

Homework:

Write a story, or draw a picture, about the class trip to the farm.

Name _____

RURAL MURAL

Draw or list the things you saw at the farm in the following categories:

1. With my class I visited a _____ .

2. I saw the following buildings:

3. I saw the following animals:

4. I saw the following people:

5. This was the favorite thing I saw:

Activity 4

PICTURES AND POETRY

Aim:

Can a picture tell you something about a poem?

Performance Objectives—Students will be able to:

- recognize that pictures are a form of communication in print.
- illustrate a poem.
- perceive that illustrations help us to understand written material.

Performance Objectives for the Special Child:

- recognize that pictures in books are called illustrations
- identify the person who draws the illustrations as an illustrator

Materials Needed:

- PICTURES AND POETRY Activity Sheet
- chart tablet
- crayons
- drawing paper
- illustrated poetry book, such as *The Mother Goose Treasury*, by Raymond Briggs, Dell Publishing Company, Inc.: New York, 1980

Motivation:

Tell students they will be making their own illustrations to a poem today.

Do Now:

Think of a poem or nursery rhyme you remember. Draw a picture to go with the poem in your notebook.

Development:

1. Read aloud a poem or nursery rhyme. Here is a sample from *The Mother Goose Treasury*

   TERENCE McDIDDLER
   Terence McDiddler,
   The three-stringed fiddler,
   Can charm, if you please,
   The fish from the seas.

2. Show the children the illustration in the book that goes with it. In this case it's a fiddler playing on the shore while a school of enchanted fish leap from the water.

3. Discuss the illustration. Ask children if they feel it tells them about the story.

4. Point out that an *illustration* is a picture that goes with a poem or story. Explain that an *illustrator* is the person who creates the picture.

5. Pass out PICTURES AND POETRY Activity Sheets. Display a poem written on a chart tablet. (Write out the poem in advance.)

6. Read the poem aloud to the children. Ask volunteers to discuss what visual images they get with the poem. Write them on the board and ask the children to make notes on their Activity Sheets. They can copy the ones on the board or create their own.

7. Have the children create an outline of their illustration for the poem on the PICTURES AND POETRY Activity Sheet.

8. Pass out crayons and drawing paper. Have children put their final illustrations on the drawing paper.

9. Ask student volunteers to come up and show their illustrations and discuss why they think the illustration helps or enhances the poem.

10. Create a bulletin board called "Pictures and Poetry." Place the chart tablet poem in the center. Put the children's illustrations around the poem.

Individual Project for the Special Child:

- Send the special child to the class library. Ask him or her to pick out an illustrated book.

Summary:

1. What is a form of communication in print?
2. Can you point to or show me the illustration you made for the poem?
3. What does an illustration help us to do?

Summary for the Special Child:

1. What are pictures in books called?
2. What is the person called who creates the picture in the book?

Homework:

Read a poem or story and make an illustration for it.

Name _____

Activity 4
PICTURES AND POETRY

List below all the different things you think of when you
hear the poem being read.

1. _____

2. _____

3. _____

4. _____

5. _____

Now draw a picture that you think describes the poem you read.

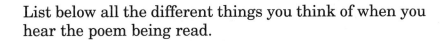

Activity 5
BOOK BONANZA

Aim:

Can we make a book?

Performance Objectives—Students will be able to:

- understand that publishers produce books.
- recognize that books have many uses.
- create a book.

Performance Objectives for the Special Child:

- observe various shapes and sizes of books
- name different types of books

Materials Needed:

- BOOK BONANZA Activity Sheet
- a variety of books in different subjects and sizes and on a variety of topics such as: *Sing a Song of Popcorn*, edited by Beatrice Shenk de Regniers et al. Scholastic, Inc.: New York, 1988; *Mouse Cookies: 10 Easy-to-Make Cookie Recipes*, by Laura Numeroff and Felicia Bond, HarperFestival: New York, 1995; *C is for City,* by Nikki Grimes, Lothrop, Lee and Shepard: New York, 1994
- construction paper
- staplers
- masking tape and glue
- markers and crayons
- picture magazines
- safety scissors

Motivation:

Tell students they will be making their own books today.

Do Now:

Look around the room and draw or list in your notebook as many books as you can find in the room.

Development:

1. In the front of the room, display a variety of published books, as well as samples of homemade books constructed prior to the lesson.

2. Review the "Do Now." List the books on the board that the children cited.

3. Display two or three different sizes, shapes, formats, and contents of books (see examples mentioned). Show the titles and describe the contents.

4. Ask children to describe the differences. List the differences on the board for example, a column for size and a column for content (e.g., nonfiction versus poetry).

5. Discuss the many uses of books, including how-to's to learn how to do something, or poetry for relaxation.

6. Discuss where books come from and how they are made. Describe what a publisher is and how a book is put together.

7. Pass out the BOOK BONANZA Activity Sheets. Ask children to draw or list four different books on their sheets and how they are different from one another.

8. Give children the freedom to explore the class library and choose books to put on their Activity Sheets, or make arrangements to bring them to the school library for this activity.

9. After the children complete their Activity Sheets, have volunteers come to the front of the room and share them.

10. Display the homemade books and tell students they will be making their own books today. Language experience stories, poetry, how-to, and alphabet books are all good choices for homemade books.

11. Pass out the magazines, glue, scissors, markers, paper, and crayons. Hold the stapler and tape until the children are ready to bind.

12. Assist children in putting things together, and pair writers with nonwriters. Children can draw, write, or cut out and paste pictures for their books.

13. As children complete their books, staple them together for a binding and tape over the staples lengthwise for safety.

14. Add a "Homemade Books" section to the class library. Put the students' books there for future lending and reading.

Individual Project for the Special Child:

- Give the special child the few books you have brought to display to the class. Ask him or her to draw the books and label the type of book each one is.

Summary:

1. Who produces books?
2. What are some of the uses for books?
3. Can you show me the book you made?

Summary for the Special Child:

1. Can you show me your drawing of books in different sizes and shapes?
2. Can you tell me what type of book each one is?

Homework:

Go home and list or draw some of the books you can find in your home.

Name _____

Activity 5
BOOK BONANZA

For each of the four sections below, list or draw one type of book. Label the type of book after you finish.

_____   _____

_____   _____

My favorite book is _____ .

Activity 6
SOCK PUPPETS

Aim:
Can we make sock puppets?

Performance Objectives—Students will be able to:
- recognize that puppets can be made from everyday objects.
- create a sock puppet.
- make puppets move.

Performance Objectives for the Special Child:
- draw pictures of sock puppets
- compare their characteristics

Materials Needed:
- SOCK PUPPETS Activity Sheet
- old socks
- rags or stockings for stuffing
- cardboard rollers from toilet paper
- buttons
- string
- safety scissors
- glue
- felt scraps

Motivation:
Tell students they will be making sock puppets today.

Do Now:
Draw or list any puppets you have seen.

Development:
1. Review the "Do Now." List any puppets the children can name on the board.

2. Display a premade puppet. Tell children they will be making their own puppets today.

3. Pass out SOCK PUPPET Activity Sheets.

4. Ask students to design the face they want on their sock puppets.

5. Have children share their SOCK PUPPET Activity Sheets.

6. Demonstrate how to make the sock puppet. Pass out the sock puppet materials.

7. Have children stuff their socks with stuffing materials. Fill the sock up to two inches from the opening.

8. Push a cardboard roller into the sock to make a stick.

9. Wrap string around the sock several times to secure it to the stick.

10. Children can decorate the socks, making any faces they wish. Have them glue on the felt and buttons where they want them to appear.

11. Have children make up plays with their sock puppet characters.

Individual Project for the Special Child:

- Ask the special child to make sketches of the different sock puppets. Ask him or her to compare them.

Summary:

1. What can we make from everyday objects?

2. May I see the puppet you made?

3. Can you make it move?

Summary for the Special Child:

1. Can you show me the drawings of the sock puppets that you made?

2. Can you tell me how they are different?

Homework:

Go home and find scrap materials. Draw or describe the puppet you could make from them.

Activity 6
SOCK PUPPET

Draw the face you would like to make on your puppet. Remember to think about what materials you will use to make the face.

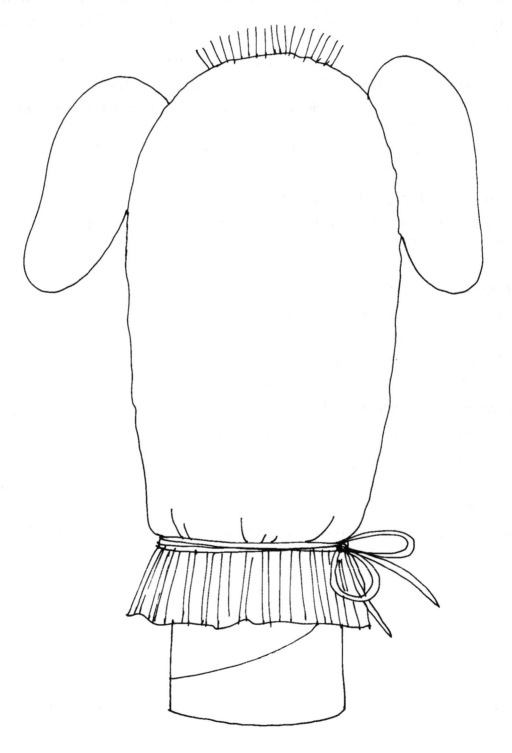

Activity 7
PRINTING PRACTICE

Aim:
Can we learn to print?

Performance Objectives—Students will be able to:
- recognize what printing is.
- recognize the uses of printing.
- print something.

Performance Objectives for the Special Child:
- comprehend that printing can be used to visually coordinate two items
- print some stationery

Materials Needed:
- PRINTING PRACTICE Activity Sheet
- finger paints
- markers
- felt-tip pen
- paper plate
- books
- magazines
- advertising circulars
- a newspaper

Motivation:
Tell children they will be doing some of their own printing today.

Do Now:
List or draw in your notebook all the different things you can think of that are printed.

Development:
1. Review the "Do Now." List on the chalkboard any things the children can think of that are printed, such as books, newspapers, signs.

2. Display the different print materials that you have for the class. Pass them around for the children to see.

3. Discuss with students the different uses for printing, such as disseminating information, advertising, art, and so forth.

4. Pass out the PRINTING PRACTICE Activity Sheet to the children. Explain that they will be doing their own printing today. Read the instructions aloud.

5. Pass out finger paint and paper plates. Pour finger paint into the plates for children. Have them press a fingertip into the paint. Then press that finger onto the PRINTING PRACTICE Activity Sheet. Wait for it to dry, then have children repeat the fingerprints into a row or pattern.

6. After the paint dries, have the children use a felt-tip pen or fine-line marker to add to the fingerprint design.

7. Have children share their designs with the class when they finish.

8. Make a bulletin board entitled "Printing Practice" and hang the class pictures.

Individual Project for the Special Child:

- Have the child create his or her own stationery from paper and an envelope. Take the design from his or her PRINTING PRACTICE Activity Sheet and place it on a sheet of paper and on the envelope. Draw lines on the sheet with a ruler and pencil.

Summary:

1. What is printing?
2. What is printing used for?
3. Can you show me what you printed?

Summary for the Special Child:

1. Can you show me your stationery?
2. Can you tell me why they match?

Homework:

Go home and find some samples of printed things in your house. Bring them in and share with the class tomorrow.

Name _____

Activity 7
PRINTING PRACTICE

Put finger paint in a plate. Put your fingertip in and then print your fingerprint in the space below. Do this several times in a pattern. Then take markers or pens and make a drawing.

Activity 8
MUSIC AND ART

Aim:

Can we make art from music?

Performance Objectives—Students will be able to:

- listen to "mood music."
- create a piece of abstract art based on the music.
- understand that there is a relationship among all the arts.

Performance Objectives for the Special Child:

- identify a piece of music by name on hearing it
- identify the composer of the same piece

Materials Needed:

- MUSIC AND ART Activity Sheet
- cassette player
- tape of mood music, such as Vivaldi's *Four Seasons*, Tchaikovsky's *Nutcracker Suite*, and Bach's *Brandenburg Concertos*
- crayons
- a book on the composer of the piece you choose

Motivation:

Tell children they will be doing their own drawings based on some music today.

Do Now:

List in your notebook your favorite songs and music.

Development:

1. Play the piece you have chosen for this lesson for the class.
2. Tell the students the name of the composer and the name of the piece. Write it on the board. Pass the book about the composer around the room.
3. Discuss with the class how music evokes feelings in people. Elicit from the class their reactions to the music and write them on the board.

4. Discuss how people react differently to music and how they will feel different things when listening to the same music.

5. Discuss how people can also draw different things when listening to the same music.

6. Tell students they will be drawing while listening to music today. Talk about the relationship among all the arts.

7. Pass out the MUSIC AND ART Activity Sheets and crayons. Read the directions aloud to the children.

8. Play the mood piece you selected again for this lesson.

9. Tell children to listen and draw what they feel on the Activity Sheet. Abstract or literal art is equally acceptable. Discuss this with the children.

10. Have volunteers share their drawings with the class and talk about their drawings.

11. Design a bulletin board called "Music and Art." Hang up the children's MUSIC AND ART Activity Sheets on the bulletin board.

Individual Project for the Special Child:

- Give the cassette player and tape to the special child. Ask him or her to listen to it with earphones. Give him or her the case for the tape and show him or her the name of the piece and the composer.

Summary:

1. Can you listen to this music on the cassette player?

2. Can you show me the drawing you made from the music?

3. What is common among all the arts?

Summary for the Special Child:

1. What is the name of the music you listened to?

2. What is the name of the person who wrote the music?

Homework:

Go home and listen to music on television or radio, or on tapes, CDs, or records your family may have. Write down the name of a piece of music and the composer.

Name _____

Activity 8
MUSIC AND ART

Music brings out different feelings in different people. Listen to the music and draw below whatever you think of as you listen:

Activity 9
FUN WITH RHYTHM

Aim:

Can we make our own rhythms?

Performance Objectives—Students will be able to:

- identify rhythm as a musical facet.
- develop their own rhythms.
- recognize and name certain rhythm instruments.

Performance Objectives for the Special Child:

- identify a rhythm in a song
- clap the rhythm to music

Materials Needed:

- NATURAL RHYTHMS Activity Sheet
- tape of different music with different rhythms
- cassette player
- instrument, such as a piano, if available
- rhythm instruments: drums, tambourine, triangle, bell, sticks, maracas, cymbals

Motivation:

Tell children they will be playing their own music today.

Do Now:

Name any songs, with rhythm, that you like in your notebook.

Development:

1. Play the tape, or play on the piano, some rhythm songs for the class.
2. Review the "Do Now." List any songs that students name on the board.
3. Discuss the fact that music can communicate feeling to us. Play different rhythms on the piano or cassette player and ask children to talk about their emotional responses to the rhythms.

4. Tell children to feel the music in their bodies. Have the children stand and move to the music.

5. Next, discuss the fact that there are different ways of making musical sounds; for example, clapping hands.

6. Ask students to suggest different ways to make rhythms.

7. Play another song on the cassette player or piano. Sing the song. Have the children sing it after you until they learn it.

8. Now clap as you sing the song.

9. Have the class sing the song inside their heads and just clap the rhythm as they go. You should clap along with them. Pass out NATURAL RHYTHMS Activity Sheets and ask children to make notes.

10. Display the rhythm instruments in the front of the class. Name them and demonstrate the sounds they make.

11. Pass out rhythm instruments to children. Play a rhythm and encourage children to join in.

12. Encourage children to develop their own rhythms. Have them make notes on their Activity Sheets.

13. Finish off with a march around the classroom, with children making rhythm to a marching song.

Individual Project for the Special Child:

- Have the child listen to the song on the cassette player, then identify the rhythm and clap it out.

Summary:

1. What is rhythm?
2. Can you choose an instrument and make a rhythm?
3. Can you point to each instrument and tell me its name?

Summary for the Special Child:

- Can you listen to the song I'm playing and clap out its rhythm?

Homework:

Go home and make a rhythm instrument out of common objects at home; for example, two spoons, and bring them in tomorrow to share with the class.

Name _____

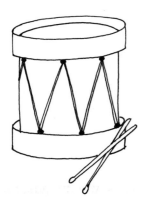

Activity 9
NATURAL RHYTHMS

Listen to a song and draw hands below to help you clap out the rhythm:

Now create a rhythm without a song. Draw hands to show when you clap.

Activity 10
MY OWN ORCHESTRA

Aim:

Can you make a musical instrument?

Performance Objectives—Students will be able to:

- comprehend that an orchestra has four sections: strings, brass, woodwinds, and percussion.
- create a musical instrument.
- produce sound from a musical instrument they've made.

Performance Objectives for the Special Child:

- work with a partner musically
- identify a percussion instrument

Materials Needed:

- MY OWN ORCHESTRA Activity Sheet
- tissue box
- paper fasteners
- rubber bands
- hose piping (clear, can be found in most science labs)
- funnels
- paper straws
- safety scissors
- empty yogurt containers
- seeds
- classical music tape with full orchestra
- tape
- crayons

Motivation:

Tell students they will be making their own instruments today.

Do Now:

Draw your favorite instrument in your notebook. Label it.

Development:

1. Play the music tape for the class.

2. Review the "Do Now." Draw four columns on the board and mark them: strings, woodwinds, brass, and percussion. List the children's favorite instruments on the chalkboard under the correct column.

3. Discuss the fact that there are four types of instruments in an orchestra and review them.

4. Create four instruments prior to class. To make a guitar for strings, remove the perforated cardboard from the top of a tissue box. Empty the box. Fold the perforated cardboard to make a "bridge" by placing it to one side of the hole and tape it down. Affix six paper fasteners at each end of the box and stretch six rubber bands across the box and bridge, winding them around the fasteners.

5. Next, make a horn for brass by attaching a funnel to the end of a piece of hose piping.

6. Next, make a straw whistle for woodwinds. Take a paper straw (a plastic straw won't work) and flatten one end. Cut the flattened end into a point. This is the end to blow through.

7. Finally, make maracas for percussion from empty yogurt containers. Place seeds in the containers. Seal the ends with tape.

8. You can show the instruments in a warm-up lesson and have children choose the instruments they would like to make. Then ask children to bring in materials to make the instruments they want.

9. Pass out MY OWN ORCHESTRA Activity Sheets. Have students match up the instruments in each of the four sections.

10. Demonstrate how to make each of the four instruments. Tell children to make one of their own. They can choose one of yours as a model, or they can create their own.

11. Have volunteers come to the front, display and identify their instrument and the category it falls in, and then play a note on it.

Individual Project for the Special Child:

- Have the special child choose a friend to work with. Ask the special child to use the percussion instrument. Ask the other child to choose another instrument and have them make up a rhythm together.

Summary:

1. What are the four sections of the orchestra?

2. Can you show me the instrument you made?

3. Can you make a sound from your instrument?

Summary for the Special Child:

1. Can you tell me which child you worked with?
2. Can you identify the percussion instrument here? (Show the different instruments to the child.)

Homework:

Listen to music on the radio, tape player, or television. Draw and label any instruments you hear. Name which section of the orchestra the instruments are from.

Activity 10

MY OWN ORCHESTRA

The four sections below—strings, brass, woodwinds, and percussion—are the names of the instruments in the orchestra.

 Draw a line from the name of the section in Column A to the picture of the instrument it matches in Column B. Then color in the instruments.

Column A	Column B

1. Strings

2. Brass

3. Woodwinds

4. Percussion

Activity 11
SONG SENSATION

Aim:

Can we learn a song?

Performance Objectives—Students will be able to:

- recognize that songs have many uses, like entertaining us and telling us a story.
- learn a song.
- learn a new language from a song.

Performance Objectives for the Special Child:

- listen to the words and phrasing of a new song
- learn that songs are sung in different languages

Materials Needed:

- SONG SENSATION Activity Sheet
- cassette player
- tape of songs in different languages

Motivation:

Tell students they will be learning some new songs today.

Do Now:

List in your notebook your favorite songs.

Development:

1. Play the cassette tape of songs for the class. It would be helpful if the tape included "Frère Jacques" and "Dona Nobis Pacem," but any tape of appropriate songs will do.

2. Review the "Do Now." List on the board the students' favorite songs.

3. Ask volunteers what the purpose of songs is. Elicit from the class things like telling stories, passing culture, entertaining, and so forth.

4. Discuss with the class the fact that songs are sung in many languages. For instance, the two songs the class will be learning today are in French and Latin.

5. Sing the song "Frère Jacques" for the class in French and then in English. If you have an instrument, play the music. Discuss the meaning of each line.

6. Pass out SONG SENSATION Activity Sheets. Read the song aloud to the class from the sheet.

7. Sing the first line. Have the class sing it. Go on to the second and have the class sing it after you. Finish with each of the third and fourth lines.

8. Continue to sing the song through together a few times.

9. Repeat the procedure with the English part of the song. Then sing as a group.

10. Introduce "Dona Nobis Pacem." Tell the class that in Latin this means "Give us peace."

11. Repeat the song-learning procedure with the class.

12. After the children have learned the songs, have them perform them for relatives or another class. Both songs are particularly good performed in rounds.

Individual Project for the Special Child:

- Give the special child the cassette player to listen to. Ask the child to repeat or tell you about a song he or she has learned from the tape.

Summary:

1. Can you tell me some of the uses songs have?

2. Can you sing a song that you learned?

3. Can you tell me one word that you learned from a song in a different language and what that word means?

Summary for the Special Child:

1. Can you repeat to me or tell me about a new song that you learned?

2. Can you tell me the languages "Frère Jacques" and "Dona Nobis Pacem" are in?

Homework:

Take a survey of the people at home. Find out their favorite songs and report back to the class tomorrow.

Activity 11
SONG SENSATION

Frère Jacques

Frère Jacques, frère Jacques,
Dormez-vous, dormez-vous,
Sonnez les matines, sonnez les matines,
Ding, ding, dong; ding, ding, dong.

Are you sleeping, are you sleeping,
Brother John, brother John,
Morning bells are ringing, morning bells are ringing,
Ding, ding dong; ding, ding, dong.

Dona Nobis Pacem

Do - na no-bis pa-cem pacem. Do-na no-bis pa———cem.

Do-na no-bis pacem.   Do-na no-bis pa———cem.

Do-na no-bis pa-cem.   Do-na no-bis pa———cem.

Activity 12
DRAMATIZING A SONG

Aim:

Can we show a story through a song?

Performance Objectives—Students will be able to:

- learn a song.
- dramatize the actions in a song.
- work cooperatively toward a common goal.

Performance Objectives for the Special Child:

- understand that music is a form of communication
- recognize that songs can tell us about people, places, and things

Materials Needed:

- STORY SONG Activity Sheet
- chart tablet
- markers
- tape of children's songs
- cassette player

Motivation:

Tell children they will be making their own songs today.

Do Now:

List in your notebook your favorite songs.

Development:

1. Play the cassette tape of children's songs for the class.
2. Ask the children if they can "visualize" anything from the songs.
3. Review the "Do Now." List the children's favorite songs on the board.
4. Introduce the song "Five Monkeys Jumping on a Bed." If you can find the song on a tape, play it for the children. If not, sing it for them. (See the words on the STORY SONG Activity Sheet.)

5. Have five volunteers come up and dramatize the five monkeys as the class sings the song with you.

6. Pass out STORY SONG Activity Sheets.

7. Put a blank Activity Sheet up on the chart tablet.

8. Ask students to create a song to the tune of "Five Monkeys Jumping on a Bed." For example:

> Five kittens sitting on a gate.
> One kitten left 'cause it was getting late.
> Mama called the others and they just sat.
> Then she said, "That's the end of that."

9. Tell children to copy the new song on their STORY SONG Activity Sheets or create one of their own.

10. Ask children to draw on their sheets how they would act the song out.

11. Divide children into groups and have them choose a song to dramatize together.

12. Have each group perform their song.

Individual Project for the Special Child:

- Have the child draw a picture or write a story about one of the songs he or she hears performed in the class.

Summary:

1. Can you sing the song you learned?

2. Can you act out the song?

3. Can your group act out the song?

Summary for the Special Child:

1. What is a form of communication?

2. What do we learn from songs?

Homework:

Go home and ask your family to name a favorite song of theirs. See if they can teach it to you to perform for the class tomorrow.

Activity 12
STORY SONG

FIVE MONKEYS JUMPING ON THE BED

Five monkeys jumping on the bed
One fell off and broke his head.
Mama called the doctor and the doctor said,
No more monkeys jumping on the bed.

(Can be repeated with four, three, two, and one monkey.)

On the lines below, write the words to your song. Then write or draw instructions on how to act it out.

_____

_____

_____

_____

This is how I would act it out:

Activity 13
DANCING OUT

Aim:

Can we develop a dance movement?

Performance Objectives—Students will be able to:

- develop a dance movement.
- develop a pantomime.
- perform a dance movement in front of an audience.

Performance Objectives for the Special Child:

- take notes, in words or pictures, on a dance performance
- evaluate a dance performance

Materials Needed:

- DANCE STORY Activity Sheet
- different hats
- a ball
- a cassette player and music tape without words
- crayons

Motivation:

Tell students they will have the opportunity to develop their own dance.

Do Now:

Think of a story you could tell without words. Draw it in your notebook.

Development:

1. Play the music tape on the cassette player. Tell children they will be dancing to the music today.
2. Review the "Do Now." Have children come to the front of the room and show their story pictures. See if the class can guess the stories from the pictures.
3. Have the children gather their chairs in a circle. Take out the ball and ask them to pretend the ball is a newborn kitten, a hot potato, or a holiday present. Tell children they cannot use language to express what the object is.

4. Next, have the children pull back the chairs and stand in a semicircle facing you. Demonstrate a series of simple steps, such as moving your right arm, left arm, right leg, and left leg. Have the students repeat what you do. Repeat the same steps several times. Play the music on the tape.

5. Explain to students that they are performing a dance where the steps are in sequence, or repeated in the same order over and over.

6. Ask children to create their own dance steps in order. Have some volunteers demonstrate them after they have developed them.

7. Next, have students go back to their desks. Pass out the DANCE STORY Activity Sheets and tell children they will be developing a story through dance. Write the word "pantomime" on the board and explain that it's a story told with the body's movement without words.

8. Display the hats to the class. Ask them if they would like to borrow a hat to pantomime their story. Also make the music available to them. Model one pantomime; for example, wear a fire hat and model a firefighter with a hose at a fire.

9. Read the directions of the DANCE STORY Activity Sheets to students. Tell them to draw their stories in sequence in the boxes.

10. When the children have finished, ask volunteers to come to the front and perform their dance stories. See if the class can guess the stories. Have as many children perform as time allows.

Individual Project for the Special Child:

• Give the special child some extra DANCE STORY Activity Sheets. Ask the child to draw the story he or she sees the other children performing. Ask the child to write down what he or she understands of the story.

Summary:

1. Can you perform your dance for me?

2. Can you perform your story for me?

3. Can you perform it for the class?

Summary for the Special Child:

1. May I see the DANCE STORY Activity Sheets of the dance stories you evaluated?

2. Can you tell me what you liked about the dance?

Homework:

Draw a dance story about your family. Perform it for the class tomorrow.

Name _____

Activity 13
DANCE STORY

Draw your dance story, in order of the steps, in the boxes below:

My dance story is about _____.

1.	**2.**
3.	**4.**
5.	**6.**

Continue on the back if you run out of room.

Activity 14
SHIPS AHOY

Aim:

Can you perform a series of body movements?

Performance Objectives—Students will be able to:

- perform a series of body movements.
- recognize opposites, such as up/down and slow/fast.
- play imaginatively.

Performance Objectives for the Special Child:

- work with a small group of children
- create a dance based on movement

Materials Needed:

- MOVEMENT Activity Sheet
- large box
- nautical gear—skipper's hat, model ship, steering wheel
- cassette player and music tape with water sounds
- blue, yellow, green, and red markers

Motivation:

Tell children they will be creating their own series of body movements today.

Do Now:

Draw or write down everything you know about ships.

Development:

1. Review the "Do Now." Write down on the board everything children know about ships.
2. Display nautical gear. Show model ship.
3. Play cassette tape with water sounds.
4. Before the class, put the steering wheel on the box and draw red, green, yellow, and blue buttons on it. Display the box to the class.

5. Discuss with the class what opposite means. Give some examples: hot/cold, up/down, over/under, slow/fast.

6. Tell children that the box is where the ship is steered from. Give the following commands as you press the following buttons:
   - red—move slowly
   - green—move in a silly way
   - yellow—move fast
   - blue—move up and down

7. Pass out the MOVEMENT Activity Sheets. Ask children to draw each of the four movements described by the colored buttons on their MOVEMENT Activity Sheets. Ask student volunteers to come to the front and display their drawings.

8. Play the music with the water sounds. Ask a student volunteer to be "skipper."

9. The "skipper" comes to the front of the room and operates the box panel.

10. Ask the children to move back desks and chairs and respond to the commands of the skipper.

11. Repeat the process with various "skippers."

Individual Project for the Special Child:

- Ask the special child to choose two or three friends to work with. Give the group the tape and cassette player. Ask the group to create a dance to go with the music to perform for the class.

Summary:

1. Can you show me the body movements you made on the ship?
2. What is the opposite of up and of fast?
3. Can you take the box and pretend you're steering a big ship?

Summary for the Special Child:

1. Can you show me the group you worked with?
2. Can you perform the dance you made up for the class?

Homework:

List as many opposites as you can think of.

Activity 14
MOVEMENT

Draw a slow movement in the first square and color it red. Draw a silly movement in the second square and color it green. Draw a fast movement and color it yellow. Draw an up-and-down movement and color it blue.

1. Slow	2. Silly
3. Fast	**4. Up-and-Down**

Activity 15
ACTING OUT

Aim:

Can you act out a common situation?

Performance Objectives—Students will be able to:

- develop spontaneous language.
- problem solve.
- work cooperatively in groups.

Performance Objectives for the Special Child:

- make notes, in words or pictures, on a class dramatization
- evaluate a class dramatization

Materials Needed:

- PROBLEM-SOLVING PLAY Activity Sheet
- keys
- coins
- rings
- paper cups

Motivation:

Tell students they will be creating their own plays today.

Do Now:

We are going to play a game called "Can You Guess What I Am?" Think of something to be that you can act out without telling anyone who you are.

Development:

1. Review the "Do Now." Ask volunteers to come to the front and act out what they are without talking. Have the children guess what they are. (Don't call on children to do this, as many are shy about performing in front of a group.)
2. Tell children that what they just did is a dramatization, or pretending something in front of an audience. Tell children they will be working out several dramatizations today.

3. As a warm-up, divide the children into groups. Pass out the small objects to the groups. Ask them to work together to create a dramatization about the object. (Objects like coins, cups, and keys should distract children from their self-consciousness.)

4. Have each group perform a story.

5. Next, pass out the PROBLEM-SOLVING PLAY Activity Sheets. Read the directions aloud. Have children prepare solutions to the problems in dramatic story form, using their Activity Sheets as scripts.

6. Have children from each group perform one problem of their choice and their solution. They can make up their own dialogue for this.

Individual Project for the Special Child:

- Have the special child watch the class dramatizations and take notes on them. The child should evaluate what he or she liked about the story. Did the child think it was performed well, and what suggestions does he or she have to improve the skit?

Summary:

1. Can you tell me the words your group used to solve the problem you chose for your dramatization?

2. How did you solve your problem?

3. Did you work in a group?

Summary for the Special Child:

1. Can you tell me from the notes you took, what you liked about the stories that were performed?

2. Were they performed well?

3. How do you think the stories could be better?

Homework:

Choose a famous person you would like to meet. Create a story about what you would say to that person and perform it in class tomorrow.

Name _____

©1997 by The Center for Applied Research in Education

Activity 15
PROBLEM-SOLVING PLAY

Create a solution to the following problems. Then choose one situation and act it out.

1. You are on the cafeteria line waiting to get your lunch. On two separate occasions, students get ahead of you. What do you do the third time this happens?

_____

_____

_____

2. You are walking home from school and your bookbag gets stolen. You run to the local police station, but the police doubt your story.

_____

_____

_____

3. You are in class and the principal announces over the loud speaker that you have to come to the main office immediately. The principal wants to know what you know about a stolen watch. What do you say?

_____

_____

_____

4. You get a Walkman for your birthday. You show it to your friends. They want to borrow it. Your father has asked that you not lend it out. How do you handle the situation?

_____

_____

_____

Activity 16
PLAYING A ROLE

Aim:
Can we play different roles?

Performance Objectives—Students will be able to:
- develop language and abstract thinking.
- perform with other children.
- perform a role play.

Performance Objectives for the Special Child:
- watch a role play
- develop audience skills

Materials Needed:
- ROLE PLAY Activity Sheet
- books on a variety of subjects, such as: *Home Lovely*, by Lynne Rae Perkins, Greenwillow Books: New York, 1995; *How I Was Adopted*, by Joanna Cole, Morrow Junior Books: New York, 1995; *When You Go to Kindergarten*, Morrow Junior Books: New York, 1994; *There's an Owl in the Shower*, by Jean Craighead George, HarperCollins Children's Books: New York, 1995
- materials to make quick costumes, such as construction paper, hats, capes, safety scissors, glue

Motivation:
Tell children they will have the opportunity to play a role today.

Do Now:
List or draw in your notebook some of your favorite characters from books or television.

Development:
1. Read an excerpt from a book with several characters; for example, *There's an Owl in the Shower* is a good one for this.
2. Review the "Do Now." List on the board all the children's favorite characters and their characteristics.

3. Ask volunteers to role-play the owl and two characters, Leon and Borden. Have the children role-play the owl riding on the handlebars of Borden's bike. Tell children they will be doing a role play from one of the books they choose.

4. Divide the class into groups. Pass out the books and ROLE PLAY Activity Sheets.

5. Ask each group to choose a role play, with several characters, from one of the books.

6. Read over the directions from the ROLE PLAY Activity Sheet. Ask the children to make notes on the Activity Sheet about the character they will be playing, what the characters will say, how they will act, stage directions, and how they will put together a costume.

7. Pass out materials. Have each group make costumes.

8. When each group is ready, have them perform a role play.

9. After each role play, have the class discuss what they saw. Remind them that the purpose is to share and discuss the behavior of the characters. The observers should discuss what was said or what might have been said.

10. When all groups are finished, discuss possible future role plays to give children the opportunity to use a variety of reactions and verbal responses.

Individual Project for the Special Child:

• Have the child watch a role play, then participate in the audience discussion.

Summary:

1. Can you describe to me how you played your character and what you said?
2. Can you tell me what role you played?
3. Can you perform it for me with the group?

Summary for the Special Child:

1. Can you tell me about the role play you saw?
2. Can you tell me what a good audience does?

Homework:

Go home and pick a role play from a book. Write or draw a story about it.

Name _____

Activity 16
ROLE PLAY

My character is _____ .

My character looks like: _____

_____

_____

My character will say: _____

_____

_____

My character will wear: _____

_____

_____

This is the character I would like to play next: _____

_____

_____

Activity 17
DRAMATIC SPEAKING

Aim:

Can we speak dramatically?

Performance Objectives—Students will be able to:

- learn a poem.
- arrange the dramatic reading for performance.
- work in a group.

Performance Objectives for the Special Child:

- listen to a dramatic reading
- compare dramatic readings

Materials Needed:

- DRAMATIC SPEAKING Activity Sheet
- various books of poetry, such as: *Sing a Song of Popcorn*, edited by Beatrice Shenk de Regniers et al. Scholastic, Inc.: New York, 1988; *"There's an Awful Lot of Weirdos in Our Neighborhood" and Other Wickedly Funny Verse*, by Colin McNaughton, Simon and Schuster Books for Young Readers: New York, 1987; *Rhymes for Annie Rose*, by Shirley Hughes, Lothrop, Lee and Shepard: New York, 1995; *Gingerbread Days: Poems by Joyce Carol Thomas*, HarperCollins Children's Books: New York, 1995

Motivation:

Tell students they will be dramatizing poems today.

Do Now:

List any poems you know in your notebook.

Development:

1. Pick a poem that would be good dramatically and read it to the class. (See the list of suggested books.)
2. Review the "Do Now." List the children's favorite poems on the board.
3. Tell children they will be dramatizing or "acting out" a poem today.

4. Divide children into groups. Give each group a book from the poetry collection.

5. Pass out the DRAMATIC SPEAKING Activity Sheets. Ask the groups to make notes on their sheets of the poems they want to use for their dramatic reading, and directions on how they will dramatize their parts.

6. Ask children to pass the books around as they finish with them, so each group will get to choose from a variety of books.

7. Remind children, before they start, that it is the pleasure of the participants, not the audience, that's important.

8. Choose a leader for each group to start, cue, and direct different speakers.

9. Explain that each member of the group must participate individually or in the group as a whole.

10. Have the groups perform their poems.

Individual Project for the Special Child:

- Have the child listen to the different groups speak, then compare the different readings.

Summary:

1. Can you tell me the poem you learned?
2. Can you recite it for me?
3. Can you recite it with your group?

Summary for the Special Child:

1. Did you listen to your group recite poems?
2. Can you tell me two things about it?
3. Can you recite any part of it?

Homework:

Go home and choose a poem you like. Read it to the class tomorrow or describe it.

Name _____

Activity 17
DRAMATIC SPEAKING

Choose a poem or series of poems. Write them here:

_____

_____

_____

_____

_____

_____

_____

Make notes here about how you would act it out:

©1997 by The Center for Applied Research in Education

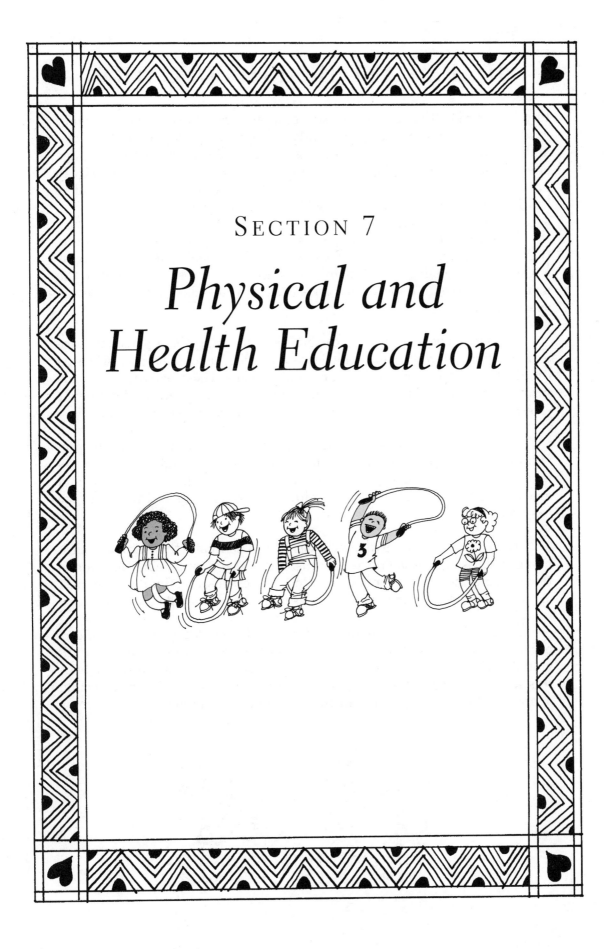

SECTION 7

Physical and
Health Education

PHYSICAL AND HEALTH EDUCATION

Physical and health activities constitute an important area for the primary grades special child. Some special children excel in sports; others have disabilities that keep them from excelling. Special children have a wide range of abilities and limitations in physical education, and you must be ready to handle them all in your primary classroom. Basic living skills related to health can be a formidable challenge for the special child.

In this section, physical activities do not stress competition, but direction following and a feeling of confidence. The health activities stress engendering a feeling of well-being and success in the special child in the primary classroom. All activities are suited to whole-class activities for the special child.

The section begins with basic exercises in learning about personal space and direction following. Next come lessons in such basic safety procedures as fire drills, and following verbal and auditory cues. These activities are particularly good for the beginning of the year when you're setting the tone for classroom management of the whole class, including the special child.

The physical education activities then go on to learning body parts, providing a basis for health activities later in the section, and basic exercises and movements through games. A minimum of equipment is used, and everyday items like balloons and jump ropes are emphasized to encourage easy recess skills.

The health section introduces basic health concepts, then explores such living skills as hand washing, teeth brushing, and sun protection. Good nutrition at home and school is emphasized in a few lessons, and finally, the impact of environmental pollution on our bodies and what we can do about it.

As always, activities provide whole-class lessons that can easily incorporate the special child, while also providing projects that can be used individually by the special child. Direction following is emphasized throughout this section in whole-class and individual activities, to help the special child adapt well behaviorally in the inclusive primary classroom.

Activity 1
GETTING TO KNOW YOU

Aim:

Can we become aware of personal space?

Performance Objectives—Students will be able to:

- become aware of personal space.
- learn how to shake hands.
- follow directions.

Performance Objectives for the Special Child:

- learn how to get acquainted with another child in the class
- play with his or her new friend during "free" time

Materials Needed:

- MY HOME SPACE Activity Sheet
- markers
- hoops

Motivation:

Tell children they will be playing friendship games today.

Do Now:

Write or list in your notebook a description of where you do your homework at home.

Development:

1. Review the "Do Now." Ask children to name the places where they do their homework.
2. Explain that this place is a *personal space*. A personal space can be a place that you take over as your own, even if it's for a limited period of time.
3. Pass out the MY HOME SPACE Activity Sheet and markers.
4. Explain to children that a personal space at home can be a room, a place where they do homework, a reading place, or any place that they claim for their own.

5. Read directions aloud from the Activity Sheet. Have children draw their personal spaces.

6. Ask volunteers to share their MY HOME SPACE Activity Sheets.

7. Pass a hoop to each student. Have them each pick a personal space and put their hoop there. Have each student sit cross-legged within his or her own hoop. Explain that this is that student's personal space.

8. Have each child step out of his or her hoop and shake hands with another child. Tell children this is a way of greeting or meeting someone. Model shaking hands with a student, look into the student's eyes, and smile. Have them return to their hoops.

9. Next, ask all the girls to leave their hoops, shake hands, and introduce themselves by telling another girl their names. Have the girls return to their hoops.

10. Next, have all the boys leave their hoops, shake hands, and tell one other boy something they like (for example, I like to play cards or I like to go to the supermarket with my father). Have the boys return to their hoops.

11. Finish off with each child sitting quietly in his or her hoop, enjoying the peace and quiet. Have students return the hoops to the play area.

Individual Project for the Special Child:

- During the course of the "hoop" exercise, ask the child to pick a friend to spend time with during "free" time.

Summary:

1. Where is your personal space?

2. How do you shake hands with a new friend?

3. (Give a direction and ask the child to follow.) Can you get your hoop and go to your personal space?

Summary for the Special Child:

1. Did you make a friend in the class?

2. Did you play with him or her during "free" time?

Homework:

Go home and talk to a family member. Ask the family member about his or her personal space. Write about the family member's personal space or draw a picture of it.

Activity 1
MY HOME SPACE

We all have a personal space where we do homework, sleep, or just like to be alone. Draw your personal space in your home below. Then write under it any details you want to share about it.

Activity 2
SAFETY TIPS

Aim:

Can we follow safe rules during an emergency?

Performance Objectives—Students will be able to:

- practice fire drill procedures.
- learn to line up single file.
- discuss safety rules.

Performance Objectives for the Special Child:

- cite a safety rule
- draw a picture of himself or herself on a safety line

Materials Needed:

- SAFETY Activity Sheet
- crayons
- marching tape
- cassette player
- safety scissors
- manila folders or cardboard
- glue

Motivation:

Tell students they will be learning safety procedures today.

Do Now:

Write or draw in your notebook any emergency situations where safety might be a special consideration.

Development:

1. Review the "Do Now." List on the board any emergency situations the children come up with—fire, medical, emergency, and so on.
2. Tell children that they will be playing games to prepare for emergency procedures. Review emergency situations and what to do in them, for example, fire or a lightning storm.

3. Tell children that fire drills help keep us safe by teaching us what to do in case of fire.

4. Review fire drill procedures for your school with the children.

5. Stress these safety points:
   - Stop everything you're doing, including talking, when alarm sounds.
   - Line up in single file (this can be difficult for young children because they are usually trained double file).
   - Follow directions.

6. Pass out the SAFETY Activity Sheet. Read the directions aloud. Pass out crayons, glue, cardboard, and scissors.

7. Assist children in gluing their SAFETY Activity Sheets to the manila folders or cardboard.

8. After coloring, assist the children in cutting the figures out of the Activity Sheets.

9. After everyone has the figure cut out, play the march music. Line the children up one by one, holding their figures above their heads. Have them march around the room single file.

10. Stop the music and collect the figures.

11. Take the class outside to the designated area and have them practice procedures for a fire drill.

Individual Project for the Special Child:

- Ask the special child to draw a picture of safety procedures during a fire drill.

Summary:

1. Can you tell me what the safety rules are for a fire drill?
2. Can you tell me how to line up single file?
3. Can you practice fire drill procedures?

Summary for the Special Child:

1. Can you show me the picture you drew of the fire drill?
2. Can you tell me one safety rule you learned from the fire drill?

Homework:

Go home and talk to your parents about an emergency situation at home, such as a fire, and what safety rules you could develop at home to deal with the emergency.

Activity 2
SAFETY

Glue the sheet to a manila folder or cardboard. Color it in to look like you. Then cut it out:

Activity 3
FORMATIONS

Aim:
Can we go into the right formation when we hear and see the signal?

Performance Objectives—Students will be able to:
- listen to and follow directions.
- stop and become quiet on signal.
- form a line on signal.
- form a circle on signal.

Performance Objectives for the Special Child:
- follow individual instructions
- on signal, walk to a free space in the play area and sit cross-legged, facing the teacher

Materials Needed:
- FORMATIONS Activity Sheet
- markers

Motivation:
Tell students they will get to play a game today and some will be chosen as leaders and co-leaders.

Do Now:
List or draw in your notebook any ways in which you think the class could move together in a cooperative way.

Development:
1. Review the "Do Now." Elicit from the class that it would be helpful if the class could learn to line up or form a circle or become quiet in an efficient, cooperative way.
2. Tell students they will be playing a game today with leaders and co-leaders, but first they must learn some basic signals.
3. Pass out the FORMATIONS Activity Sheet and markers. Tell children to write down the signals and formations as you go through them.

4. The first signal is the Quiet Signal. Put your right hand overhead with the index and middle finger raised. Take the other hand and put your index finger to your lip. Tell children this means that everyone should stop moving, stop talking, and listen. Draw the two signals on the board and have the children do the same on their sheets.

5. Give the quiet signal to the class and wait until everyone is quiet and paying attention.

6. The next signal to introduce is the Line Signal. Extend the right arm sideways at shoulder length. The right hand should have your index finger pointing to the place where you want the first child to line up. Draw this signal on the board and have the children note it on their Activity Sheets.

7. Next, give the line signal and have the children line up. Organize the children into a line the way you want them to learn how to line up, for example, in size order.

8. Next do the Circle Signal. The right hand should be raised overhead while it makes a circle with the index finger and thumb, while the left hand points down with the index finger indicating where you want the circle formed. Draw the signals on the board and have the children note this on their Activity Sheets.

9. Go through the circle signal. Show the children where they should sit in the circle and how they should seat themselves cross-legged on the floor. Wait until the entire class is seated properly in the circle before stopping.

10. Next, divide the class into four groups. Designate a leader and co-leader for each group. Give each group a color and an area. Have the group sit cross-legged on the floor, facing the leader.

11. To play the game, have leaders and co-leaders switch giving the formation signals. If the group responds correctly, they get a point. The group with the most points wins. Have children take turns being leaders and co-leaders so everyone has a chance to give the signals.

Individual Project for the Special Child:

- Give the special child a "home" space in the free or library section. The signal is to point to the special child with the right index finger and point to the home space with your left index finger. Have the child go to his or her space and sit on the floor cross-legged facing you. This is a particularly good behavior management technique if the child is experiencing problems interrelating with the class.

Summary:

1. Can you sit down in that chair?

2. Can you stop and become quiet (give the quiet signal)?

3. Can you form a line (give the line signal)?

4. Can you form a circle (give the circle signal)?

Summary for the Special Child:

1. Can you follow the directions I'm about to give?
2. Can you go to your "home space" (give the signal)?

Homework:

Write or draw some of the activities your family does to cooperate together, for example, cooking or washing dishes.

Name _____

In the spaces below, draw the signal that means each formation:

Quiet	Line	Circle

Activity 4
MOVEMENT WITH PATTERNS

Aim:

Can we follow verbal and auditory cues?

Performance Objectives—Students will be able to:

- demonstrate a pattern by snapping fingers and clapping hands.
- listen, repeat, and move to patterns.
- follow verbal and auditory cues.

Performance Objectives for the Special Child:

- choose a partner
- find ways to move the whole body to a new pattern

Materials Needed:

- MOVEMENT WITH PATTERNS Activity Sheet
- cassette player
- music tape
- markers

Motivation:

Tell children they will be learning some patterns today and making up their own.

Do Now:

Look around the room and name any patterns you can see. Draw them in your notebook.

Development:

1. Play the music tape for the class. Ask the class if the music makes them want to do anything with their bodies, like dance, snap their fingers, tap their feet.
2. Review the "Do Now." Explain that a pattern is a way in which colors, lines, or shapes are repeated in order. List all the patterns that children find on the board.
3. Demonstrate a pattern by clapping hands, snapping fingers, or tapping feet.

4. Have children repeat the pattern after you.

5. Have student volunteers come to the front and demonstrate a pattern that you name, for example, one clap and two hops.

6. Pass out the MOVEMENT WITH PATTERNS Activity Sheets and markers. Read instructions aloud to students.

7. Have students draw and create their own patterns on their Activity Sheets.

8. Ask student volunteers to come to the front and display their Activity Sheets and demonstrate their patterns.

9. Create a bulletin board entitled "Movement With Patterns." Hang students' MOVEMENT WITH PATTERNS Activity Sheets on the bulletin board.

Individual Project for the Special Child:

• Ask the special child to choose a partner. Have both children use their whole bodies to create a pattern.

Summary:

1. Can you demonstrate a pattern?
2. Can you move to a pattern?
3. Can you hop twice and skip once?

Summary for the Special Child:

1. Can you show me your partner?
2. Can you and your partner show me the pattern you created?

Homework:

Find some materials at home, for example, buttons, and make a pattern. Bring it in to share with the class tomorrow.

Name _____

Activity 4
MOVEMENT WITH
PATTERNS

Draw below the pattern you want to make. Then
demonstrate it from the Activity Sheet:

Activity 5
STORY WITHOUT WORDS

Aim:
Can we tell a story without words?

Performance Objectives—Students will be able to:
- express themselves in movement without words.
- move in a particular space.
- act out a specific story in sequence.

Performance Objectives for the Special Child:
- find a partner to work with
- work cooperatively with a partner on developing a story pantomime

Materials Needed:
- STORY WITHOUT WORDS Activity Sheet
- markers
- music tape without words
- cassette player
- group of story books familiar to the children, such as *The Mother Goose Treasury*, by Raymond Briggs, Dell Publishing Co.: New York, 1980; *Arabian Nights*, Retold by Deborah Nourse Lattimore, HarperCollins: New York, 1995; *Tales From Moominvalley*, by Tove Jansson, Farrar, Straus & Giroux: New York, 1995; *Sofia and the Heartmender*, by Marie Olofsdotter, Free Spirit Publishing Inc: Minneapolis, MN, 1993; *The Book of Dragons*, Selected by Michael Hague, Morrow Junior Books: New York, 1995

Motivation:
Tell children they will be acting out a story today.

Do Now:
Draw or write a story in sequence in your notebook.

Development:
1. Play the music tape and read one of the stories from the storybooks you have assembled.

2. Review the "Do Now." Write a few story sequences on the board.

3. Review the concept of personal versus general space. Discuss moving in those spaces.

4. Explain to the class what a pantomime is. Have a few volunteers pantomime some simple acts like running, eating, and so forth.

5. Have volunteers come to the front and make up their own pantomime while the rest of the class guesses what they're doing.

6. Pass out the storybooks, markers, and STORY WITHOUT WORDS Activity Sheets.

7. Tell children to choose a story they would like to tell without words.

8. Read the instructions on the Activity Sheet aloud. Have children draw or write in their pantomime instructions.

9. Have volunteers share their Activity Sheets and perform their pantomimes.

Individual Project for the Special Child:

- Have the special child choose a partner. Then have them work out a story without words together.

Summary:

1. Can you choose an action and act it out without words?

2. Can you find your personal space to act out a story?

3. Can you act out your story without words?

Summary for the Special Child:

1. Can you get a partner to do your story with?

2. Can the two of you act out your story?

Homework:

Choose a different story to sequence and draw or write it out.

Activity 5
STORY WITHOUT WORDS

Choose a story. Imagine telling the story without words. Draw or
make notes on how you would tell the story and in what order you
would do it.

1. Name of Story _____

2. First Panel	3. Second Panel
4. Third Panel	5. Fourth Panel

Activity 6
BODY PARTS

Aim:

Can we name our body parts?

Performance Objectives—Students will be able to:

- listen and follow directions.
- name the parts of the body.
- point to a body part that is named.

Performance Objectives for the Special Child:

- draw a body with all its parts
- label body parts on a drawing

Materials Needed:

- BODY PARTS Activity Sheet
- beanbags
- crayons
- large sheet of paper (like newsprint)
- safety scissors
- glue
- construction paper

Motivation:

Everyone will play a game using body parts today.

Do Now:

Write or draw in your notebook as many body parts as you can think of.

Development:

1. Review the "Do Now." Write the different body parts on the board and have children demonstrate where they are as they write them.
2. Draw a body outline on the board.
3. Have volunteers name and demonstrate the body parts. Label the parts on the body outline you drew on the board.

4. Tell children they will be playing a game about body parts, but first they will have to learn the names.

5. Pass out the BODY PARTS Activity Sheet, crayons, glue, construction paper, and scissors. Read the directions aloud.

6. Ask children to cut the Activity Sheet into body parts and glue them in the correct order on the construction paper. Model one for them in the front of the room.

7. Children may finish by completing the drawing and making the body themselves or have someone else do it.

8. Have volunteers share their BODY PARTS Activity Sheets with the class.

9. Push back the desks and chairs. Tell children they will be playing a game.

10. Pass out beanbags to each child. Ask children to balance the beanbags on their body parts as you call out the names; for example, if you call out head, they will all balance beanbags on their heads.

11. After you've reviewed basic body parts with the bean bag exercise, collect the beanbags.

12. Prepare them to play a new game called "Simon Says."

13. Tell children they must listen carefully to directions during the game. If they hear, "Simon says touch your toes," they must touch their toes. If they just hear, "Touch your toes," they must not touch their toes.

14. Play the game, going through all the body parts covered in the previous exercises.

15. Repeat the game, letting student volunteers be Simon.

Individual Project for the Special Child:

• Lay a piece of newsprint as long as the special child on the floor. Have the special child lie down on the sheet while another child traces the special child's body on the sheet. Have the special child label the body parts and put his or her name on the sheet.

Summary:

1. Can you listen to directions and follow them?

2. Can you name body parts?

3. Can you touch your head, arms, feet, eyes, and nose?

Summary for the Special Child:

• Can you draw an outline of the body and label its parts?

Homework:

Think of your favorite body part. Draw it and label it.

Activity 6
BODY PARTS

Cut out the different body parts on this Activity Sheet. Then paste them in the right order on a piece of construction paper. Label the parts with crayon. Last, draw it into a real person:

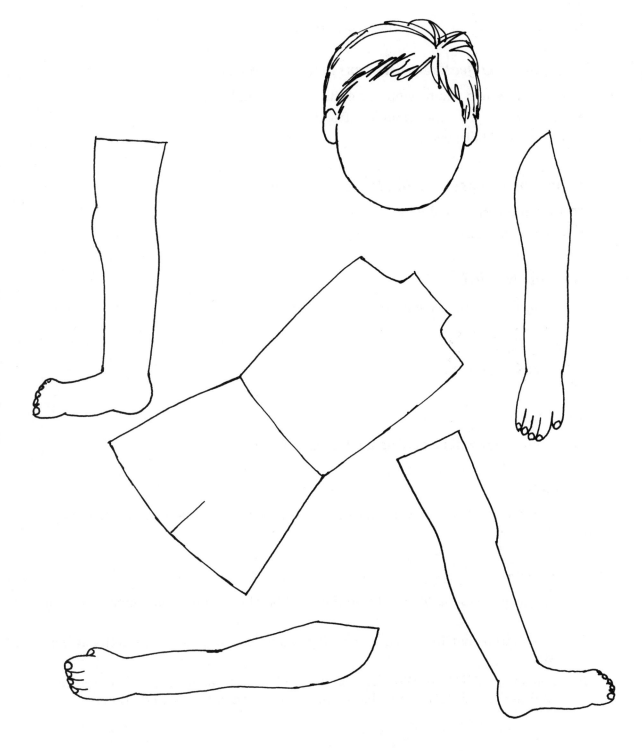

387

Activity 7
ANIMAL WORKOUT

Aim:

Can we develop leg, arm, and shoulder strength?

Performance Objectives—Students will be able to:

- develop sounds and movements of different animals.
- improve leg, arm, and shoulder strength.
- follow verbal directions.

Performance Objectives for the Special Child:

- stretch the arms and legs
- follow directions

Materials Needed:

- ANIMAL WALKS Activity Sheet
- markers
- music tape
- cassette player

Motivation:

Tell students they will be playing an animal game today.

Do Now:

In your notebook, list or draw as many animals as you can think of. Describe the way they move.

Development:

1. Play the music tape. Tell children they will be playing an animal game to music today.
2. Tell children that before they can play the game, they must learn the animal walks.
3. Pass out the ANIMAL WALKS Activity Sheets and markers. Tell children they will first draw the animal walks on their sheets, then they will do them.

4. Read the directions aloud from the Activity Sheet. Tell students to draw the motion as they see it on their Activity Sheets. Read each one, for example, Dog Walk. Have a student demonstrate the motion in the front of the room.

5. Next, demonstrate the Gorilla Walk. Have students draw it on their Activity Sheets. Go through this procedure with each animal walk.

6. After you have completed the Activity Sheets, have some volunteers come to the front and share their drawings.

7. Ask the children who demonstrated each animal walk to come to the front and demonstrate it again. This time have the students get up and practice what the student demonstrates.

8. Play the music tape. Have a volunteer come to the front and call out the animal walk for the children to do. The volunteer should not demonstrate it.

9. Vary the game with different volunteers.

Individual Project for the Special Child:

- Ask the special child to do a cat walk. Ask the child to get down on all fours. Have him or her slowly lift the middle section upward, taking the weight off the toes and hands and stretching like a cat.

Summary:

1. Can you show me how some different animals move and sound?

2. Can you move your legs, arms, and shoulders like a specific animal?

3. Can you demonstrate one of the walks you learned in the animal walk game?

Summary for the Special Child:

- Can you demonstrate the cat walk for me?

Homework:

Think of a different animal from the ones in the animal walk game. Develop a walk and a sound for that animal and demonstrate it in class tomorrow.

Activity 7
ANIMAL WALKS

Below are listed different animal walks you will be learning. Please draw pictures in each box to go with the animal walk that shows how the animal walks:

1. Dog Walk

   Walk on your hands and one foot, holding the other foot off the floor, to imitate a lame dog.

2. Gorilla Walk

   Bend over and hold onto the front of your foot while keeping your legs as straight as you can. Walk forward in this position.

3. Bear Walk

   Get down on all fours and put your weight on your hands and feet. Move forward by moving the right hand and the right leg at the same time.

Name _____

ANIMAL WALKS, *continued*

4. Seal Walk

Bend over, leaning on your hands for support. Move forward, dragging your feet behind like a seal.

5. Chicken Walk

Get into a squatting position, put your arms between your legs and grasp your ankles. Strut around like a chicken.

6. Duck Walk

Squat the way you did in the chicken walk, but this time, tuck your hands under your armpits and walk around like a duck.

Activity 8
JUMPING ROPE

Aim:

Can we jump rope?

Performance Objectives—Students will be able to:

- turn a jump rope.
- jump with a jump rope.
- jump to rhythm.

Performance Objectives for the Special Child:

- work with a partner
- develop a jumping pattern

Materials Needed:

- JUMPING ROPE Activity Sheet
- one jump rope per child (ask children to bring in prior to the lesson)
- crayons
- tape of music with a 4/4 beat
- cassette player

Motivation:

Tell children they will be jumping rope today.

Do Now:

List any songs you can think of in your notebook.

Development:

1. Review the "Do Now." List any songs the children cite on the chalkboard.
2. Play the cassette tape of the 4/4 rhythm song you are using for the lesson for the children.
3. Pass out the JUMPING ROPE Activity Sheet and crayons. Read directions aloud and ask children to work on their Activity Sheets.
4. Ask student volunteers to share their Activity Sheets with the class.

5. Push back the desks or, go to the gym or, weather permitting, take children outside to the schoolyard.

6. Ask children to find a personal space. Make sure that there is enough space to turn a rope without touching anyone.

7. Tell children to stand tall with knees slightly bent and heads up.

8. Tell children to turn the rope, using small, circular wrist movements.

9. Tell children to start turning the rope, swing it overhead and backward, and catch it under their heels.

10. Tell children to start with the rope behind them. Swing it overhead and forward, and catch it under their toes.

11. Play the cassette tape. Tell children to hold the rope, one end in each hand, just off the floor. Allow the rope to swing back and forth, just off the floor. Have them jump over the rope each time it passes under them.

12. Collect the jump ropes for use at recess time.

Individual Project for the Special Child:

• Choose a friend to work with. Develop your own jumping pattern; for example jump once, catching it with your toes and jump again.

Summary:

1. Can you take this jump rope and turn it?

2. Can you jump with this jump rope?

3. Can you jump to the music?

Summary for the Special Child:

1. Can you show me the friend you worked with?

2. Can you take this jump rope and show me the pattern that you and your friend worked out?

Homework:

Go home and jump for sixty seconds. Count the number of jumps and write them down.

Name _____

Color the first child jumping rope red, the second child blue, the third child yellow, the fourth child green, and the fifth child orange.

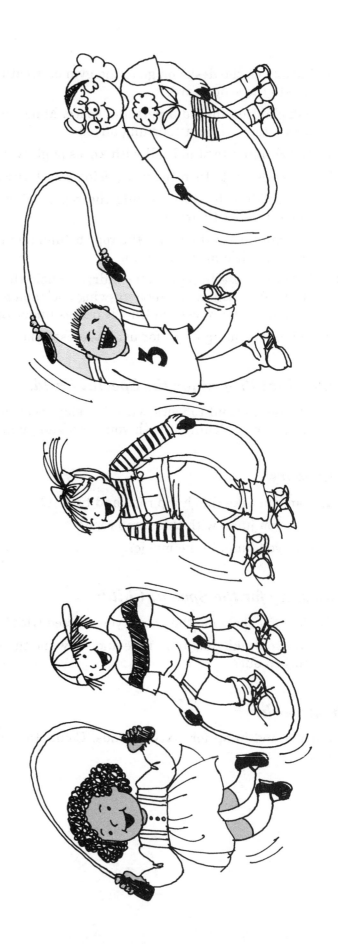

Activity 9
BALLOON FUN

Aim:

Can we follow directions with balloons?

Performance Objectives—Students will be able to:

- develop skills to be used in ball sports, such as soccer.
- follow directions.
- visually track a balloon.

Performance Objectives for the Special Child:

- share a balloon with a partner
- invent an exercise with the balloon

Materials Needed:

- BALLOON FUN Activity Sheet
- colored markers
- balloons (Purchase durable ones in bulk. Have children blow them up prior to the lesson and knot them. Store them in a large garbage bag—and be sure to have extras!)
- a whistle

Motivation:

Tell students they will have their own balloon to play with today.

Do Now:

List or draw as many ball games as you can think of in your notebook.

Development:

1. Review the "Do Now." List the ball games that the children name on the board.
2. Tell children that they will be playing a balloon game today that will help them with ball games in the future.
3. Pass out the BALLOON FUN Activity Sheets and markers. Read the directions aloud. Have children color the balloons.

4. Have student volunteers share their Activity Sheets with the class.

5. Push the desks back in the classroom. Have children find a personal space.

6. Give a balloon to each child.

7. Give the children specific instructions to manipulate the balloon. First ask them to tap the balloon with their left hand, then with their right hand, then tap it from one hand to the other.

8. Have the children tap the balloon up in the air and turn around once. Then blow the whistle to have them catch it with their two hands.

9. Have the children keep the balloon in the air without using their hands, like a soccer player. Have them use their knees, feet, head, and so on.

10. Have students interlock fingers and keep their arms long in front. Then have them bat the balloon upwards, keeping their arms straight, as in volleyball.

11. Last, have them bat the balloon, making believe their hands are tennis racquets.

12. Have student volunteers collect the balloons and store them in the garbage bag.

Individual Project for the Special Child:

• Have the special child choose a partner. Give them one balloon and have them invent an exercise together; for example, lie on your back and use your hands and feet to bat the balloon.

Summary:

1. Can you select a balloon and follow my directions?

2. Can you see where the balloon is going?

3. Can you bat the balloon like a baseball, keep it going without your hands like a soccer ball, and serve it like a volleyball?

Summary for the Special Child:

1. Can you show me the partner you chose?

2. Can you show me the exercise you two made up with the balloon?

Homework:

Interview the people in your family and find out which ball games each has played. Report back to class tomorrow.

Activity 9
BALLOON FUN

Color the first balloon red, the second balloon yellow, the third balloon green, the fourth balloon blue, and the fifth balloon orange.

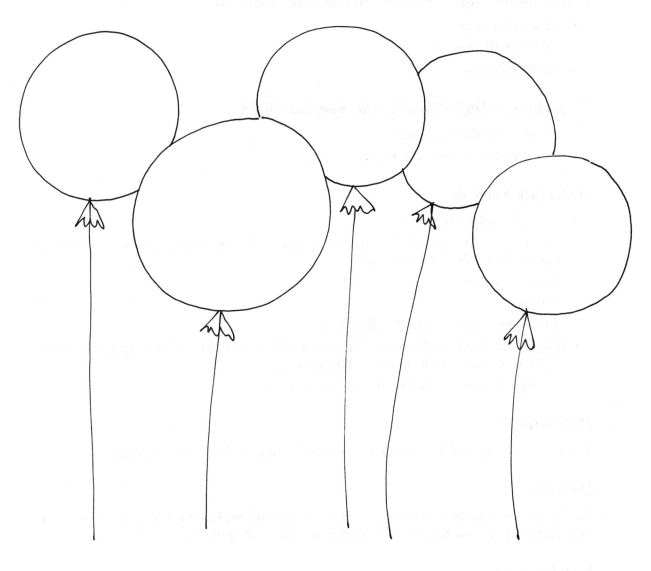

Activity 10
TOSSING AND CATCHING

Aim:

Can we toss and catch a ball?

Performance Objectives—Students will be able to:

- toss a ball in place.
- catch a ball in place.
- follow directions.

Performance Objectives for the Special Child:

- follow individual directions
- toss a ball in a hoop or basket

Materials Needed:

- BALL TOSS Activity Sheet
- music tape (A spirited 4/4 march is good, for example, "Stars and Stripes Forever" by John Philip Sousa.)
- cassette player
- crayons
- a ball per child (a Nerf™ ball is best)
- *This Is Baseball*, by Margaret Blackstone, Henry Holt and Company: New York, 1993, or some other book about ball playing
- a hoop (An empty wastepaper basket will also do.)

Motivation:

Tell children they will be playing a game with their balls and music today.

Do Now:

Do this problem in your notebook. If Sally tosses her ball seven times and Bert tosses it eight times, how many ball tosses were there altogether?

Development:

1. Review the "Do Now." Have a student volunteer do it in number form on the board and have students check their answers.
2. Read aloud the book *This Is Baseball*, or another book about ball playing. Discuss what you read with the class.

3. Explain to students that they will be playing a ball game today with music. They will also be practicing some skills that will help them later on when playing ball games, such as baseball.

4. Pass out the BALL TOSS Activity Sheet and crayons. Read the directions aloud. Explain that Rodney Raccoon needs to get the ball in the hoop and ask the children to find the path through the maze from the ball to the hoop.

5. After the children finish their Activity Sheets, have some volunteers come to the front and share their solutions.

6. Push back the desks or move to the gym or schoolyard. Tell the children to listen to instructions and find a personal space.

7. Pass out the balls. Tell children to toss them up gently and catch the balls again. After they have accomplished this, have them form a circle.

8. Play the march for the children on the cassette player. Tell children to march around in a circle with their balls quietly until they hear the music stop. Then they are to stand still and toss their balls in the air and catch them until they hear the music start, when they will hold their balls and begin marching again.

9. Those children who do not follow instructions will be eliminated. The children who follow instructions all the time will be the winners. (There can be more than one.)

10. Those children who are "winners" should be rewarded by being allowed to lead the game. They should decide when to put the music on and off on the cassette player.

Individual Project for the Special Child:

- Give the individual child a Nerf™ ball and hoop or empty wastebasket. Have the child practice tossing the ball until he or she can successfully land it in the hoop or wastebasket on three successive tries. (If the child has trouble accomplishing this task, move the hoop or basket closer. If it's too easy, move it farther away from the child.)

Summary:

1. Can you follow my instructions?
2. Can you toss a ball in place?
3. Can you catch a ball in place?

Summary for the Special Child:

1. Can you follow these special instructions?
2. Can you toss a ball in the wastebasket three times in a row without missing?

Homework:

Take your ball home and practice the toss and catch in place.

Name _____

Activity 10
BALL TOSS

Rodney Raccoon wants to put the ball in the hoop, but he needs to get through the maze. Can you help him? Draw a path from Rodney to the hoop, and then color in Rodney and the hoop.

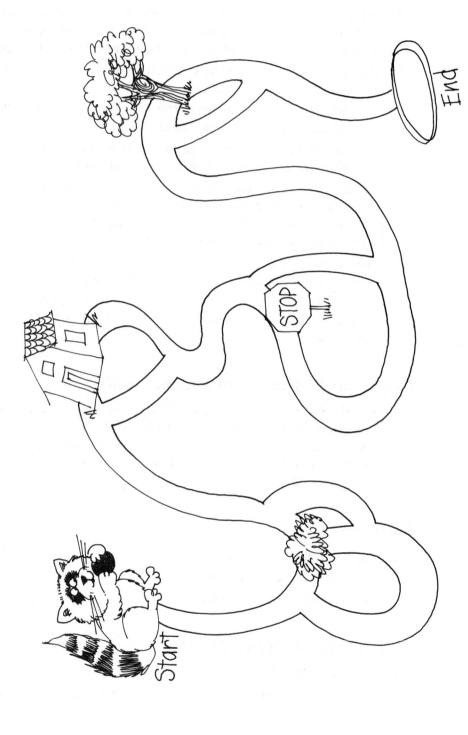

Activity 11
BALLS OF FUN

Aim:

Can we throw and dodge a ball?

Performance Objectives—Students will be able to:

- throw a ball.
- dodge a ball.
- switch roles in a ball game.

Performance Objectives for the Special Child:

- catch a ball from another player
- throw a ball to another player

Materials Needed:

- MONKEY WITH A BALL Activity Sheet
- *Dulcie Dando, Soccer Star*, by Sue Stops, Henry Holt and Company: New York, 1992, or some other ball game story
- two Nerf™ balls
- crayons

Motivation:

Tell students they will be playing "Monkey in the Middle" today.

Do Now:

Name as many ball games as you can think of.

Development:

1. Review the "Do Now." List all the ball games the class can think of on the board.
2. Read aloud the book *Dulcie Dando: Soccer Star*, or another book about a ball game.
3. Discuss the book and different ball games with the class. Tell the class they will be playing a ball game today.
4. Pass out the MONKEY WITH A BALL Activity Sheets and crayons.

5. Read directions aloud and ask students to color in the monkeys with the balls and cross out the monkeys without balls.

6. Have student volunteers share their Activity Sheets with the class. Check them for accuracy.

7. Explain that they will be playing a game that will help them develop skills they can use in ball games, such as throwing a ball and dodging a ball.

8. Push back the desks, or move to your play area in the gym or schoolyard. Bring the two Nerf™ balls.

9. Divide the class in half. Tell the first half to form a circle around the second half.

10. Explain that you will be playing "Monkey in the Middle," in which the children in the middle are the monkeys. The children on the outer circle will take turns throwing one Nerf™ ball at the "monkeys." If the "monkey" successfully dodges the ball and doesn't get hit, he or she goes to the outer circle and the child who threw the ball becomes a "monkey in the middle." If the "monkey" gets hit, he or she stays in the middle.

11. After the children have been playing for awhile, introduce the second Nerf™ ball and have two balls going at once.

Individual Project for the Special Child:

- Ask the special child to choose a friend to play ball with. Give them one Nerf ball. Have them throw it to each other and catch it.

Summary:

1. Can you throw a ball?

2. Can you dodge a ball?

3. Were you the "monkey in the middle" and in the outer circle?

Summary for the Special Child:

1. Can you throw the Nerf™ ball to me?

2. Can you catch the Nerf™ ball when I throw it?

Homework:

Go home and throw a ball around with your family.

Name _____

MONKEY WITH A BALL

Some of the monkeys on this page have a ball. Some do not. Color in the monkeys that have a ball. Cross out the monkeys that do not.

Activity 12
WEALTH OF HEALTH

Aim:

How can we be at our healthy best?

Performance Objectives—Students will be able to:

- recognize that it is in everyone's best interest to be healthy.
- identify good and bad habits.
- learn behaviors that are good health habits.

Performance Objectives for the Special Child:

- describe how he or she feels when sick
- describe how he or she feels when well

Materials Needed:

- WEALTH OF HEALTH Activity Sheet
- crayons
- *Good Night, Feet* by Constance Morgenstern, Henry Holt and Company: New York, 1991, *Lunch* by Denise Fleming, Henry Holt and Company: New York, 1993, or some other book about the body or food.

Motivation:

Tell students they will be developing their own plans for good health today.

Do Now:

List or draw in your notebook any habits you have.

Development:

1. Read *Lunch* or some other book about the body or food aloud to the class. Discuss the book.

2. Review the "Do Now." List on the board any habits the children name.

3. Explain that a habit is something we do so often that after awhile we do it without thinking about it. Clarify that habits can be good or bad.

4. Make two columns on the board for good and bad habits. Have the child who names the habit classify it as good or bad.

5. Explain that good habits lead to good health. Add to the good habits list and make sure it includes: exercising daily, eight hours of sleep a night, a good breakfast, brushing teeth at least twice a day, washing hands before meals and after the bathroom, choosing healthy snacks, wearing a helmet on a bike and a seatbelt in the car, talking about feelings, eating a good lunch and a good dinner, spending time with family and friends, bathing daily.

6. Pass out the WEALTH OF HEALTH Activity Sheet and crayons. Read directions aloud and ask students to list or draw healthy habits on their Activity Sheets.

7. Have student volunteers share their Activity Sheets with the class.

8. Make a "Wealth of Health" bulletin board. Hang the students' Activity Sheets and drawings about health on the board.

Individual Project for the Special Child:

- Ask the special child to do a "talking picture" of the last time he or she was sick. (This is a picture with a bubble of dialog from the character in the picture.) Then ask the child to make another "talking picture" about when he or she got well again.

Summary:

1. Why is it good to be healthy?
2. Can you describe some good and bad health habits?
3. Can you describe some of the good health habits you practice?

Summary for the Special Child:

1. Can you describe to me your "talking picture" of when you were sick?
2. Can you describe to me your "talking picture" of when you got well?

Homework:

Bring home your WEALTH OF HEALTH Activity Sheet. Share it with your family.

Activity 12

WEALTH OF HEALTH

Below, list all of the things you should do to keep your body healthy. Draw pictures and label them.

Activity 13

SLOSHING AND WASHING

Aim:

Can we wash our hands?

Performance Objectives—Students will be able to:

- wash their hands effectively.
- get an understanding of germs.
- learn the appropriate times to wash their hands.

Performance Objectives for the Special Child:

- understand that keeping clean helps prevent health problems
- work cooperatively with a partner

Materials Needed:

- LET'S REMEMBER TO WASH OUR HANDS Activity Sheet
- copy of *The Velveteen Rabbit,* by Margery Williams, Simon and Schuster Books for Young Readers: New York, 1994, or some other book about illness
- crayons
- sink with warm water or a bowl of water
- soap
- paper towels

Motivation:

Tell children they will have the opportunity to wash their hands in class today.

Do Now:

Draw in your notebook a picture of your favorite doll or stuffed animal, or one belonging to a friend.

Development:

1. Review the "Do Now." Have volunteers share pictures of their stuffed animals.
2. Show the class the picture of *The Velveteen Rabbit* on the front of the book.

3. Explain to the class that stuffed animals or dolls can be very nice, but in the upcoming story, they became a problem for the main character.

4. Read the story *The Velveteen Rabbit*, or some other book about illness or germs, aloud to the class.

5. Discuss with the class the concept of germs and how they got on the rabbit and other possessions the boy had. When he got ill, the possessions needed to be washed or destroyed to destroy the germs.

6. Ask children when they think they should wash their hands to avoid germs. Elicit from them, and write on the board, after they sneeze or cough, after using the toilet, before they eat, and anytime their hands get dirty.

7. Remind children that the germs are there even though they can't see them.

8. Tell children that they will be working on an Activity Sheet today to help them remember to wash their hands.

9. Pass out LET'S REMEMBER TO WASH OUR HANDS Activity Sheets and crayons. Read directions aloud and ask children to draw themselves washing their hands.

10. Ask student volunteers to share their Activity Sheets.

11. Set up soap, paper towels, and water for class. Have each child, including the special child, wash his or her hands and dry them.

Individual Project for the Special Child:

• Choose a partner to work with. Discuss with your partner the different ways to keep clean to keep healthy.

Summary:

1. Can you wash your hands?

2. Do you know what germs are?

3. Do you know when you should wash your hands?

Summary for the Special Child:

1. Can you show me the partner you worked with?

2. Can you and your partner tell me how you can keep clean and healthy?

Homework:

Take home your LET'S REMEMBER TO WASH OUR HANDS Activity Sheets and hang them in a place where it will remind you to wash your hands. (Also, hang one in the classroom.)

Name _____

Activity 13
LET'S REMEMBER TO WASH OUR HANDS

Draw a picture of yourself washing your hands:

Activity 14

TERRIFIC TEETH

Aim:

Should we care for our teeth?

Performance Objectives—Students will be able to:

- recognize that teeth are necessary for biting, tearing, chewing, and good appearance.
- brush teeth properly.
- understand the importance of regular visits to the dentist.

Performance Objectives for the Special Child:

- play a role about a tooth fairy
- write a paragraph about it

Materials Needed:

- BRUSHING RECORD Activity Sheet
- crayons
- children's toothbrushes (Have your visiting dentist bring them; dentists sometimes gets samples—or have children bring them from home.)
- *Going to the Dentist* by Stacie Strong, Simon and Schuster Books for Young Readers: New York, 1991, or similar book

Motivation:

Tell the children they will be learning to brush their teeth with their own toothbrushes today.

Do Now:

List or draw in your notebooks the things you think your teeth are good for.

Development:

1. Read aloud to the class the book about the dentist. Tell children that they will have a special guest speak with them today. (Prearrange a visit from a dentist or other dental professional.)
2. Review the "Do Now." Write on the board why children think teeth are important.

3. Introduce the dental professional to the class.

4. Pass out the toothbrushes and ask the dentist to talk about the importance of teeth and how to brush teeth properly and when.

5. Have children ask questions of the dentist. Elicit from the dentist that it is normal for children to lose their teeth.

6. Thank the dentist for coming and pass out the BRUSHING RECORD Activity Sheets and crayons.

7. Read the directions aloud to the children. Explain to them how to record their brushings on their Activity Sheets at home.

8. When the Activity Sheets have been completed and brought back to school, have student volunteers share them with the class.

Individual Project for the Special Child:

- Have the special child pretend he or she is the tooth fairy. Have the child write a paragraph or draw a picture about what he or she would do with all the teeth collected.

Summary:

1. Why are teeth necessary?

2. Why do we brush our teeth?

3. Why do we visit the dentist?

Summary for the Special Child:

1. Who did you pretend you were?

2. What did you do with all those teeth as the tooth fairy?

Homework:

Bring home your BRUSHING RECORD Activity Sheets to record brushing your teeth at home. Bring them back in two weeks.

Name _____

Activity 14

BRUSHING RECORD

On the sheet below, record the number of times you brush in a day. On the left side are the days of the week. On the bottom are the number of times you brushed.

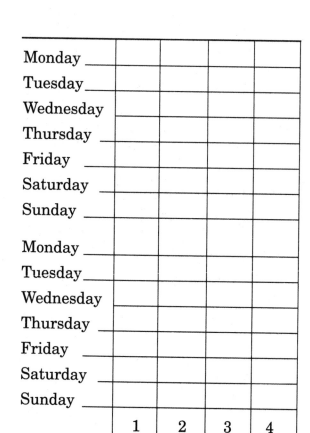

	1	2	3	4
Monday ____				
Tuesday____				
Wednesday ____				
Thursday ____				
Friday ____				
Saturday ____				
Sunday ____				
Monday ____				
Tuesday____				
Wednesday ____				
Thursday ____				
Friday ____				
Saturday ____				
Sunday ____				

	1	2	3	4
Monday ____				
Tuesday____				
Wednesday ____				
Thursday ____				
Friday ____				
Saturday ____				
Sunday ____				
Monday ____				
Tuesday____				
Wednesday ____				
Thursday ____				
Friday ____				
Saturday ____				
Sunday ____				

Activity 15
SUNNY SUNBLOCKERS

Aim:

Can we protect our bodies from sunburn?

Performance Objectives—Children will be able to:

- learn about the benefits of the sun.
- identify the ways that people can protect themselves from the sun.
- learn about sunscreen and how to apply it.

Performance Objectives for the Special Child:

- recognize that the eyes need protection from the sun
- learn one way to protect the eyes from the sun

Materials Needed:

- SUNBURN SAFETY Activity Sheet
- crayons
- a hat with a brim that shades the ears
- a bottle of sunscreen with an SPF of 15 or over
- sunglasses with UV protection
- *What Makes the Weather* by Janet Palazzo, Troll School and Library: Mahwah, NJ, 1982

Motivation:

Tell students they will be learning about the sun outside today.

Do Now:

Draw or write in your notebook the things you like to do in the sun.

Development:

1. Review the "Do Now." List on the board all the activities children like to do in the sun.

2. If the weather is good, take the class on a walk outside; if not, have the children look out the window at the sunlight. Remind children never to look directly at the sun.

3. Bring the children back to the classroom.

4. Lead a discussion with the class about how the sun makes life possible. Explain that animals, plants, and people need sunlight to live. The sun gives us warmth and light.

5. Explain that many years ago children developed different skin tones. Explain that people who lived in the hottest part of the earth developed a darker skin tone. Explain, also, that everyone, regardless of skin tone, needs protection from the sun.

6. Tell the children that there are different ways to protect our bodies from the sun. Elicit from the class ways in which they think they could do this. Make sure they include: wearing sunscreen, wearing sunglasses, staying out of the sun in mid-day, wearing a hat to protect the head, wearing a shirt to protect the upper body, and never looking directly at the sun.

7. List all the preventive measures on the board.

8. Have two volunteers come up, preferably two with different skin tones, and demonstrate on them how to apply sunscreen to the parts of the body exposed to the sun, including feet and ears.

9. Have student volunteers also model the hat and sunglasses as methods of sun protection. Talk about UV protection.

10. Read a book about the sun, such as *What Makes the Weather*.

11. Pass out SUNBURN SAFETY Activity Sheets and crayons.

12. Read directions aloud to the class. In a class discussion, have them come up with different ways to protect themselves from the sun. Then have them draw their ideas on their Activity Sheets.

13. Have student volunteers share their Activity Sheets with the class.

Individual Project for the Special Child:

• Tell the special child to pretend he or she is out in the sun. Ask the special child if he or she thinks the eyes need protection. Ask the child to choose something from the sun protection material to protect the eyes (for example, sunglasses). Then ask the child to draw a picture of himself or herself in the sun wearing the sun protection for the eyes.

Summary:

1. How does the sun help us?

2. How can we protect ourselves from the sun?

3 What is sunscreen and how can we apply it?

Summary for the Special Child:

1. Do the eyes need protection from the sun?
2. Can you name one way to protect the eyes from the sun?

Homework:

Take the SUNBURN SAFETY Activity Sheet home to share with the family.

Activity 15
SUNBURN SAFETY

Draw yourself below with sun protection. Draw yourself with everything you need for full protection from the sun:

Activity 16
LEARNING ABOUT GOOD FOOD

Aim:

Can we learn about good food?

Performance Objectives—Students will be able to:

- interview school personnel about food.
- identify the five basic food groups.
- discuss the nutritional value of food.

Performance Objectives for the Special Child:

- discuss food preferences
- exchange a snack with a friend

Materials Needed:

- FIVE BASIC FOOD GROUPS Activity Sheet
- markers
- magazines and supermarket circulars
- safety scissors
- glue

Motivation:

Tell students they will be hearing a talk by the school dietitian or kitchen manager today. (Arrange the visit beforehand.)

Do Now:

Write in your notebook questions you would like to ask the school dietitian.

Development:

1. Review the "Do Now." List on the board questions the children would like to ask.
2. Introduce the school dietitian.
3. Ask the dietitian to explain how the lunches (or breakfasts, if you have a breakfast program) are planned and why.

4. Have the children read their questions from the board for the dietitian to answer. If they don't ask about the nutritional value of food, ask the dietitian yourself.

5. Ask the dietitian to identify the five basic food groups, including: Grains, Dairy, Meat and Fish, Fruits and Vegetables, and Fats.

6. List these groups on the board.

7. Pass out the FIVE BASIC FOOD GROUPS Activity Sheet, markers, glue, scissors, and magazines.

8. Ask children to draw or choose a picture from the magazine of one food from each food group and put it in the correct category on the Activity Sheet.

9. You and the dietitian can assist the children in making appropriate choices.

10. Have the children share their Activity Sheets with the class upon completion.

11. Thank the dietitian for his or her time. After the dietitian leaves, have the class write him or her thank-you notes and do drawings.

Individual Project for the Special Child:

• Have the special child choose a partner to work with. Have them discuss their snack preferences with each other. Then have them switch snacks.

Summary:

1. What questions did you ask the school dietitian?

2. What are the five basic food groups?

3. Why is food good for you?

Summary for the Special Child:

1. What are your food preferences?

2. Can you tell me which friend you shared your snack with?

Homework:

Describe the food groups you had for dinner.

Name _____

Activity 16

FIVE BASIC FOOD GROUPS

Below are listed the five basic food groups. Draw the right food in the box, or cut out and paste a picture in the box.

Category 1: Grains

Category 2: Dairy

Category 3: Meat and Fish

Category 4: Fruits and Vegetables

Category 5: Fats and Sweets

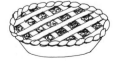

Activity 17
TAKING CARE OF OUR WORLD

Aim:

What can we do to keep the environment clean?

Performance Objectives—Students will be able to:

- understand that the environment is endangered by pollution.
- identify some of the sources of pollution.
- learn ways in which the environment can be helped.

Performance Objectives for the Special Child:

- identify recyclable versus nonrecyclable garbage
- create a sculpture

Materials Needed:

- TAKING CARE OF OUR WORLD Activity Sheet
- TAKING CARE OF OUR HOME Activity Sheet
- crayons
- *Global Warming: A Pop-Up Book of Our Endangered Planet,* by Sandy Ransford, Simon and Schuster Books for Young Readers: New York, 1992; *Garbage! Where It Comes From, Where It Goes.* Simon and Schuster books for Young Readers: New York, 1990; *Nature in Danger,* by Mary O'Neill, Troll Books: Mahwah, NJ, 1991, or other book about the environment*
- garbage bags—blue and another color (In some schools, the custodian may supply them.)
- glue

Motivation:

Tell students they will be helping to clean the environment today.

Do Now:

List or draw in your notebooks items you normally throw away as garbage.

Development:

1. Read aloud the book *Garbage* or another book about the environment, to the class. Discuss the book with the class.

2. Review the "Do Now." List on the board things children commonly throw away as garbage.

3. Explain that keeping the environment healthy is one of the things we must do to keep ourselves healthy, because we have to live in the environment.

4. Explain that "environment" means everything in the world around us and that "pollution" means dirty. Write both words on the chalkboard.

5. Ask the class for some examples of pollution—car exhaust, cigarette smoke, garbage, chemicals from factories. List these on the chalkboard under pollution.

6. Explain that pollution can hurt us. Discuss some examples, such as air pollution causing dizziness, headaches, or burning eyes; broken bottles in garbage cutting people; dirty water making it unsafe to fish.

7. Pass out the TAKING CARE OF OUR WORLD Activity Sheets and crayons. Read the directions aloud to the class. Ask them to color in the activities that help the environment as you discuss them and to cross out those that don't.

8. Elicit from the class those activities that they think would help to clean up the environment. Here are some suggestions:

   - Separate recyclables from nonrecyclables.
   - Throw nonrecyclables in the wastebasket.
   - Collect cans for recycling.
   - Turn off lights when they're not needed.
   - Don't let the water run unless you're using it.
   - Reuse things—books, plastic and paper bags, plastic containers.
   - Help out at home by keeping your room clean or washing dishes.

9. Have student volunteers share their Activity Sheets with the class. Check to see that children colored in the correct activities.

10. Discuss recyclable garbage versus garbage that cannot be recycled. Explain that recyclable garbage is gathered and packaged separately to go to a recycling center and be used again.

11. Pass out garbage bags—blue and another color. Tell children that they will be doing an activity to help the environment. Then choose a cleanup activity. (This should be prearranged with school personnel—custodian or kitchen staff—or the person in charge of another site.)

12. Bring children to the cleanup site. This can be the cafeteria following lunch, the schoolyard following recess, or a local park. Ask children to gather up the garbage and separate it into recyclables in the blue bag and nonrecyclables in the other-color bag.

13. Give the garbage to the custodian for proper disposal.

14. Have children wash their hands when they return.

Individual Project for the Special Child:

- Ask the special child to gather together some recyclables. Give the child glue and ask him or her to make a sculpture by gluing together the recyclable materials.

Summary:

1. Why is pollution dangerous?
2. What are some of the sources of pollution?
3. What can we do to clean up the environment?

Summary for the Special Child:

1. Can you show me some of the recyclables and nonrecyclables you gathered on the trip?
2. Can you show me the sculpture you made from the recyclables?

Homework:

Take home the TAKING CARE OF OUR HOME Activity Sheet and share it with your family.

Activity 17
TAKING CARE OF OUR WORLD

Below are several pictures. Some will help the environment; some will not. Color in the pictures that will help the environment. Put X's through the pictures that will not.

Activity 17 (continued)

TAKING CARE OF OUR HOME

Below are several pictures. Some will help the environment at home. Some will not. Color in the pictures that will help and put X's through the ones that will not: